Current Issues in Economic Policy

Current Issues in Economic Policy

Edited by

R M GRANT
The City University

G K SHAW
University of East Anglia

SECOND EDITION

Philip Allan

First published 1975 by

PHILIP ALLAN PUBLISHERS LIMITED
MARKET PLACE
DEDDINGTON
OXFORD OX5 4SE

Second edition 1980
Reprinted 1981

British Library Cataloguing in Publication Data

Current issues in economic policy. – 2nd ed.
1. Great Britain – Economic policy – 1945–
I. Grant, Ronald Melville
II. Shaw, Graham Keith
330.9'41'0857 HC256.6

ISBN 0-86003-029-6
ISBN 0-86003-128-4 Pbk

Set by MHL Typesetting Limited, Coventry
Printed in Great Britain at The Camelot Press Limited, Southampton

Contents

PART III MACROECONOMIC POLICY

Preface

PREFACE TO THE SECOND EDITION

The appearance of the second edition of *Current Issues* permits the editors to take account of the constructive comments and criticisms received from colleagues and students alike. In particular, in response to many appeals, the attempt is made to give the volume a more formal structure by distinguishing between micro and macro policy issues. Whilst the validity of such a dichotomy is open to question, particularly with regard to policy formation, such a division does preserve conformity with the conventional theoretical texts which the present work is designed to complement.

New material has been included and certain topics eliminated in keeping with the changing emphasis in UK policy discussion. While conceding that other topics might equally have been included, the principal objective of our present selection is to highlight the relationship between theory and policy in the context of the UK economy, rather than to attempt a comprehensive account of economic policy. Needless to say, we are indebted to the participating authors, and we are particularly grateful to Mrs Joan Reed of St. Andrews University and Mrs Sabina Harding of City University for their willing assistance.

R.M. Grant
G.K. Shaw

PREFACE TO THE FIRST EDITION

This volume evolved from a growing conviction that most introductory economics courses, as conventionally taught in universities and polytechnics, are predominantly theoretical in approach. To a large extent this is inevitable if the groundwork of the subject is to be laid adequately, especially when many first-year students have no prior contact with economics. Invariably, however, it leads to a situation where the student does not readily perceive how the theoretical structure relates to the policy issues which are at the centre of economic debate and controversy. This is particularly the case when the theoretical framework has been treated as a series of distinct component parts, as an aid to assimilation and comprehension, and its consequences are especially serious when the student does not pursue his economic training beyond the introductory level.

Current Issues is designed to remedy this defect by focusing upon some key areas of applied economics and the role of government in the economy, drawing upon the basic apparatus of elementary micro and macro economic theory. Each author has analysed a current policy issue, primarily although not wholly within a United Kingdom context, invoking no more than the conventional tools of first-year economics. Thus, the book is designed as a complement to an introductory theory text, with the hope that it may bridge the gulf between the abstractions of economic theory and the complexity of economic policy; a gulf clearly and dauntingly perceived by the student and yet a gulf which in reality does not, and should not, exist.

A word of caution is necessary. With regard to content, it was never intended that the book should be exhaustive and the decision on what to include or leave out has been purely a question of personal choice on the part of the editors, who accept responsibility for any glaring omissions. Secondly, for the most part each chapter has been written by a specialist within the field, who has approached the subject matter from his own particular vantage point. There has been no attempt to reflect all shades of opinion on any given topic, even where the subject is highly controversial. Rather, our objective has been to provoke continuing enquiry by introducing the reader to major policy issues and options and indicating how they may be further explored with the aid of contemporary analysis.

The editors wish to thank the participating authors, not only for making the present work possible, but also for their willingness to submit to editorial surgery. We also thank Mrs Joan Reed of St. Andrews University for undertaking the bulk of the secretarial work involved.

R.M. Grant
G.K. Shaw

Foreword: studying economic policy

ALAN PEACOCK
Principal and Professor of Economics,
University College at Buckingham

The traditional purpose of an introduction is to say nice things about the authors. Honeyed words will hopefully disarm criticism and promote sales. As the success of the first edition has proved, this book does not need sponsorship of this kind. It clearly fills a gap in the undergraduate literature. Books on basic theory abound and there is a growing number of undergraduate texts on applied economics displaying considerable sophistication, but it is difficult to find a *tour d'horizon* of the main areas of economic policy which is neither on the one hand too descriptive nor, on the other, too overweighted with advanced analysis. I have chosen my task as that of trying to help the reader in using this volume. I attempt to do so by considering what are the essential ingredients for a study of economic policy, leaving the reader to consider further how these ingredients are combined to fashion finished products in the chapters ahead.

A policy suggests immediately an objective or set of objectives, chosen by some method by someone. In the study of macroeconomic policy, the general procedure is to identify objectives of interest to the policy maker and which are therefore *data* to the investigator. The selection of such objectives by the economist is based on observed behaviour of governments. In the UK the objectives of macroeconomic policy are generally agreed to be full employment, price stability, economic growth and equilibrium in the current account of the balance of payments.

It may be useful for some purposes to look at objectives singly, but a growing and important field of economic analysis is concerned with the study of macroeconomic policy 'in the round', involving the construction of a government 'utility function' or 'social welfare function' analogous to the individual utility function commonly used in demonstrating the maximising behaviour of consumers or producers. This suggests that objectives must be *quantified* in some way (e.g. the unemployment percentage, the rate of economic growth) and targets set for them. In the likely event that not all targets can be simultaneously reached, the social welfare function can be redefined to indicate how these targets will be 'traded off' against one another. This approach is difficult to implement in examining actual policies because of the problems encountered in acquiring data, not so much on objectives, but on trade-offs. Governments, however formed, may not have precise ideas about trade-offs, and, if they do, may not wish to reveal them unless they are sure that the revelation will support their position (see Chapter 9). What is more, they may change them frequently in the light of the need for support. Both the shape and the position of the government's 'indifference surface' may be indiscernible and, so far as it is revealed, unpredictable. The authors of this volume who have identified targets have been wise to avoid any attempt to calculate the weights attached to individual policies, though the notion of trade-offs provides them with a useful frame of reference.

There is, however, another approach to the problem of identification of objectives and trade-offs. It is often rather misleadingly labelled a microeconomic approach, simply because it derives objectives from the behaviour of individuals faced with the usual economic constraints on resources available to them and on the development of their capacity to alter those constraints. Policy objectives to be implemented by collective action are identified as a logical consequence of individuals' maximising behaviour. The extent and form of collective action by government budgetary and other measures depends on the way in which collective decisions by individuals are arrived at. This approach is used to demonstrate which policies logically follow from individuals' behaviour (Chapters 5 and 6, for example), or may be developed into a model which endeavours to explain or even to predict how actual policies emerge (Chapter 2).

There is no logical conflict between these two approaches. Essentially the second approach goes a few stages further back in the political process which governs policy formation than the first approach. Whether or not governments who implement policy decisions take account of individuals' aspirations is a matter for empirical investigation. Where differences and potential conflict between the approaches may arise is in the appraisal of policy decisions, but this is a matter which is considered later.

Once objectives are specified, policy makers must choose instruments in order to fulfil them. In countries with mixed economies, this entails introducing policy measures which are designed to alter the economic environment surrounding private consumers and producers so that they modify their actions in line with the required objective. If it is believed that capital accumulation is the instrument to achieve the objective of growth (Chapter 12), policies will be designed to induce entrepreneurs to increase their rate of investment, for example by lowering tax rates on companies. But policy makers will be interested not only in achieving the correct direction of change but also in the magnitude of change possible within the constraints imposed on their actions, the most important being scarcity of available resources. Thus if increasing investment means reducing consumption – consumption being the rough symbol we might use for alternative objectives – attention is directed towards the problem of tracing the quantitative relationship between the increase in investment and the associated increase in economic growth. The less the increase in investment required to achieve the growth target, the less difficult it will be to achieve other objectives. This argument has been couched in very general terms, but is sufficient to demonstrate what further ingredients are needed in studies of economic policy.

The first requirement, then, is a model which traces the chain of causation between the policy instruments and the objectives. What this model contains will depend on the problem which the economist wishes to illuminate. If it is policy intervention in a single market where one objective is considered, it may be sufficient, particularly at the introductory stage assumed in this volume, to build on simple supply and demand analysis; and there are several examples of the versatility of this simple technique in this work (Chapter 4). Likewise, in examining a single macro-objective such as stemming inflation, the essential relationship between the objective and policy instruments can be illustrated using either a simple Keynesian-type or Friedman-type macroeconomic model (see Chapter 9; the monetarist approach is developed further in Chapter 11).

It is characteristic of the contributions to this volume that objectives are considered singly; though, in contrast, alternative instruments to reach single objectives are frequently considered (Chapter 8). Reference is made in some cases to the side effects of particular instruments used to achieve a single objective on other objectives, so offering a useful reminder to the reader of the complications associated with the pursuit of a unified multi-objective policy. Indeed, the very structure of the work, with single chapters on various aspects of policy, more or less imposes such a framework of analysis. The reader may find it useful to know that there has been a very striking development in economic analysis under the general label of 'the theory of economic policy' in which very sophisticated models are used to show how governments can maximise several objectives simultaneously, given the structure of the economy and the instruments available. Not the least interesting aspect of these attempts to formulate 'optimal decision rules' for government is the way in which, as we have already indicated, the terminology and to some extent the methodology of microeconomic analysis has been deployed.[1]

Most of the contributions deal with the second requirement in marrying instruments to objectives – that of establishing quantitative relationships – either by numerical illustration with reasonably realistic parameter values or by some statistical and/or descriptive background (see Chapter 10). The derivation of quantitative relationships is a highly specialised and extremely difficult area of study (econometrics) to which passing reference is made. In essence, statistical techniques are used to calculate the value of parameters – for example, the average and marginal propensity to import and consume, the incremental capital-output ratio – using data from the past. As policy decisions involve consideration of what the quantitative relations between instruments and objectives will be in future time, the question arises as to how far past relationships, hopefully significant ones, can be a guide to future ones and, if this is only likely to be approximately so, what further methods can be used to improve forecasts of expected values.

Here we enter an area of considerable professional controversy. All will agree that errors in estimation of parameters and of lags in adjustment to policy changes have often rendered policies inappropriate. Then the paths divide. There are those economists who maintain that these errors are endemic to any exercise in forecasting and that professional effort should be concentrated more on devising policy measures which dispense with, or at least reduce reliance on, forecasts. There are others who maintain that model building and associated estimation procedures are only in their infancy and that technical progress in economics and econometrics will result in improvements. Sometimes this debate has ideological overtones, for it clearly strengthens the case of those who object to widespread policy intervention on political grounds if such intervention will be ineffective because it must rely on imperfect forecasts. It follows that the nearer one approaches perfect forecasting, the weaker the technical objections become. There is no way of resolving this debate in a satisfactory way, and the practical issue is this: what should economists be doing in the period up to the point when its resolution seems possible? It says much for the intellectual resilience of economists that this issue has been very thoroughly discussed, albeit at an abstract and highly technical level. In broad terms, these investigations endeavour to identify decision rules for government faced with the problem of uncertainty surrounding both the specification of the right economic relationships in the economy and the effects of policy instruments used to attempt to influence these relationships. The rules attempt to distinguish between those situations where the government would be advised to act *as if* the estimated values of parameters will be correct and those where this 'certainty equivalence' approach would not be appropriate. Little of this discussion has so far penetrated the introductory texts in economics and the only purpose in mentioning it here is to underline the importance of uncertainty in decision making, about which perhaps too little is said in expository works in economics.

This suggested framework for studying economic policy is based on purely positive foundations: that is to say, no judgement need be made about the desirability or otherwise either of the policy objectives or the measures which are designed to achieve them. As the reader will be well aware, popular writing on economic policy problems in the financial press is full of references to 'sound' and 'unsound' economic policies and reflects disagreement on policy matters which does little to consolidate the reputation of economics as a scientific discipline, at least in the public eye. These disagreements are inevitable and are healthy if they reflect differing views about the choice of policy objectives and trade-offs between them. After all, there is nothing in a scientific discipline which obliges its members to agree on value judgements. They are perhaps more serious when disagreements concern facts and logic. However, let us assume that the facts and logic are agreed, or at least that there is agreement about how disagreements about them can be resolved, e.g. by statistical and analytical techniques. What then?

Granted the assumption, appraisal of economic policy is possible without recourse to judgement on the policy aims themselves by asking the question: do the instruments achieve the desired ends? In other words, within the limits of our knowledge as economists, policies can be tested for consistency. It should be possible, for instance, to offer at least an informed judgement about whether a particular policy measure will achieve the desired objective, having regard to any possible side effects it may have on other objectives considered relevant. A large part of the time of economists in government is taken up with the task of giving advice, not on whether the objectives are the right ones, but on whether the policy instruments are appropriate for achieving the objectives. Their task may be made more difficult when no known instruments employed in any combination are likely to achieve what their political masters would wish. Thus the 'objectives/economic model/instruments' logic may help to achieve consistency in policy making, both through the choice of instruments and adaptation in policy aims which may be a necessary consequence of the constraints on the effectiveness of the instruments themselves. It may also point in the direction in which instrumental innovations might be sought. There are several examples in this book which introduce the reader to the problem of consistency of ends and means (Chapter 13 for example) and with the related question of minimising resource use in the process (the discussions of cost–benefit and cost-effectiveness in Chapters 6 and 7).

It would do less than justice to the authors of this volume to let the matter of appraisal end at this point.

Economists frequently judge policy measures by reference to the postulates of welfare economics (which are expounded in Chapter 1). Broadly speaking, and with due regard to circumstances in which competitive markets may not conform with their interests, a very large proportion of the economics profession would judge any policy measures in terms of their effects on the welfare of individuals. They would have to admit that, in the last analysis, the famous Paretian axioms are value judgements. They justify support for them on various grounds, the principal one being that the informed judgement of 'reasonable men' would lead to a consensus view that individuals must be the ultimate judges of their own welfare. Practical expression of the application of these axioms is exemplified (Chapter 3) by such devices as showing the effect of government measures on consumers' surplus. The implicit conclusion of this approach is that if consumers' surplus is reduced by some policy measures then, whether or not governments act consistently in achieving their own stated objectives, Paretian welfare criteria pronounce these measures as inappropriate because individuals' welfare is decreased. Furthermore, this approach employs a model of the economy in which governments act completely independently of individual decision makers, who appear to have no part in the political process. Its relevance depends on whether such a model is consistent with the political decision making system actually in existence. If it is, and political decisions are beyond the control of individuals, then it is difficult to reconcile Paretian welfare economics with the condition that individual preferences are sovereign. If, as 'liberal Paretians' believe, the implications for political decision making of the Paretian welfare must be fully explained, appraisal of policies must depend on which policies are sanctioned by political arrangements consistent with these axioms. Individual decisions through the market place and through the political process cannot then be segmented.[2]

The analysis of the ingredients which form a study of economic policy tempts me to conclude as follows.

Firstly, there is obviously no fundamental difference between a macroeconomic and a microeconomic approach to policy issues. Both require the delineation of objectives, the use of economic models, the specification of parameter values and the identification of policy instruments. The macro/micro distinction simply emphasises in a rough-and-ready way the scale of policy operations.

Secondly, the conventional distinction between 'theory' and 'applied' wears thin when policy issues, as in this volume, are properly analysed. All that one can say is that different policy issues may require different degrees of abstraction in explaining them properly and different degrees of technical input, though this is less obvious at an introductory level. Such statements that an economist is a good theorist but not a good applied or policy-oriented economist are thoroughly misleading, suggesting a false dichotomy between the creative innovator and the plodding tool-user. Apart from the fact that several contributors to this volume move easily between different levels of abstraction, the creative mind can find plenty to test it in the design of policy instruments as well as in improving the models in which their effects are manifested.

Thirdly, it is possible to offer an appraisal of economic policies, allowing for human frailty, without the author having to pass judgement on policy objectives. Policies can simply be tested for consistency between objectives and instruments. Despite this, many members of the economics profession are still committed to Paretian axioms, which are used to judge policy measures independently of the objectives to which they are directed. But whether objectives are treated as data or as axioms to which the economist is committed, they must be made explicit if rational discussion of policy issues employing economic analysis is to proceed.

Alan Peacock
August 1979

Notes

1. For an extended treatment at a more advanced level see Peston, M.H., *Theory of Macroeconomic Policy*, Philip Allan 1974. For an enlightening analysis of its practical limitations, see *Report of the Committee on Policy Optimisation* (Ball Report), Cmnd. No. 7148, 1978.
2. For a discussion of these issues and other difficulties associated with the application of Paretian axioms to political questions see Rowley, C.K., and Peacock, A.T., *Welfare Economics: A Liberal Re-Statement*, Martin Robertson 1975.

PART I

Introduction

1. The role of government in the UK economy

R.M. GRANT
Lecturer in Business Economics, The City University

Despite a half century of virtually uninterrupted economic expansion[1] accompanied by reductions in unemployment, poverty, illiteracy and ill-health, dissatisfaction over the performance of the British economy has never been greater. Concern arises principally from a comparison of the progress of the British economy with that of other countries. Of the major western nations the UK has had by far the lowest rate of economic growth since 1950 and although the UK rate of unemployment has been below that of many countries, the rate of inflation has exceeded that of most. At the beginning of this century Britain accounted for 32.5% of world manufactured exports; by 1954 this share had fallen to 20.4%, and by 1977 to 8.3%. The relative decline of Britain has tended to accelerate during the past two decades. As recently as 1960 Britain's GNP per head of population was exceeded in Europe only by Sweden and Switzerland. By 1976 Britain had been overtaken by France, Germany, Austria, the Netherlands, Belgium, Luxembourg, Denmark, Norway and Finland. The lack of international competitiveness of the economy is indicated by the recurrent balance of payment crises and the fall in the value of the pound sterling. In spite of considerable appreciation since 1977, between 1960 and mid-1979 the pound fell by 29% against the US dollar, 36% against the French franc and 67% against the German mark.

Table 1. *Growth of the public sector*

	Public authorities current expenditure	*Government revenue*	*Public administration and defence as a % of total employment*
	as a % of GNP at market prices		
1900	11.7	8.4	2.4
1910	10.2	10.6	3.0
1920	22.1	23.7	3.7
1930	23.3	20.7	2.6
1938	26.2	23.1	5.1
1950	33.2	38.4	6.7
1960	32.5	31.8	5.7
1970	38.5	48.2	6.2
1978	47.0	48.0	7.1

The increased attention accorded to economic affairs reflects also the greater interdependence of the modern economic system, which has meant that economic welfare has become increasingly dependent on the performance of many different parts of the economy. Increased interdependence has resulted from the increased specialisation that has accompanied technological advance and capital accumulation. As a consequence the vulnerability of the economy as a whole to disruption due to strike, bankruptcy or technical failure in any part of the system, is increased. The increasing importance of international trade and financial flows has meant increased economic interdependence at world level, so that essentially national problems such as the weakness of the US dollar and political upheaval in Iran can have world-wide economic repercussions.

The elevation of economic matters to a central position in current affairs and political debates is a result also of the growing importance of government as an employer and a producer and consumer of goods and services. The result is that government now occupies a dominant position in the national economy. The expanding role of government in the economy has been one of the most significant features of the twentieth century economic development of Britain. Some indication of the growing importance of government in the economy is shown in table 1.

This expansion of the role of government has involved the growth of the public sector of the British economy through direct provision of goods and services (such as transport, energy, communication, education and health and welfare services) and also intervention into and regulation of the private sector of the economy. Such interventions include pollution controls, consumer protection, the regulation of employment contracts and conditions of work, competition policy, prices and incomes controls, and a great variety of legislation which influences almost every facet of economic life.

The expansion of the functions of government and the scope of economic policy reflects a profound change in prevailing attitudes towards economic problems. During the 19th century the problems of unemployment, poverty, inflation and urban squalor were seen as the result of the operation of the laws of economics and a lack of the moral virtues of thrift and enterprise. Today, although most of the economic and social problems – of unemployment, poverty, inflation and urban squalor – remain the same, it is government which is held responsible. Two factors of particular significance may be identified in this change of attitude. First, the development of economic science has increased knowledge of the working of the economy, thereby enabling the diagnosis of economic problems and the prescription of corrective action. Second, the demand for government intervention to ameliorate and remedy the economic problems which arise from the uncontrolled operation of the economic system has increased with the progressive democratisation of the British political system and the increased prominence of political pressure groups representing particular economic interests.

It is these two forces with which this chapter is concerned. In the light of the principal developments in economic theory, the problems of the market economy are examined and the rationale for government intervention to increase economic welfare is established. We then proceed to consider the forces within the political system which have influenced the choice and application of economic policies and survey some of the major trends in economic policy during the past two decades.

The Efficiency of the Market Mechanism and the Policy of Laissez-faire

The emergence of Britain as the world's wealthiest and most powerful industrial economy during the 19th century was paralleled by an increase in the understanding of the operation of the market mechanism and the process of economic development. The foundations for this analysis were laid by Adam Smith in his *Inquiry into the Nature and Causes of the Wealth of Nations* (1776). From the viewpoint of economic policy, the most exciting and influential discovery of Smith was the mechanism of the *invisible hand* – the process by which individual decisions of self-interest are coordinated by the price mechanism to promote the common good of all. The implication was that the government can best promote the economic welfare of society by limiting its intervention in the economy. To understand this argument it is necessary, in the light of modern economic analysis, to consider first what is meant by the economic welfare of society and, second, how it can be maximised in the competitive market economy.

From Jeremy Bentham writing at the beginning of the 19th century to Alfred Marshall at the end, social welfare was treated as the sum of cardinally measurable utilities of the individual members of society. Yet clearly, to quantify and aggregate individuals' subjective experiences of pleasure is impossible. Even if, following Marshall, the utility which consumers derive from their consumption of goods and services is measured according to their willingness to pay, aggregating individuals' utilities assumes that the utility of money is constant between persons. Vilfredo Pareto's major contribution was to derive criteria for society which did not depend upon comparisons of individuals' utilities (Pareto 1908). Starting from the premise that social welfare depends solely upon the welfare of each and every individual in society, *Pareto's criterion* for any increase in social welfare is that *the welfare of at least one person is increased without any other person experiencing a decrease in welfare.* A *Pareto optimum* is therefore reached where it is *impossible to increase any person's welfare without reducing that of someone else.*

It can be shown that in a perfectly competitive economy utility maximisation by households and profit maximisation by firms results in the establishment of an equilibrium position which is also a Pareto optimum:

utility-maximising consumption decisions by households result in an optimal distribution of goods and services, insofar as no redistribution could make any one consumer better off without making anyone else worse off;

cost-minimising production decisions by firms result in a distribution of factors of products between firms and industries which is optimal, since no redistribution of factors could increase the production of any one good without reducing the output of some other good;

in competitive equilibrium the allocation of factors of production to different industries results in optimal levels of output for different goods and services, since no re-allocation of factors between industries could produce a more preferred combination of different goods and services.

In the 19th century the precise analytics of welfare maximisation under perfect competition had yet to be demonstrated; nevertheless the theory of the invisible hand was remarkably influential as the scientific basis for the philosophy of *laissez-faire* – the view that production, exchange and foreign trade should in the interests of prosperity and growth be free from the interventions of government. A typical mid-19th century *laissez-faire* view is expressed in Frederic Bastiat's account of his visit to Paris in 1845:

> How does each succeeding day manage to bring to this gigantic market just what is necessary – neither too much, nor too little? What then is the resourceful and secret power that governs the amazing regularity of such complicated movements? . . . That power is . . . the principle of free exchange. We put our faith in that inner light which Providence has placed in the hearts of all men, and to which has been trusted the preservation and the unlimited improvement of our species, a light we term 'self-interest', which is so illuminating, so constant and so penetrating, when it is left free of every interference. Where would you be, inhabitants of Paris, if some

> cabinet minister decided to substitute for that power contrivances of his own invention? . . . Although there may be much suffering within your walls . . . it is certain that the arbitrary intervention of the government would infinitely multiply this suffering and spread among all of you the ills that affect only a small number of your fellow citizens. (Quoted in Kohler 1970)

Echoes of the *laissez-faire* philosophy are heard in the free-enterprise views of certain conservative economists and politicians today. It must be emphasised, however, that the arguments of Milton Friedman and F.A. Hayek for a contraction in the economic role of government are based not on faith in the perfection of the competitive market economy, but on a belief in the inherent inefficiency of government and the threat to individual liberty posed by extensive and arbitrary government intervention in the economy (see Friedman 1962 and Hayek 1976).

Imperfections of the Market Economy: Considerations of Equity and Justice

A principal advantage of Pareto's approach to social welfare is that it allows us to distinguish considerations of *efficiency* from considerations of *equity*. A Pareto optimum is not an absolute welfare maximum; only an efficient as compared with an inefficient equilibrium position. There are an infinite number of possible Pareto optima each corresponding to a different initial distribution of resources in society. Since interpersonal comparisons of utility are not possible on the basis of any objective criteria, welfare economics does not enable us to rank different Pareto optima involving different income distributions. By either redistributing resource ownership or redistributing final income among consumers, the government can achieve a range of different income distributions, all of which are welfare maximising in the Pareto sense. Thus we have two criteria for evaluating social welfare: a positive criterion which enables us to identify an efficiency maximisation in the economy (a Pareto optimum) and a normative criterion for evaluating the impact of redistribution of income.

Indeed, the idea that the distribution of income that arises from the free operation of the market economy is in any way optimal is difficult to reconcile with any political or social philosophy. In the market system an individual's income depends upon the price he can obtain for his labour services and the amount of wealth he owns. Those who cannot offer productive labour and possess no wealth receive no income. The market economy will thus tend to concentrate poverty upon the old, the young, the handicapped and the unemployed. A redistribution of income by government will cause the economy to move to a new point of general equilibrium; so long as redistribution does not involve distortions of prices, then the new equilibrium will also be Pareto optimal. Normally, however, taxes on income and goods will affect market prices and so cause the economy to depart from the Pareto optimum. In this case government must balance an increase in social welfare resulting from a more desirable distribution of income, against a fall in social welfare resulting from a decline in efficiency.[2]

In a democratic society value judgements by government are made by society as a whole through the electoral process. Extension of the franchise gave the poorer members of society the political power to demand greater equality. The framework for income redistribution was established by the 1906 to 1914 Liberal Government which introduced surtax, national insurance for old age, sickness and unemployment, and raised income tax to the unprecedented level of 6%. Since 1914 governmental redistribution of income has increased largely as a result of the burden of taxation on the better-off arising from the expansion of public expenditure. The principal conscious effort by government to achieve a major re-ordering of incomes was that of the 1945–50 Labour administration, which expanded the scope of national insurance and introduced national assistance, family allowances and the National Health Service.

Another aspect of equality which has motivated government intervention in the economy is the desire for *equality of opportunity* in economic matters. Since 1964 legislation has been introduced to prohibit discrimination in employment on the grounds of race and sex. In educational policy the extent to which governments should try to create equality of opportunity by providing a common educational framework for children up to the age of 16 has been a topic of considerable controversy (see Chapter 6).

The pursuit of greater equality has not been the only area where normative judgements by government have provided the motivation for intervention in the economy. Paretian welfare economics is based on the assumption that the individual is the best judge of his own welfare. This assumption is open to challenge and a further value judgement which has been used to justify state intervention is the belief that in certain instances governmental decision making is superior to private decision making. The assumption that consumers take decisions that maximise their welfare requires not only that consumers are *rational* but also that they are *informed* of the whole range of choices available and the consequences of these choices. Legislation restricting the free choice of individuals was one of the most important areas of government intervention during the 19th century and was a response primarily to pressure from social reformers. Examples are the Factory Acts limiting hours of work and prohibiting child employment, the licencing laws restricting the opening hours of public houses and the Education Acts which made schooling up to a minimum age compulsory. A more topical issue is whether motor car passengers should be obliged to wear safety belts. The justification for these limitations on freedom of choice lies in the presumed inability of some individuals to make choices that maximise their long-term welfare due to short-sightedness or lack of adequate information. The extent to which the State should undertake a paternalistic role in encouraging the consumption of certain goods and services by providing them free of charge remains an important issue between the two major parties. For example, while the income redistribution policies advocated by the Conservative Party emphasise the direct transfer of money income, the Labour Party has tended to favour the subsidised provision of medical services, council housing and even food (1974–76), together with a wide range of special benefits to meet the particular needs of individual groups.

Imperfection of the Market Economy: Inefficiencies in the System

Considerations of equity and justice are only one source of stimulus for the rapid 20th century growth of state economic intervention. Developments in economic theory this century have revealed the assumptions implicit in the conclusion that the competitive economy maximises efficiency and so reaches a welfare optimum in the Pareto sense. The development of welfare economics by Pigou during the 1920s, the analysis of imperfect competition by Chamberlin and Robinson during the 1930s, the theory of public goods, Lipsey and Lancaster's theory of second best (1956) and most importantly, Keynesian macroeconomic analysis, were all directed towards analysing failures of the market mechanism. We proceed by identifying some of the major sources of imperfection of the market economy, indicating the types of problem to which they give rise and outlining government policies that have attempted to remedy these problems.

The Problem of Monopoly

The maximisation of efficiency by the market economy is dependent on the existence of perfect competition. Perfect competition requires that buyers and sellers in markets are so numerous that no individual buyer or seller can influence market price, buyers and sellers all have full knowledge of the alternatives open to them, and there is complete mobility of resources. In practice, of course, these conditions can never fully be met. Moreover there is always an incentive among sellers and buyers to co-operate so as to limit competition. As Adam Smith noted: 'People of the same trade seldom meet together, even for merriment or diversion, but the conversation ends in a conspiracy against the public, or in some contrivance to raise prices.' (Smith 1910, p. 117)

But while the dangers of monopoly have long been recognised, legislation to maintain competition was not introduced until 1948 (the Monopolies and Restrictive Practices Act).

Even since then the attitudes of some governments to competition policy have been curiously ambivalent. While all governments have opposed the abuse of market power by large companies, there was a consistent trend between 1960 and 1979 to rely upon direct intervention by government into private industry rather than upon competition as a means of improving industrial performance (see Chapter 2).

Complex problems are posed in industries where economies of scale are present. For the government to prevent the emergence of monopoly in such industries will involve inefficiency through sub-optimally sized firms. One solution for the problem of these 'natural monopolies' is a government-regulated monopoly which enables exploitation of economies of scale without monopoly pricing. In Britain the problem of natural monopolies such as railways, postal services and the supply of electricity, gas and water has been dealt with by nationalisation of these industries (see Chapter 3).

Externalities

The operation of the invisible hand requires that individual welfare-maximising decisions by consumers and firms simultaneously maximise social welfare. The necessary condition is that the costs and benefits of any action to the individual (private costs and benefits) as measured by market prices are identical to the costs and benefits to society.

The identity will not hold where one individual's action affects the welfare of another individual and the external welfare effect is not taken into account in the individual's cost-benefit calculation. Externalities may be *external costs* – when a factory's smokey chimneys impose higher laundry and cleaning bills on neighbouring residents; or *external benefits* – when the eradication of insect pests on one farmer's land leads to higher crop yields for surrounding farmers.

The presence of externalities prevents the attainment of a Pareto optimum in the economy due to non-optimal output levels of different goods[3] and the adoption of inefficient techniques of production.[4] Two solutions to the problem of externalities are available to governments. First, externalities can be internalised so that private costs and benefits are made equal to social costs and benefits. This can be achieved either by legislative change forcing those responsible for external costs to provide compensation to others and allowing the propagators of external benefits to charge the beneficiaries, or by the adjustment of market prices by taxes and subsidies to take externalities into account. While the law of liability has not undergone any major changes as a result of the increasing awareness of the problem of externalities, adjustment of market prices by taxes and subsidies has been a growing area of government intervention. The imposition of petrol tax and road tax ensures that the motorist bears some of the costs of highway maintenance, pollution and congestion for which he is responsible. One area where external benefits are particularly important is innovation. To encourage the optimal quantity of productive resources into research and development, the government boosts the rewards from invention by the granting of patents, and reduces the cost of research by tax allowances and research grants.

Secondly, the government can calculate what is the socially optimal level of output to an activity where externalities are important and choose the socially least-cost technique of production and, by taking charge of the production of the good or service, directly determine the allocation of resources to the activity. The public provision of education and health services may be justified on the basis of the importance of external benefits to society from a skilled, healthy and well-educated populace. Chapters 6 and 7 discuss the rationale for the state provision of education and health services and the problems of determining output and securing efficiency in the absence of the profit motive. Nationalisation of certain unprofitable industries may also be justified with reference to externalities: railways confer external benefits in the form of reduced road congestion; coal-mining offers benefits to the economy as a whole by reducing imports of oil.

Public Goods

A special case of externalities relates to public goods. These are goods whose benefits are spread over the whole community irrespective of who actually purchases the good. For this reason public goods are sometimes called *collective* goods – they are consumed collectively by society as a whole rather than by individuals. Because an individual can benefit as much from other peoples' purchases of public goods as his own, there is little incentive for anyone to provide himself with public goods and consequently the market economy will under-allocate resources to these goods. For goods that are consumed collectively, provision must also be made collectively; since the market mechanism does not effectively operate for these goods, supply must be organised by the state.

The most important example of a public good is defence. An individual cannot protect himself from attack by a foreign power without simultaneously providing protection to the other members of his community. Consequently defence can only be effectively provided by the state and defence has traditionally been the primary function of government. During the post-war period defence spending has fallen sharply both as a proportion of total public expenditure and as a proportion of GNP. Other examples of public goods are the maintenance of law and order and the environmental benefits of clean air, unpolluted coastal waters and attractive urban planning.

A principal problem of the state provision of goods and services is the determination of the optimal allocation of resources to the activity. It is this problem that the technique of cost–benefit analysis attempts to solve by evaluating the desirability of public investment projects through the quantification of the social costs and benefits of the expenditure involved. Since almost all public investment projects generate benefits to some members of society and losses to others, cost–benefit analysis cannot unambiguously show that a project represents an increase in social welfare in the Pareto sense. Judging the net welfare effect in these cases invokes the *compensation principle*: are the gains of the beneficiaries sufficient to compensate the losers? If so, then the project represents a *potential* Pareto improvement. However, use of the compensation principle to justify the aggregation of costs and benefits necessitates inter-personal comparisons of utility which leads us from the path of positive economics into the field of value judgements.

General Equilibrium Problems

The imperfections of the market economy we have dealt with so far, although important in terms of particular problems, are of limited scope: monopoly, externality and public goods cause misallocations of resources, but they can be rectified by limited government intervention and call for the qualification rather than the abandonment of the concept of the invisible hand. By far the most important problems of the market economy, however, have arisen not from inefficiency in the employment of productive resources, but from the inability of the market economy to reach an equilibrium where all resources are employed.

Unemployment in 19th century Britain was a major source of poverty and during the course of the 19th century the business cycle, accompanied by periods of large-scale unemployment, became an increasingly apparent feature of the industrial economy. But the downturns in industrial activity of 1884–87, 1892–93 and 1921–22 proved to be only dress rehearsals for the Great Depression of the early 1930s. Government policies towards unemployment in the early years of the 20th century were directed at alleviating the hardship of unemployment rather than tackling the problem itself. In fact, any policy effectively to counteract unemployment was impossible due to the lack of understanding of the problem. The existence of large-scale involuntary unemployment was difficult to explain within the framework of price theory, for it implied a failure to reach equilibrium in the labour market. Explanations of unemployment during the first three decades of this century suggested that economic change combined with a lack of labour mobility (both occupationally and geographically), or a lack of wage flexibility due to trade union monopoly power, were to blame. Such explanations of unemployment were difficult to maintain during the inter-war years when the experience of the period not only created widespread disillusion over the usefulness of the neo-classical model in explaining the operation of the economy, but also finally discredited *laissez-faire* as a tenable basis for the role of the state.

Between 1921 and 1938 the unemployment rate never fell

below 9% and it reached a peak of 22% in 1932. The government responded by attempting to maintain confidence in the pound and the monetary system, using domestic deflation to support an overvalued exchange rate and seeking in vain to balance the public budget. The empirical weakness of a theory that assumed the automatic adjustment of the economy towards a full employment equilibrium and the failure of policies to deal with the crisis created an atmosphere receptive to new ideas. The breakthrough came with the publication of *A General Theory of Employment, Interest and Money* by John Maynard Keynes, a book that laid the structure of modern macroeconomic theory. While the significance of Keynes's contribution to economic theory is still the subject of continuing debate, the basic message for policy makers was clear: the market economy cannot be relied upon to adjust automatically to a full employment level of output; when demand from the private sector is insufficient to call forth an output that will employ all of the nation's resources, then it is up to the government to stimulate aggregate demand by expanding public expenditure to take up the slack.

Acceptance of Keynes's ideas was a gradual process. Although the 1944 White Paper on Employment Policy declared that 'The Government accept as one of their primary aims and responsibilities the maintenance of a high and stable level of employment', it was not until the 1950s that a contra-cyclical budgetary policy was consciously practised by Chancellors of the Exchequer. The detailed application of fiscal and monetary policy tools to the economy in order to achieve precise short-term targets for the major macro variables ('fine-tuning') developed during the 1960s, when the improvements in forecasting techniques resulting from the adoption of modern econometric methods by the Treasury gave increased scope for macroeconomic policy (see Chapter 10).

Economic Policy and the Political Process

So far we have viewed the increasing intervention of government in the economic system in terms of imperfections in the market mechanism and the guidelines suggested by economic analysis for action by government to increase social welfare. As an account of the forces influencing the formulation of economic policy this approach is misleading in two respects. First, advances in economic analysis have not in general been important in motivating new departures in economic policies. Extensions of the role of government have generally preceded their rationalisation by economic theory and have been in response to the pressures generated by events and politics. The public works programmes and budgetary deficits of British governments during the early 1930s occurred before the publication of the *General Theory*; the introduction of regional policies and the provision of public services preceded the development of regional development theories and the analysis of public goods. That is not to say that economics has not been influential in the realm of policy, but the role of theory has been more to improve, legitimise and clarify the working of policy tools rather than to encourage radical new departures. Where new developments in economic analysis have been influential in changing economic policy, it is generally only after a long lag. The voluntary adherence by British Chancellors of the Exchequer to money supply targets did not occur until the mid-1970s, although Friedman's restatement of the quantity theory of money was published in 1956 (Friedman 1956). More immediate impacts of economic ideas on policy can generally be accounted for by the special influence of certain individuals. The introduction in 1966 of selective employment tax and corporation tax has been attributed to the economic ideas of Lord Nicholas Kaldor, then a special adviser to government.

Second, the assumption that government policy is aimed at the furtherance of the economic welfare of society is difficult to reconcile either with the realities of the political process or the economic theory of individual behaviour which assumes utility maximisation. The analysis of government behaviour in terms of constitutional structure and the utility maximising behaviour of the various actors in the political process is a relatively new area of economic analysis associated with the work of Anthony Downs (1957), Kenneth Arrow (1963), James Buchanan (1972) and Gordon Tullock (1965).

The principal features of the British political system which influence the choice of government policies are:

(1) *The behaviour of political parties.* Political parties may be regarded as being interested principally in gaining office. Their strategy, therefore, is one of vote maximisation. In a two-party system vote maximisation will result in the policies of both parties tending to identify with the preferences of the median voter, the result being consensus politics. Convergence of the economic policies of the Conservative and Labour Parties has been a noticeable feature of the post-war period, notably during the 1950s when the term *Butskellism* was coined (after R.A. Butler, the Conservative Chancellor, and Hugh Gaitskell, the Labour leader). Policies will also reflect other influences, however, notably the influence of party members (whose views are likely to be more extreme than those of the median voter) and the sources of finance of the party (the trade unions in the case of Labour, business in the case of the Conservatives).

(2) *The political behaviour of individuals and groups.* Individuals exert influence upon the government primarily through voting but also through the formation of pressure groups and through participation in party organisation. In all cases participation involves costs to the individual, principally in time. Thus political activity will reflect the strength of individuals' motivations. Since most people's earnings are dependent upon a single activity while their expenditures are diversified, it follows that political activity is likely to reflect the producer rather than the consumer interests of individuals. The powerful influence exerted by the two major producer interests in the UK, the CBI and the TUC, on economic policy is notable in this respect. At the European level, the existence of the Common Agricultural Policy is an excellent example of government intervention to benefit a minority producer group at the expense of consumers (see Chapter 4).

(3) *The behaviour of the executive.* The executive branch of British government comprises government ministers,

drawn from the MPs of the majority party, and the Civil Service. Its motivation is of great importance since in comparison with other countries the British executive is immensely powerful: through the party system government ministers control both Parliament and the machinery of government. The economic theory of bureaucracy suggests that utility maximisation by the administrator will involve him in attempting to maximise his income, number of subordinates, status and influence – most of which will be related to the size of budget he controls. Government ministers will of course be subject to additional influences – notably the desire to further their political careers and the need for their party to be re-elected. However not only are ministers dependent upon their full-time officials, but their desire for influence and status will encourage them to support the expansionist goals of their officials. The result is a strong bias towards expansion of the public sector and a preference for government planning and intervention, as opposed to reliance upon the market economy. The trend towards detailed state intervention is apparent in many areas of public policy during the 1960s and 70s, not least in industrial policy (see Chapter 2).

Directions in Economic Policy Since 1960

Political debate over economic policy has closely reflected the ideological traditions of the two major parties. The Labour Party, with its origins in industrial trade unionism and the socialist philosophies of the turn of the century, has consistently favoured a transfer of ownership and control from the private to the public sector. This preference reflects a distaste for private profit as a medium of motivation and reward and a distrust of profit incentives as a secure basis for the long-term prosperity of society. The Conservative Party has emphasised the dynamism of the free enterprise economy and, in the interests of efficiency and the safeguarding of individual liberties, has preferred policy to operate through the market system rather than to replace markets by government planning.

During the post-war period the differences between the

parties over the economic policies have related to *means* rather than to the *ends* of policy. Unanimity over policy objectives reflects the constancy of certain major problems (such as balance of payments weakness and inflation) and the need for both parties to appeal to the 'middle ground' of political opinion. Thus both parties have accepted the macro-economic stabilisation of the economy, full employment, the welfare state, the maintenance of competition in industry, regional development programmes and the nationalisation of certain basic industries (e.g. the energy industries and rail and air transport). Even on income distribution, where the objectives of the two parties might be expected to diverge considerably, there is no consistent evidence of a greater tendency towards equality under Labour than under Conservative governments.

The divergence in the economic philosophies is more clearly reflected in election manifestos than in the policy conduct of governments. The Labour Party has been the principal advocate of economic planning and was responsible for the National Plan of 1966–67 and the Industrial Strategy of 1974–79. It has favoured expanding the public sector through nationalisation (e.g. of steel in 1965 and aircraft and shipbuilding in 1976) and the extension of public ownership into the private sector (e.g. the Industrial Reorganisation Corporation 1966–70 and the National Enterprise Board 1975–79). The Conservative Party has placed greater emphasis on the market: reductions in direct taxation aimed at encouraging individual effort and enterprise have been regarded as the most effective means of encouraging growth; income transfers rather than the universal provision of welfare benefits are the favoured means of income redistribution; indirect control of inflation through monetary restraint has been preferred to wage–price controls.

In government, however, the convergent tendencies of successive Labour and Conservative economic policies are clearly apparent. Under both parties the public sector – whether measured by revenue, expenditure or employment – has continued to grow and the extent of direct intervention by government into the economy has increased. Although economic planning is identified more closely with the Labour

Party, it was a Conservative Government which inaugurated indicative planning with the establishment of the National Economic Development Council in 1962. Despite the Conservative Party's preference for monetary restraint over wage–price controls, it was the Labour Chancellors Roy Jenkins and Denis Healey who were initially associated with strict controls over monetary growth, and it was the 1970–74 Conservative administration which introduced the most comprehensive controls over prices and incomes. During the 1970s selective industrial intervention increased under both parties. Despite pronouncements in 1970 of a tough approach to industrial 'lame-ducks', it was the 1970–74 Conservative Government which gave assistance to Rolls Royce, Upper Clyde Shipbuilders and British Leyland and established the framework for detailed industrial intervention in the 1972 Industry Act.

The tendency for governments of both parties to abandon ideology and seek similar solutions to the same problems reflects the limited room for manoeuvre in economic policy. While both parties have proposed fundamental reforms to the economic system of the country, the course of economic policy has been dictated by short-term considerations. The associated problems of inflation, balance of payments weakness and pressure on sterling occasioned the abandonment of the National Plan (1967), the introduction by a Conservative Government of wage–price controls (1972), and the progressive watering-down of the Industrial Strategy (1976–79). The political sensitivity of the electorate to unemployment has encouraged all governments to provide selective assistance to industry for the maintenance of employment.

The intractability of the problems of unemployment, low growth, balance of payments weakness and inflation has been a major factor encouraging governments to seek new and more direct methods of intervention in the economy. The use of fiscal and monetary instruments to 'fine-tune' the economy has been subject to particular criticism, with claims that Keynesian policies have been ineffective, destabilising or inflationary (see Chapter 9). The inability of macroeconomic policies to halt the rise in unemployment from 2.6% in the beginning of 1970 to a post-war peak of 5.9% at the end of

1977 resulted in direct maintenance and creation of employment through financial support to insolvent companies, temporary employment subsidies and job creation schemes. To boost economic growth, governments have taken an increasingly active role in directing resources to growth sectors. Various schemes have been introduced to subsidise research and development and to give financial help to the establishment of new projects in areas of new technology – the role of the Department of Industry and National Enterprise Board in the development of micro-electronics is a notable example. To improve the balance of trade in manufactured products and safeguard the prosperity of British industry, direct controls over manufactured imports have been proposed (Cambridge Economic Policy Review, April 1979). In the control of inflation the ineffectiveness of traditional policies of demand managements has caused governments to look in two directions for solutions. On the one hand governments have introduced direct controls over prices and incomes; on the other there has been a return to pre-Keynesian notions of price stability through monetary stability and budgetary orthodoxy (the monetarist thesis is presented in Chapter 11).

The ineffectiveness of fiscal policies and other policy instruments which operate through the price mechanism reflects in part the evolution of the UK economy from a competitively structured market economy where economic theory can be employed to predict the responses of the private sector with some degree of accuracy. Growing concentration has been a general feature of the economy – by 1972 41% of UK manufacturing net output was accounted for by the 100 largest industrial firms, while the 11 largest trade unions accounted for 63% of total union membership. Galbraith's analysis (1968) views the structure and behaviour of the modern industrial economy as determined chiefly by the need for long-term planning by monopolistic industrial corporations. Within the corporate economy not only are the effects of fiscal policy tools likely to be weak and unpredictable, but government and industry are forced into a relationship of mutual cooperation such that economic policy can succeed only with the collaboration of industry.

Whether or not the Galbraithian thesis is accepted as an accurate description of the working of the UK economic system, the trend of UK economic policy clearly demonstrates the necessity for close cooperation between government and the chief centres of economic power. Since the founding of the NEDC in 1962, economic policy has involved consultation and cooperation between government, the TUC and the CBI. Where governments have not had the cooperation of the trade unions the result has been the reduced effectiveness of economic policy (e.g. the collapse of the 5% incomes guideline in 1978) or even the collapse of government itself (e.g. the March 1974 election defeat of the Conservative Party following general union opposition to wage control and a strike by miners).

Although interventionist policies based on joint action by government, business and unions gives greater effectiveness to economic policy, the need for cooperation from industry and unions also limits the range of policy options which can be considered by government. Thus in order to gain TUC consent to wage restraint, the 1974–79 Labour Government committed itself to a number of policies desired by the unions including industrial relations, public expenditure and price control.

At the time of writing it is apparent that the benefits of North Sea oil to the balance of payments have produced a profound change in the background against which economic policy must be formulated. For virtually the whole of the post-war period successive governments have grappled with the recurring problems of the balance of payments, which have severely constrained economic policy options. The lifting of this constraint by the North Sea windfall means that the range of opportunities for medium and longer term economic policies is considerably expanded. The importance of choosing the correct policies cannot be over-emphasised. At one extreme it is possible that the respite from the short-term constraints which have dogged economic expansion in the UK could enable the economy to make the transition into a new era of productivity growth and capital accumulation. At the other extreme the temporary benefits of North Sea oil to the balance of payments, the pound sterling and to living standards could have the effect only of increasing the lack of competitiveness of British exports and accelerating the industrial decline of the UK.

Notes

1. Since 1931 GDP in real terms has declined in only 3 years: 1958, 1974 and 1975.
2. In the 1979 general election, the proposition that high marginal rates of income tax reduced national prosperity by discouraging effort and initiative was an important feature of the Conservative Party's manifesto.
3. In the above example of the farmer with crop-ravaging insects, the consumption of pesticide is too low. If the farmer could be induced financially by his neighbours to use more pesticide, then both the farmer and his neighbours could be made better off.
4. In the case of the factory's smoke emissions, if the extra cost of a smokeless production technique is less than the cost savings in laundry bills to the local residents, then the existing technique is inefficient. The residents could pay the factory owners to use the smokeless method and both groups could be made better off.

References

Arrow, Kenneth, *Social Choice and Individual Values*, Yale University Press 1963.

Bastiat, Frederic, *Economic Sophisms*, Van Nostrand 1964 (translated by Arthur Goddard) (first published 1846).

Buchanan, J.M., *Theory of Public Choice: Political Applications of Economics*, Michigan University Press 1972.

Downs, Anthony, *An Economic Theory of Democracy*, Harper 1957.

Friedman, Milton (ed.), *Studies in the Quantity Theory of Money*, University of Chicago Press 1956.

Friedman, Milton, *Capitalism and Freedom*, Chicago University Press 1962.

Hayek, F.A., *The Road to Serfdom*, Routledge & Kegan Paul 1976 (first published 1944).

Kohler, Heinz, *Economics: the Science of Scarcity*, Dryden Press 1970.

Pareto, Vilfredo, *Manuale di Economia Politica*, 1906.

Smith, Adam, *An Inquiry into the Nature and Causes of the Wealth of Nations*, Dent 1910 (first published 1776).

Tullock, Gordon, *The Politics of Bureaucracy*, Public Affairs Press 1965.

Suggestions for Further Reading

A comprehensive account of economic policy 1960–74: Blackaby, F. (ed.), *British Economic Policy 1960–74,* NIESR 1978.

On Western economic development: Heilbronner, R.L., *The Making of Economic Society* (4th edn), Prentice Hall 1972.

On the relationship between economic policy and economic thought in Britain and America during the 20th century: Winch, D., *Economics and Policy,* Hodder & Stoughton 1969.

On welfare economics in general: Bohm, Peter, *Social Efficiency,* Macmillan 1973.

On the analytics of Pareto optima under perfect competition: Lancaster, K., *Introduction to Modern Microeconomics,* Rand McNally 1969, Chapter 10.

PART II

Microeconomic Policy

2. Industry and manpower policy

KEITH HARTLEY
Reader in Economics,
University of York

The Policy Debate

Since the late 1950s, UK government policy towards industry and manpower has become more extensive and increasingly controversial. The trend has been away from general policies aimed at 'setting the rules' and then relying on market forces to allocate resources and determine industrial structure. Instead, governments have become more active in intervening within industries, culminating in greater intervention at the level of the firm. During the 1970s, controversy has raged over policy towards manufacturing industry and the public sector, reflecting concern about 'de-industrialisation'. Doubts have been expressed about the traditional emphasis on aggregate demand policies to the relative neglect of the supply side of the economy and its microeconomic foundations. There have been differences between the major political parties on the extent and appropriate form of state intervention in industry. Labour governments have preferred interventionist policies in the form of an Industrial Strategy, supported by the National Enterprise Board, state ownership, planning agreements and an extensive system of subsidies. Conservative governments have preferred market solutions, with a smaller public sector and reduced state intervention, withdrawals of industry and manpower subsidies with more emphasis on competition policy, and lower personal taxation to increase incentives for managers, workers and small firms, the aim being job creation rather than preservation. At the centre of this policy debate are increasing worries about unemployment in the 1980s and pessimism over the prospects for the UK economy's future competitiveness and growth rate. Some forecasts suggest a jobs 'gap' of 2.4 million in the early 1980s, with the need to create some 1.2 million additional jobs in order to reduce unemployment to 1 million (Manpower Services Commission, Review 1978). Conflicts are likely to arise, at least in the short run, between policies aimed at improving competitiveness and industrial efficiency, and policies aimed at job preservation. Understandably, there is concern about the employment effects of new technology, particularly micro-electronics. In the circumstances, the twin problems of unemployment and an inefficient UK economy have added new elements to the policy debate. Proposals have been made for import controls and increased worker participation to achieve industrial democracy.

How can economists contribute to this policy debate? Rather than attempt a superficial and chronological description of recent policies, this chapter will show how industry and manpower policy can be analysed as aspects of applied microeconomics. The emphasis will be on the contribution of economic theory to understanding policy issues, with the central unit of analysis being the firm as a buyer of labour and other factors, and a seller of goods and services in different market situations. Two groups of questions will be considered. First, why does the state need an industry and manpower policy? This involves the methodology of economic policy and the market failure paradigm. Second, how can economic theory be used to evaluate specific policy measures? Detailed consideration will be given to three broad policy issues, namely government policies towards industry, competition and subsidies.

Why do Governments Intervene in Industry and Labour Markets?

Policy debates always involve questions about the 'proper'

role of government in the economy. In particular, should the state intervene, in which sectors, to what extent and in what form? For example, should governments intervene in the micro-electronics industry or favour the manufacturing sector; should policy be applied to all firms or a selected group, and should intervention be in the form of subsidies (to firms, capital or labour), nationalisation, competition or merger policy, or import controls? The methodology of economic policy provides a framework for answering these questions (Hartley 1977a, Ch. 1). Applied to a policy such as the Industrial Strategy, it would require consideration of the objectives of the Strategy, the causes of de-industrialisation and the choice of the Strategy as the preferred solution from a range of alternatives. Economic theory approaches these issues *starting* from Paretian welfare economics. If society wishes to achieve an optimum allocation of resources, within a private enterprise economy, then economic theory suggests that 'properly functioning' competitive markets are 'desirable'. This provides the basis for some broad guidelines for industry and manpower policy. State intervention might be required whenever product and labour markets are failing to work properly (i.e. where there are substantial departures from the competitive ideal). Such failures are likely where there are imperfections in the form of monopolies, oligopolies and restrictive practices, and where there are beneficial or harmful externalities (See Chapter 1, pp. 21–26). At this point, the economist has to be careful in distinguishing between the *technical* issues, concerned with the causes of market failure, and the *policy* issues, concerned with the choice of the most appropriate solution. Even if imperfections are identified as the main source of market failure, policymakers have to choose between such alternative measures as increased competition, reduced tariff barriers, price and profit controls on monopolies and the regulation of trade union restrictive practices. Similarly, externalities might be 'corrected' through tax-subsidy policy, legislative changes in property rights or public ownership. However, problems arise in 'operationalising' Paretian welfare economics and relating it to the declared objectives of British governments with their full employment, price stability, balance of payments, growth and distributional targets. An integration (if somewhat tenuous) can be achieved by regarding these policy targets as a general social welfare function showing the 'bundle of goods' which contribute to the utility or welfare of individuals in society. In this way, industry and manpower policy form the microeconomic foundations of macroeconomic policy objectives.

Traditionally, the rationalisation by economists of state intervention has been in terms of market failure. Recent developments in the economics of politics and bureaucracies provide, however, an alternative explanation of industry and manpower policy. The economics of politics recognises that governments operate in a political market place of voters, parties and bureaucracies. As vote-maximisers, parties offer policies in return for votes, whilst bureaus supply information, goods and services to governments and aim to maximise their budgets. Four predictions of the model are relevant to explaining UK industry and labour policies. First, in a two-party democracy, there will be consensus politics with both parties agreeing on any issues favoured by a majority of voters. This was evident, for example, between 1970 and 1975 when both major political parties developed similar policies towards 'lame ducks' (e.g. Rolls Royce, British Leyland) and towards training and manpower policy (e.g. Manpower Services Commission and the 1973 Employment and Training Act). Second, parties do attempt to differentiate their policies, but movements towards the political extremes of complete *laissez-faire* or total collectivism are likely to be constrained by the potential losses of moderate voters. The Labour Government's 1974 Regeneration of British Industry policy with its proposals for a 'powerful' National Enterprise Board (NEB), an extension of state ownership and the large-scale use of planning agreements is an example of an attempt at 'differentiation': it was subsequently modified and appeared in 1975 in a different, and less radical, form as 'An Approach to Industrial Strategy' (HMSO 1974 and 1975). Third, producer interest groups are dominant since they have the most to gain from influencing government policy in their favour. The Sector Working Parties of the Industrial Strategy can be regarded as interest groups comprising industrialists and trade unionists. Fourth, bureaucracies aiming to maximise their budgets have every incentive to over-estimate the demand for, and under-estimate the costs of, preferred policies. On this basis, there is a presumption that industry and manpower activities which are directly supported by the Department of Industry and the Manpower Services Commission will be 'too large' (Hartley, 1977a, Chs. 3 and 11). In total, the economics of politics recognises that the actual operation of economic policies cannot be divorced from the motives and behaviour of both politicians and bureaucrats. As a result, it is being recognised increasingly that whilst markets can fail, solutions involving state intervention also have potential for failure!

It remains to be shown how this methodology can be used to assess current policy debates. The examples selected are topical and embrace both industry and manpower. Should a government have policies towards industry, competition and subsidies? Initially, it is necessary to consider views about the policy problem and its causes before assessing the appropriateness of different solutions.

The Policy Problem and its Causes

Policy-makers are aiming at a high-output–high-wage economy. Given this objective, it is generally agreed that the policy problem is the relative decline of UK industry, especially the manufacturing sector, and the need to reverse this decline. The evidence is persuasive. The UK's share of world trade in manufactures has declined from around 20% in 1955 to under 10% in the late 1970s. Rising imports into the home market have cast doubts on the competitiveness of UK firms and their supply responsiveness. Examples include cars, domestic electrical appliances, footwear, motorcycles and textiles. This increasing import penetration has meant that changes in aggregate demand have had less effect on UK output and hence employment and a greater effect on the balance of payments. Other studies have shown that labour productivity in the USA is over 50% higher than in the UK, whilst in Germany it is 35% higher and in France over a quarter higher. Whilst variations in scale and capital equipment might explain about one-half of the difference in productivity between the UK and Germany, the remainder reflects efficiency differences between the two countries – i.e. variations in the extent of competition, managerial motivation, overmanning, strikes and restrictive work practices (Pratten 1976). In the case of motor vehicles, it was found that, compared with West European firms, British manufacturers were at a unit cost disadvantage of some 10% on volume-produced cars (CPRS 1975). Such evidence suggests that, on average, there is more inefficiency or 'slack' in the UK. Does this constitute a problem requiring state intervention and, if so, is some type of industrial policy required or is competition policy a more appropriate solution to a general inefficiency? In the circumstances, it is even more fascinating to contemplate the relevance and role of subsidy policy!

The advocates of interventionist policies of the Industrial Strategy type (Labour Government, 1975–9) maintain that: 'the health of manufacturing industry is of vital importance to our national economic performance. Our manufacturing industry has not done as well as its competitors. In particular, it has not responded adequately to changes in the pattern of world trade and suffers from structural rigidities which show themselves in bottlenecks both of manpower and components in the early stages of economic upturns' (HMSO 1975, p. 4). This is by no means a clear and unambiguous statement of the policy problem and the first task for the economist is to seek clarification. For example, it is alleged that industry has not responded 'adequately'. But what would be an 'adequate' response and why has industry failed to respond adequately: is it because of 'structural rigidities'? If so, what are these rigidities, where do they exist and why? The assertion seems to be that these rigidities show themselves in 'bottlenecks'. But if a 'bottleneck' means excess demand in labour and product markets, relative prices might be expected to adjust to clear the market. Are upward adjustments prevented because of market imperfections or are they policy-created through government controls on prices and incomes? And if the bottlenecks are in manpower, this suggests that a manpower policy is required rather than an industrial policy. Indeed, there is a potential conflict between a state commitment to job saving and 'lame duck' firms on the one hand, and, on the other, a desire to raise the economy's growth rate with the required re-allocation of resources, especially manpower, from the declining to the expanding sectors (with the implications for job information, training and labour mobility). Nevertheless, the advocates of an Industrial Strategy argue that it aims to increase '. . . the national rate of growth through regenerating our industrial structure and improving efficiency' (HMSO 1975, p. 6). Consideration must now be given to policy-makers' views about the causes of the problem.

In the late 1970s, the general policy view was that if left to themselves, market forces will fail to improve our economic performance. Indeed, one model suggested a circular and cumulative chain of causation: the prediction that once a nation starts on a decline, it will continue to contract and experience a vicious downward spiral (Blackaby 1979, Ch. 9). Difficulties arise in determining whether the UK economy is trapped in a vicious downward spiral or is experiencing a period of resource re-allocation and structual adjustment resulting from changing demands and changing comparative advantages in world markets. The policy analysis of the late 1970s specified capital and labour markets together with public policy as the main causes of the poor performance of UK manufacturing industry (HMSO 1975, p. 5).

Within capital markets, emphasis was placed on investment and finance. Investment was believed to be 'too low' and 'poorly' chosen, with capital being utilised inefficiently. But what constitutes the 'correct' rate of investment, why is it low and why is it being used inefficiently? Nor is it clear what is a 'good' investment choice, especially when such decisions are *ex ante* and made under uncertainty. As for finance, the policy view seems to be that the capital market is imperfect and 'fails' to give priority to the 'needs' of industry. But what are the causes of capital market failure, what are the 'needs' of industry and whose interpretation of 'need' is being used? Within labour markets, the government has diagnosed market failure in the form of skilled labour shortages, and low labour productivity, reflecting 'poor' management, 'inadequate' consultation, restrictive practices, overmanning and disruption by industrial action. Once again, attention is given to *effects* rather than *causes*. Questions have to be asked about the causes of 'poor' management, the reasons for restrictive practices, overmanning and strikes; and the contribution, if any, of public policy to 'solving' these problems. Finally, government policy was identified as a cause of our poor performance. 'Stop–go' policies were believed to make it difficult for companies to plan ahead. However, it is not obvious how improvements can be made in government *ex ante* decision-making under uncertainty. The employment contract in the Civil Service provided little incentive to efficiency, and no monitoring of performance. Civil servants have every incentive to be risk-averse, delegating all decisions and responsibility to the amorphous committee. Policy was also criticised because of the 'pre-emption of resources by the public sector and by personal consumption to the detriment of industry's investment and export performance' (HMSO 1975, p. 5). The emphasis on the public sector being 'too large' resembles the de-industrialisation hypothesis: too few producers. This explains Britain's economic performance in terms of the growing shift of resources from the production of goods and services which can be *marketed* at home and overseas to the provision of *unmarketed* public services. According to the de-industrialisation thesis, the shift to non-marketed public services 'explains' the economy's low growth rate, its balance of payments and investment performances, as well as 'obstructive' trade union behaviour (Bacon and Eltis 1978).

Some general comments and criticisms can be made of this analysis of industrial problems. First, evidence suggests that Britain's low productivity is to a large extent due to factors concerning *motivation and efficiency* and has little to do with factors such as *scale* and *capital stock*. Nor is industrial structure a cause of the British problem. A comparison of UK and West German manufacturing industry found similar industrial structures in both countries and yet the difference in performance was substantial (Panic 1976). In other words, the relative failure of UK industry was one of performance rather than structure. Significantly for selective industrial policy, the relatively poor UK performance was not confined to a few industrial groups but was spread throughout Britain's manufacturing sector. Second, in assessing the alleged causes of the problem, we need to ask if there is anything 'special, unique or different' about manufacturing industry. Services and the 'dynamic' nature of manufacturing cannot be ignored. A policy emphasis on production tends to neglect the service and other non-manufacturing sectors with their potential contributions to employment, balance of payments and growth. However, the supporters of manufacturing argue that it is the *dynamic* sector of the economy. It is reputed to be the sector with the greatest potential for technical progress and increasing returns to scale and hence for productivity growth. In other words, the growth model is one in which the UK's growth rate depends on the growth of its manufacturing sector. However, the possibility arises that some of the beliefs about the relative lack of technical progress in non-manufacturing activities reflect the problems of measuring productivity and output in these sectors. Certainly technical progress occurs outside manufacturing. Examples include the application of computers in offices, banks and foreign exchange markets; high-speed trains and jumbo jets; automation in hotels and underground transport; supermarkets and hypermarkets; the use of vehicles and radios to replace policemen 'on the beat' and the substitution of capital for labour in the Armed Forces and in the household. Such examples show that consideration has to be given to the concept of an 'optimum' economic structure.

Welfare economics suggests that an optimal economic and industrial structure can be determined by market forces in the form of British and foreign consumer preferences, and the competitiveness of domestic and foreign firms. In this way, a properly working competitive market will determine the optimal allocation of resources between manufacturing and services and between regions, as well as the optimum size of both firms and the manufacturing sector. However, private markets might fail to determine the optimum size of the public sector. Some products and services desired by society might not be provided by private markets or might be under-provided. Examples include public goods such as national defence, law and order and arrangements for regulating and administering the operation of markets such as state agencies for competition, anti-pollution and health policies (see Chapter 1, pp. 22–24). These sources of market failure do not, of course, imply that the existing public sector in the UK is of optimal size (whatever this might mean). Even if the arguments for state finance of some activities were acceptable (which activities and why?), there remain extensive possibilities for the *private provision* of services which in the UK are publicly provided: examples include government skill-centres, job-centres, road and air transport, public utilities, education, health and local authority services such as refuse collection and direct works departments for housing and road projects. Nor is it sufficient to argue that many state activities are justified by decreasing costs, since the economics of bureaucracies predicts this outcome from bureaucrats trying to estimate the government's demand curve for the activity when, in fact, they could be operating under constant or increasing costs!

Industry Policy

Given the policy problem and its perceived causes, one solution was an Industrial Strategy of the type operated by the Labour Government between 1975 and 1979. This policy aimed to '. . . remove obstacles to the growth of some of our key industries . . . ' (HMSO 1975, p. 3). These are not easy to define once we recognise the inevitable interdependencies associated with any general equilibrium framework. However, policy defined 'key' industries in terms of size and export performance, their importance to the rest of the economy (e.g. components) and their potential success. Some forty Sector Working Parties were formed covering industries such as clothing, domestic electrical appliances, electronics, machine tools, office machinery and telecommunications. Each Sector Working Party operated within NEDC and consisted of businessmen, trade unionists and civil servants. As such, they formed an interest group where producers and bureaucrats have every incentive to combine so as to protect or raise their incomes. This can have implications for the ways in which interest groups and bureaucracies present information to government decision-makers. Thus, the Department of Industry and Manpower Services Commission and Sector Working Parties can use the 'national interest' to justify greater state involvement in 'protecting' the nation's industrial base and in 'maintaining' jobs. It can be argued that a scheme (e.g. Concorde) is 'vital' to prevent the country 'sliding down the league table', and that we must 'go ahead and subsidise a project because our rivals have done so' (e.g. shipbuilding). References will be made to 'social benefits' of schemes in the form of their contribution to balance of payments, employment and high technology targets. On the cost side, estimates might not be presented on a consistent price basis with, say, 1975 expenditures simply added to 1980 outlays: this, plus the omission of interest charges and the neglect of any social costs, will under-state the true opportunity cost of a project. Then, further 'pressure' can be placed on government decision-makers by arguing that if the project does not 'go ahead' and is cancelled, all the previous expenditure will be 'wasted' and 'valuable' research teams and skilled labour forces will be 'broken-up and lost for ever'.

Persuasive though many of these arguments appear, they tend to be long on emotion and short on economic analysis and empirical support. For example, use of the word 'vital' invites such questions as: vital to whom, and is it vital regardless of cost? The argument that 'rivals are subsidising' is dubious, since if they wish to offer free gifts, we could respond by accepting them and specialising elsewhere. Indeed, in evaluating any scheme, consideration has to be given to the likely costs and benefits of alternatives, including a 'do nothing' option. Nor is the social benefit argument convincing in the absence of empirical support showing that the alleged benefits are greater than could be obtained from alternative uses of the resources. After all, any economic activity involves jobs so, if governments are obsessed with employment targets, they have to consider whether a proposed scheme results in more employment than could be obtained from alternative projects. This involves a comparison between, say, state aid for British Leyland compared with similar expenditures for other firms, or for labour mobility, re-training and job information policies. Arguments about cancellation are also confusing, since previous expenditures are 'sunk' costs, where sacrifices have already been incurred. Nor is cancellation necessarily 'wasteful': it may be cheaper than continuing with the project and past expenditures can provide benefits through adding to society's stock of information and knowledge. The general point to be made is that there are opportunities for analysing the behaviour of bureaucracies and committees, such as the Sector Working Parties. These groups usually lack efficiency incentives to achieve the declared policy objectives. Indeed, they usually have discretion in interpreting objectives and, normally, committee members do not have an employment contract which rewards success and penalises failure. Unlike private firms, such committees are not at risk. If they are 'wrong', the impersonal committee is to blame and the tax-payer finances the cost of failure! This is particularly worrying since uncertainty is a major problem for any industrial policy. Today's bottlenecks might be tomorrow's surpluses.

Uncertainty will always exist about future changes in demand and supply in both the UK and in world markets. The comparative advantages and disadvantages of UK industries is not fixed forever. But if industrial policy involves the state in 'picking the winners', it cannot avoid choices under uncertainty. Which are likely to be the new growth sectors over the next five, ten or twenty years? The debate about high technology is a good example. The supporters of advanced technology, such as aerospace, computers, electronics, micro-processers and nuclear power, maintain that competition in world markets has resulted in the loss of many of Britain's traditional exports (e.g. textiles, ships, cars, motorcycles, TVs). It is asserted that in the future we shall be increasingly unable to compete with low-wage countries in established products: hence, it is claimed that Britain's future competitive-ness depends upon greater specialisation in advanced tech-nological goods. But what is the role of the state in high technology: should it intervene, and, if so, why and in which sectors? To economists, the general issue involves the most appropriate institutional and policy arrangements for respond-ing to uncertainty. One solution would be to allow private markets to operate with governments 'correcting' any major market failures. Where there are a large number of private economic agents with a diversity of views about the future and with their funds at risk, some are more likely to guess the future more accurately, and there are always opportunities for new entrances and exits. On the other hand, if there is only one central decision-making body – and this is the worry with an Industrial Strategy – there is a greater chance of it being wrong! And here, the state's record in high technology projects is far from impressive (e.g. aerospace, nuclear power). Nevertheless, there is analytical support for a public policy towards research and invention. Competitive markets might under-invest in research because of the difficulties of establishing complete property rights in marketable ideas, the risk of research and increasing returns in the use of information (marginal cost pricing problem). But even if this analysis is accepted, it does not necessarily constitute a *prima facie* case for state support of any specific sector, such as micro-electronics or aerospace.

Industrial policy also involves debates about the form of state intervention. Whilst there might be general agreement about the policy problem and its causes, disagreements arise over the most appropriate solution. Supporters of an Industrial Strategy favour state agencies, such as the National Enterprise Board, designed to re-structure British industry through encouraging mergers, supporting lame ducks and promoting new enterprise. In the late 1970s, the NEB was a major shareholder in such firms as British Leyland, Fairey, Ferranti, Inmos and Rolls Royce, embracing aerospace, cars, electronics, engineering, machine tools and micro-electronics. State involvement in re-structuring industry is often justified in terms of increased efficiency. Critics maintain that competition policy is more appropriate for removing imperfections and improving efficiency in product, capital and labour markets.

Industrial Re-structuring and Competition Policy

Some critics of the UK economy maintain that in many sectors of industry firm sizes are too small to obtain the benefits of scale economies and to undertake the research and development required to compete in world markets. It is then alleged that the capital market will fail to undertake the 'desired' re-structuring, so that a state intervention (through, for example, an agency such as the Industrial Reorganisation

Corporation or the National Enterprise Board) is required to correct market failure. What evidence might be used by such a state agency? A starting point must be the determinants of firm size and industry structure.

Theory explains the size of a firm in terms of its objectives (e.g. profits, sales or managerial satisfaction) and the underlying demand and cost conditions. The traditional U-shaped long-run average cost curve, reflecting economies and dis-economies of scale, represents the cost factors determining firm size and industry structure. Where scale economies are substantial, the UK market might only be able to support one or a relatively small number of firms, so that there will be a conflict between efficient scale ('optimum' size of firm) and competition. The price of efficient scale might be a domestic monopoly, with possible adverse effects on prices, outputs, technical efficiency, consumer choice and innovation. To clarify such policy conflicts, evidence is required on the extent of scale economies in the UK and the cost implications of substantial departures from efficient scale.

In general, the evidence on long-run average cost curves in the UK, Western Europe and the USA shows that typically they are L-shaped, sloping downwards at first and then tending to become horizontal. The point at which scale economies are largely exhausted is called the *minimum efficient scale* (mes). There is little evidence of dis-economies of scale: this may reflect their complete absence, or that firms have chosen to avoid such sizes. Or, it might reflect the difficulties of estimating long-run average cost curves. British evidence indicates that for manufacturing industry as a whole, unit costs might fall by about 10% when output is doubled from one-half of *mes*. Actual experience is varied, as shown in table 1. Clearly, the supporters of NEB-type industrial re-structuring will tend to focus on industries where *mes* is a large percentage of UK output and where departures from *mes* involve substantial cost penalties. But such re-structuring is likely to create domestic oligopolies and monopolies. British legislation defines a monopoly situation where a firm has a market share of 25% or more. Table 1 shows industries where scale efficiency requires high levels of seller concentration (group I) and those where scale efficiency is compatible with a competitive

Table 1. *Scale economies in the UK*

Industry	*Minimum efficient scale of plant as a percentage of UK output*	*Percentage increase in unit costs at 50% mes compared with costs at mes*
Group I: mes ⩾ 25% of UK output		
Turbo-generators	120–200	5
Aircraft	100+	20
Electronics (radar, computers, calculators)	100+	8–10
Machine tools	100+	5
Dyes	100	22
Refrigerators, washing machines	50–69	8
Electric motors	60	15
Diesel engines	56	4
Cars	29–57	6
Chemicals	27–31	9
Steel	8–37	5–10
Group II: mes ⩽ 10% of UK output		
Cement	7–11	9
Oil refining	10	5
Bicycles	8	small
Bread	0.5–1.0	15
Bricks	0.5	25
Footwear	0.2	2

Sources: C. Pratten, *Economies of Scale in Manufacturing Industry*, Cambridge University Press 1971.
Cmnd 7198, *A Review of Monopolies and Mergers Policy*, HMSO 1978.

structure (group II). However, the evidence from individual industry studies can give a misleading impression that scale economies for a country's manufacturing industry as a whole are more important than is the case on average. After all, if there are major cost reductions from larger scale, why do they remain unexploited? In many instances, the cost penalty of operating below *mes* is quite small. One study found that at one-third of optimal scale, a cost penalty of under 5%

was found in nearly half of the products studied, and of less than 10% for three quarters of the sample (Scherer 1973).

The standard analysis of scale economies is static and it neglects the possible relationship between the size of a firm and cost-reducing dynamic factors. Technical progress and learning economies are the dynamic sources of lower costs. Supporters of large firms in monopoly or oligopoly markets maintain that they promote technical progress. For example, in the UK between 1954 and 1970, large firms (employing 1,000 or more) accounted for 80% of all innovations, being especially dominant in such capital intensive industries as cars, cement, dyes, glass, plastics and steel, as well as in aerospace, electronics and shipbuilding. Even so, small firms and independent inventors play an important innovatory role in some industries such as footwear, furniture, scientific instruments and textile machinery. Nor does the evidence show that one particular market structure has exclusive claim to be the 'best' environment for innovation. Indeed, empirical works suggests that 'a variety of firm sizes and market structures provides the best balance between stimulating a flow of research and invention and the subsequent development of . . . innovation' (HMSO 1978, p. 121). There is more convincing empirical support for learning economies as a source of lower costs. In fact, some of the estimates of (static) scale economies include learning effects. Learning curves show the extent to which unit costs decline with increases in *cumulative* output. The basic idea is that labour and management will learn-by-doing, so that they will become more efficient the more frequently they perform a task. Learning economies are substantial in labour intensive operations (e.g. assembly work) and they have been observed in aerospace, machine tools, shipbuilding and silicon transistors. For policy purposes, learning economies are relevant in explaining productivity differences between UK and foreign industries. For example, in aircraft manufacture, an 80% learning curve is typical, showing that direct labour input declines by 20% for each doubling in the cumulative output of one aircraft type. Typically, the US aircraft industry produces over 1,000 units of a combat aircraft, sometimes extending to 5,000 units, at rates of 12–14 aircraft per month, with up to 30–45 aircraft per month not unknown. In the UK, a typical production run is 200–300 at rate of 2–4 per month. Such differences in scale have been used to support European collaboration in aerospace projects, with a number of nations 'pooling' their orders in an effort to approach US output levels (e.g. Anglo-French helicopters and Jaguar, European Airbus and British-German-Italian collaboration on the Tornado). Learning also provides a justification for the protection of an infant industry, allowing the new entrant to move down the learning curve until it is able to compete with established rivals who have already exploited the benefits of learning (e.g. Japanese cars and motorcycles). Finally, learning gives the basis for a more dynamic, and alternative, explanation of industrial structure. It is argued that using the learning curve approach, 'concentration is the outcome of a process which confers on the leading producer a real cost advantage and it is this real cost advantage which maintains its superior profitability rather than exploitative behaviour in the market or improper restraints on competition' (HMSO 1978, p. 86). In other words, competition provides an incentive for firms to exploit cost reductions from learning, with superior cost improvement by one competitor resulting in the elimination of rivals. There is support for this view, one US study showing that, compared with their smaller rivals, firms with over 40% of the market had a unit cost advantage of some 10%. Whilst this analysis and evidence might apply to dominant firms, it is less applicable to mergers.

For the UK, there is not much support for the hypothesis that take-overs result in improved efficiency. A study of over 200 UK mergers concluded that, 'In general, a mild decline in profitability did typify these mergers – if market power was typically unchanged as a result of the merger, the profitability decline reflects a fall in efficiency. And if . . . market power was more often enhanced by merger, then the profitability decline is likely to under-state the loss in efficiency' (Meeks 1977, p. 25). This study also found that mergers encounter managerial dis-economies and that bigger plants have worse strike records and enjoy a less favourable utilisation of their labour force due to absenteeism and sickness. In other words, even where mergers lead to the scale economies desired by industrial re-structuring policy, the advantages might be more than offset by less competition and other dis-economies, resulting in higher prices and a mis-allocation of resources. Certainly, concentration in the UK increased rapidly in the post-war period, with mergers contributing to at least one-half of the rise. Moreover, it is now recognised that firms will not minimise costs for a given output unless competition or environmental factors compel them to do so. This X-inefficiency results because employment contracts are usually incomplete, allowing both managers and workers discretion in interpreting what they should do for the firm, with varying opportunities for 'on-the-job' leisure and 'shirking'. Where such discretion exists, any activities which impose costs on the organisation are passed on to others and ultimately to shareholders, consumers or government, where governments provide subsidies. In the circumstances, an official review recommended a more critical policy towards mergers, shifting from the 1970s policy of favouring mergers to a more neutral position (HMSO 1978, p. 35). More surprisingly, in view of the evidence on 'slack' in the UK economy, this same review concluded that 'there is no strong case for abandoning the traditional UK pragmatic approach to competition policy of treating each case on its merits' (HMSO 1978, p. 22).

Casual empiricism shows that in Britain departures from competition are extensive and are not confined to private industry. Monopolies and imperfections exist in the markets for capital, labour and land, as well as government bureaucracies, the nationalised industries and in the rules for tendering for government contracts. It is, for example, interesting to speculate on the implications of applying existing legislation on monopolies, mergers and restrictive practices to trade unions. If the behaviour of union monopolies and mergers were to be examined in the same way as private firms, consideration would be given to such performance indicators as the rate of return on human capital and union membership (c.f. excessive prices and profits), scale economies in unions, entry conditions (e.g. 'closed shops'), tariff protection and the union's contribution to technical efficiency, including innovation. Similarly, 1976 restrictive practices legislation might require that restrictive labour arrangements be registered and, ultimately, be subject to the judgement of the Restrictive Practices Court. In the 1976 legislation, there is a general presumption that restrictive agreements are against the public interest (HMSO 1979, p. 108). However, unions and professional associations might defend a restrictive practice by using one of the approved 'gateways' and arguing that the arrangement protects the public against injury (e.g. doctors, teachers) or that it benefits consumers, or provides countervailing power or maintains local employment or contributes to the balance of payments. Problems arise because there is a general lack of UK evidence on the extent of the monopoly power of unions, the sources of union power, the extent of restrictive labour practices and their effects on prices, efficiency and technical progress. We know that in *product* markets, the abolition of restrictive practices contributed to improved industrial efficiency (HMSO 1979, p. 25). The monopoly power of trade unions is limited by the possibilities of substituting union labour by machinery and non-union labour, technical progress leading to unskilled replacing skilled labour (e.g. craft workers), as well as UK consumers buying substitute products either from domestic or foreign firms. Predictably, unions respond by acting on the substitution possibilities through, for example, supporting tariff protection and subsidies for domestic industries, picketing, closed shops, lengthy apprenticeships, restricting factor substitution and imposing minimum manning requirements (e.g. firemen on diesel locomotives). The whole union movement also forms an interest group to influence vote-sensitive governments to introduce legislation which establishes and protects a worker's property rights in his job. During the 1970s, examples included industrial relations and employment protection legislation. As a result, unions might establish up to a 20% wage differential, although such estimates can be 'too high' if they ignore both training and entry costs. As for productivity, what little tentative evidence there is indicates that unionisation adversely affected productivity in the UK coal industry with a totally unionised coalfield producing some 20% less output than a completely non-unionised field; and that this estimate 'will tend to be a lower bound on that prevailing in the British economy today' (Pencavel, 1977, p. 145). But vote-conscious governments seem to regard unions as policy-created constraints (second-best), so that any pro-competition policy applied to product, labour and other markets is unlikely to be introduced and enforced because of opposition from producer interest groups. Moreover, if a government adopted a pro-competition policy, there would be some re-allocation of resources from inefficient to efficient firms. Questions arise about the adequacy of arrangements for promoting resource re-allocation in the UK and the contribution of subsidy policy.

Subsidy Policy

During the 1970s, British governments introduced a variety of subsidies. There were subsidies to individual companies facing financial difficulties; to particular outputs, notably machine tools, aircraft and shipbuilding; to factor inputs namely capital, in the form of investment assistance, and labour subsidies for employment, training, mobility and job search, as well as to research and development. Initially subsidies were employed primarily as incentives for regional development. The 1972 Industry Act however conferred wide powers on government to offer financial assistance in almost any form to virtually any industry or enterprise so long as the assistance was 'in the public interest'. The election of a Labour Government in 1974, which coincided with economic recession, resulted in a great increase in subsidisation aimed chiefly at the maintenance of employment. These subsidies included direct assistance to industries both within and outside the assisted areas and labour subsidies in the form of the temporary employment subsidy and job creation schemes aimed at particular groups such as school leavers. By 1975, UK subsidy expenditures exceeded £2,500m. With such an extensive range of subsidies, it might reasonably be asked whether there are any firms, activities or groups in the UK which would *not* qualify for a subsidy? Theory might help by providing guidelines for subsidy policy.

Subsidies are rationalised either by marginal cost pricing in decreasing cost activites or by substantial social benefits, and it is the latter argument which is most popular. Frequently, it is claimed that subsidies are required for reasons of jobs, advanced technology, balance of payments and defence, although rarely is any attention given to whether the resources would yield greater social benefits if they were used elsewhere in the economy. Nor does it follow, as is sometimes alleged, that the capital market is 'failing' if funds cannot be obtained (at the ruling price) for high-risk projects of the micro-electronics and Concorde type: this might be evidence that the market is working properly and takes the view that there are more profitable alternative users of its scarce funds. The capital market is likely to take a similar view of 'industrial invalids, experiencing temporary difficulties, but capable of being restored to health' (British Leyland?). Even if state assistance were required for such firms (why?), it could take the form of loans rather than subsidies although 'if the future health of the invalids is so blindingly obvious, why cannot loans be raised on private capital markets?' (Burton 1979, p. 36). Other examples of the confusions on subsidy policy emerge at the level of policy objectives. Consider subsidy policy in its job preservation and training roles.

In the late 1970s, the UK economy was characterised by both substantial unemployment and skill shortages. Subsidies were used, on the one hand, to preserve jobs and, on the other, to increase the quantity of training and the supply of skilled labour. Conflicts are inevitable between the static short-run employment targets of job subsidies and the dynamic, long-run growth objectives of training subsidies. Job subsidies are likely to interfere with the re-allocation of resources from the declining to the expanding sectors of the economy. They will tend to perpetuate the existing geographical and skill pattern of jobs in the economy and so maintain demands for training in the subsidised activities. In other words, employment subsidies allow firms to continue in business and avoid or postpone contraction. Here, governments cannot avoid a decision on society's attitude to change. Choices are required between the *status quo* and differing amounts of change, none of which is costless. However, the aims of training subsidy policy are far from clear. Some policy-makers stress its contribution to long-run competitiveness and growth targets through the provision of skills to reduce 'bottlenecks' (contraints on growth) and allow the labour force to adapt to the changing skill requirements of new consumer demands and new technology. Others regard training subsidies as a means of achieving distributional, as well as price stability and employment 'ends'. For example, it is believed that training policy will reduce poverty through increased skill provision (human capital) to specific groups. Furthermore, it can be one element of a manpower policy aimed at improving the operation of the labour market and so leading to a favourable shift in the short-run Phillips curve and in the natural unemployment rate. Training subsidies can also have a short-run direct job creation and skill-experience effect during the period of training. Even if such policies do not reduce long-term structural unemployment, they may have an impact (social) effect which could justify the schemes, especially if the training is aimed at preferred groups or regions. These objectives of training subsidy policy seem to ignore the possibility of trade-offs or conflicts between targets. Growth, for example, might have adverse consequences for income distribution if the costs of job change are borne by the poor! Similarly, increased productivity through competition, technical change and the substitution of capital for labour might create unemployment. Where conflicts exist, the theory of economic policy states that governments require as many policy instruments as they have objectives. Thus, whilst training subsidies might achieve one policy target, other policy instruments are required for the remaining objectives.

Assuming that governments are concerned with employment creation, are job subsidies and/or training subsidies the most efficient method of achieving this target? Certainly there are alternative policy options. For example, job-creation can be achieved with public works programmes or an expansion of aggregate demand, or through manpower policies aimed at improving the operation of the labour market (e.g. mobility and employment agencies to improve search and assist market clearing). Similarly, skill shortages can be caused by trade union entry barriers, labour immobility, lack of information, the effect of pay policies in 'squeezing' wage differentials between the skilled and unskilled, as well as 'inadequate' training. In this case, training subsidies might not be the most efficient solution to skill shortages. Evidence is required on both the causes of policy problems and the relative effectiveness of policies. Superficially, job subsidies appear attractive since their impact is immediately apparent and they seem to 'save' on unemployment benefits. But appearances are no substitution for analysis, predictions and evidence.[1] Job subsidies are likely to have a 'displacement effect' in that employment preservation in subsidised firms is purchased at a cost of jobs lost in nonsubsidised firms. Care must also be taken to ensure that the number of jobs 'saved' in subsidised firms are net additions, directly attributable to subsidies. With the youth employment subsidy (1976–78), approximately one in eight of the subsidised jobs was created as a result of the subsidy, and 75% of subsidised young people would have entered their employment regardless of the subsidy (*Gazette*, 1978). There is also the apparently persuasive argument that subsidies will save state expenditure on unemployment and social security benefits. Such an argument tends to neglect the unemployment payments for any 'displacement effects', as well as the marketability of workers who might otherwise be subsidised. Studies of redundancy show that many redundant workers find other jobs without unemployment, whilst for those who do register as unemployed, the median duration of unemployment is low. In assessing the budgetary effect of job subsidies, the crucial question is the 'time duration of job subsidisation relative to the time duration of worker-employment' (Burton 1979, p. 22). However, criticism of job subsidies does not imply that training subsidies are desirable. If it is agreed that some form of public policy towards training markets is required, it does not follow that training subsidies are 'appropriate'. Training markets might fail because of monopolies, human capital financing difficulties, restrictive practices and entry barriers (e.g. apprenticeships).[2] Or, externalities might result in 'too much' on-the-job training and 'too little' off-the-job training.

In the late 1970s, UK training policy emphasised Training for Skills, which aimed to increase the amount and quality of training in industry and to prevent persistent shortages in vital skills (Manpower Services Commission 1978). The policy instruments were the Industrial Training Boards, with their levy–grant–exemption system, and Manpower Services Commission subsidies. It was generally believed that because of poaching, firms have 'under-provided' training in general skills which have value to a large number of enterprises. But this interpretation of poaching is incorrect. It uses the general and specific skills classification and assumes incorrectly, that all training costs are borne by firms. Human capital theory predicts that general or transferable skills will tend to be worker-financed, whilst specific or non-transferable training will be firm-financed. If poaching applies to specific skills, and the training firm offers its specific-trained labour a wage rate higher than the next best alternative, how do rivals poach? Indeed, why do they poach, if specific skills have no value to rival firms? If, as policy implies, poaching refers to general or worker-financed skills, doubts arise about the nature and extent of any loss which firms experience from the 'theft' of skilled labour. At the same time, under-investment in transferable skills can arise if individuals are unable to finance worthwhile training investments. This suggests a policy-emphasis on finance for trainees, including loans, as distinct from training subsidies to firms (Hartley, 1977b).

Conclusions

British governments have adopted a variety of industry, competition and subsidy policies embracing product and labour markets and involving different state agencies. The relationship between policies and ultimate objectives is a potential source of confusion and one which could be clarified with the use of a comprehensive programme related to policy objectives and show the life-cycle costs of each programme, as well as the resulting outputs. For illustration, a simple structure might be based on two major programmes, employment and efficiency. Job subsidies administered by the Department of Industry, the Manpower Services Commission and other state bodies would be a major input into the employment programme, and possible output measures might be savings in the number of jobs or man years. Similarly, the efficiency programme would show life-cycle inputs into industrial re-structuring and competition policies as administered by the Department of Industry, the Office of Fair Trading and government contracting agents, and the resulting outputs in such forms as lower prices, technical progress and increased exports. It is, however, recognised that programme budgets only provide an information framework. They focus on the relationship between policies and targets (Williams 1967). Ultimately, policies cannot be separated from the behaviour of the agencies entrusted with their implementation. The creation of state agencies such as the Manpower Services Commission and the Industrial Training Boards, each with special responsibilities for training policy, resulted in the establishment of interest groups of trainers and educators. These groups tend to regard all training as 'good' and more as 'desirable', regardless of costs! There are no simple solutions. In many cases, the abolition of state agencies, government aid and subsidies is likely to impose substantial costs on the 'protected' groups. Compensation of the losers is a possibility, but the transactions costs of identifying the potential gainers and losers from a policy change might be so large that compensation might not be worthwhile for society. And, of course, vote-sensitive governments are unlikely to ignore major interest groups. Perhaps the lesson is that in future we should try to avoid this kind of trap and be more critical of proposals for state intervention.

Notes

1. It has been reported that seven job projects initiated in late 1978 might involve the UK in losses of up to £800m. The projects included a new Rolls Royce aero-engine, Polish orders for British ships, collaborative airliner and missile projects and an aluminium scheme. The report commented that 'we seem bent on going ahead with projects which seem likely to waste economic resources' (*The Guardian*, 28.2.79).
2. By 1979 the Sector Working Parties were generally agreed that pay restrictions and the erosion of differentials were major causes of skill shortages.

References

Bacon, R. and Eltis, W., *Britain's Economic Problem: Too Few Producers,* Macmillan 1978.
Blackaby, F. (ed.), *De-Industrialisation*, Heinemann 1979.
Burton, J., *The Job Support Machine*, Centre for Policy Studies, 1979.
Central Policy Review Staff, *Future of the British Car Industry*, HMSO 1975
Department of Employment, Youth Employment Subsidy, *Gazette*, April 1978.
Hartley, K. (a), *Problems of Economic Policy*, Allen & Unwin 1977.
Hartley, K. (b), Training and Retraining for Industry, *Fiscal Policy and Labour Supply*, Institute for Fiscal Studies 1977.
The Regeneration of British Industry, Cmnd 5710, HMSO 1974.
An Approach to Industrial Strategy, Cmnd 6315, HMSO 1975
Review of Monopolies and Mergers Policy, Cmnd 7198, HMSO 1978.
Review of Restrictive Practices Policy, Cmnd 7312, HMSO 1979.
Manpower Services Commission, *Review and Plan 1978*, HMSO 1978.
Meeks, G., *Disappointing Marriage: A Study of the Gains from Merger,* Cambridge University Press 1977.
Panic, M. (ed.), *The UK and West German Manufacturing Industries 1954–72,* NEDO 1976.
Pencavel, J., 'The distributional and efficiency effects of trade unions in Britain', *British Journal of Industrial Relations,* July 1977.
Pratten, C.F., *Labour Productivity Differentials Within International Companies,* Cambridge University Press 1976.
Scherer, F., 'The determinants of international plant size in six nations', *Review of Economics and Statistics*, 1973.
Williams, A., *Output Budgeting and the Contribution of Micro-Economics to Efficiency in Government,* HMSO 1967.

Suggestions For Further Reading

Trade Unions: Public Goods or Public Bads, Reading 17, Institute of Economic Affairs, 1978.
Leibenstein, H., 'On the basic proposition of X-efficiency theory', *American Economic Review*, May 1978.
Prais, S.J., *The Evolution of Grant Firms in Britain,* NIESR 1976.
Reekie, D., *Industry, Prices and Markets*, Philip Allan 1979.
Tullock, G., 'The transitional gains trap', *Bell Journal of Economics,* Autumn 1975.
Whiting, A. (ed.), *The Economics of Industrial Subsidies*, HMSO 1976.
Wragg, R. and Robertson, J., *Post-War Trends in Employment*, HMSO 1978.

3. The nationalised industries

M. H. PESTON
Professor of Economics,
Queen Mary College, University of London

What is a nationalised industry? This is by no means a simple question, as the House of Commons Select Committee on Nationalised Industries discovered in 1968 when it enquired as to whether the Bank of England was a nationalised industry in a sense which enabled it to examine the Bank. When the Committee was set up in 1956 its terms of reference were defined as follows: 'to examine the Reports and Accounts of the Nationalised Industries established by Statute whose controlling Boards are appointed by Ministers of the Crown and whose annual receipts are not wholly or mainly derived from monies provided by Parliament or advanced from the Exchequer.' What this amounts to is (a) that the industries are wholly owned by the state or sufficiently owned by the state to be controlled by it; (b) that the industries operate in such a way as to gain most of their revenue other than from direct Parliamentary or Treasury subsidy; and (c) that they are run by Boards of Directors. The obvious examples, British Airways, the National Coal Board, the Electricity Council, the Central Electricity Generating Board, the North of Scotland Hydro-Electric Board, the Gas Council, British Rail, the British Airports Authority, the Post Office, the Waterways Board, the British Transport Docks Board, the British Steel Corporation, come pretty easily within the heading of nationalised industries. In addition London Transport did, before it was taken over by the Greater London Council. On the other hand, the BBC is not a nationalised industry because it receives its income directly from the Exchequer as is voted by Parliament. Similarly the Stationery Office does not operate with an independent Board, although it does get most of its income from sales to the public.

It is interesting to note that the Select Committee did decide that the Bank of England was also a nationalised industry. Indeed, it would have been extraordinary if it had come to an opposite conclusion, since the government in 1946 was under the impression that it had nationalised it. Similarly, they decided that the Independent Broadcasting Authority, and quite a number of other small corporations and firms, were also nationalised industries. A full list of these can be found in the Report which the Select Committee published.

In recent years there have been a great many changes. Under the Labour Government of 1974–79 the aircraft and shipbuilding industries were taken into public ownership as were several individual companies including British Leyland and Alfred Herbert. A substantial amount of public money has been invested in a variety of private enterprises without necessarily obtaining a controlling interest. Under the present Conservative administration it appears that the post-war trend towards greater public ownership of industry will be reversed. The government has announced its intention of completely or partially divesting itself of its shareholdings in many private companies (including British Petroleum) and the sale of shares in British Airways and British Aerospace has been proposed.

For the purposes of the present discussion we shall take the Select Committee's definition of nationalised industries as appropriate. Nevertheless, while there is a basic list of nationalised industries which we shall be referring to, much of what we have to say is of broader applicability and, in particular, the fact that London Transport is no longer defined as a nationalised industry in a legal sense does not mean that the same economics is no longer relevant to it. On the other hand, most of the mixed enterprises which are only partially owned by the state and in which it does not necessarily have a controlling interest may be regarded as commercial in the ordinary sense of that term, and are not the subject of the present essay.

There is a further complication to be mentioned concerning definition. In the National Accounts Statistics of the United Kingdom which are referred to below, reference is made to the public corporations and a great many tables of statistics are published with data on their operations. The public corporations define a wider variety of institutions than the nationalised industries, including, for example, the BBC. The composition of the public corporations has also changed a great deal in the 1970s, which adds to the point that the statistics must be treated with great care. From 1974 the regional Water Authorities were included in public corporations. Late in 1975 the National Enterprise Board was established (although the companies which are its subsidiaries are classified in the companies sector). In 1976 the British National Oil Corporation was set up, followed in 1977 by British Aerospace and British Shipbuilders. It is also worth noting that such bodies as the Royal Ordnance Factories and other trading bodies used to be defined neither as nationalised industries nor as public corporations because they lacked even the independence to borrow, or to retain their own trading surpluses. But in the 1970s they have been re-classified as public corporations having been established as *trading funds* under the Government Trading Funds Act, 1973.

In sum, there is therefore an extraordinary range of related activities which come into the public sector which are of interest to the economist. There is a spectrum from the well-defined nationalised industry right across to things like the Royal Ordnance Factories, the selling of postcards in the National Gallery, etc. The important thing to bear in mind is that statistics are published under various headings which look as if they must refer simply to the nationalised industries, but may not. Great care must be exercised in interpreting the figures that are published.

Reasons for Nationalisation

The extent of nationalisation differs between nations. In almost all countries of Western Europe and in North America the postal services are nationalised; but it is not necessarily the case that the telephone or the telegraph services are in public ownership. They are certainly so in the United Kingdom and in France, but they are under private ownership in the United States. Railways are publicly owned in a great many countries of Western Europe; they are not publicly owned in the United States, and they are only half publicly owned in Canada. The electricity industry and the gas industry are publicly owned in almost all of Western Europe, but not always as complete public monopolies. In Sweden, for example, some electricity is generated by private enterprise and some by local municipal enterprise. Coal mining is a state monopoly in Austria, Great Britain and France, whereas in Italy, Sweden, Norway, Finland and West Germany the state merely owns a large share. Similar remarks can be made about iron and steel. The aluminium industry is to a large extent state owned in Norway, but not in many other countries. The firms producing cigarettes and tobacco and matches are state owned in a number of countries but not in the United Kingdom. We can find examples of state ownership of cars, aircraft, oil, armaments, alcoholic beverages, salt and forestry in different countries, but none of these is nationalised in all the countries of Western Europe. In other words, with the exception of the Post Office it is impossible to find any industry which is a state monopoly in every country of Western Europe and North America. It is also impossible to find an important industry in which there is not some degree of public ownership in one of these countries.

The heterogeneity of experience suggests that there have been many reasons for nationalisation, and that some of them may be peculiar to the countries in question. In the United Kingdom and in Austria and to some extent in Italy, nationalisation has taken place in order to fulfil explicit political programmes. In Austria again, in Italy and also to a considerable extent in Germany, nationalisation has happened by chance and is often a left-over phenomenon from a previous era. Bank failures on the continent of Europe in the inter-war period, together with the fact that the banks were important financiers of industry, meant that when government stepped in to rectify the situation they often found themselves as owners of particular industrial or commercial enterprises. Public enterprise has emerged in some countries not as a political programme, or at least not as a consequence of one party's political programme, but simply as a commitment to planning. Electricité de France is in the public sector and is part of the French commitment to a very special planning procedure. Despite the fact that right-wing governments very sympathetic to free enterprise have been in power in France for almost two decades, there has been no attempt on the part of the central government to give up these commanding heights of the economy or to abandon the planning process. The public transport system in Paris is in public ownership; and again this is not for ideological reasons, but simply as part of the commitment to plan Paris transport.

Although in many countries of the Western world nationalisation is connected with state interference in industry, other methods of state interference exist as well. It would therefore be wrong to identify the mixed economy simply with state ownership of particular enterprises. In many countries there is a wide variety of other methods of controlling industries, including those in private ownership. In several Western European countries wage and price controls are well established and are applied to private enterprise as well as to public enterprise. In Italy there is a central government National Holding Company which owns outright, or nearly outright, a wide variety of different industrial enterprises; and there is a great deal of other government interference with the rest of the economy. Governments can interfere and plan the economy without 100% nationalisation, although it can still be argued that planning and control is much assisted by public ownership.

The chance element in nationalisation is exemplified by the state management districts in Carlisle, which were nationalised simply as a result of the attempt to cut down alcoholism in World War I. They remained in public ownership for 50 years until the Conservative administration of 1970 sold them back to the private sector for what were alleged to be purely doctrinaire reasons. At that point there may have been no particular reason why they should have been in state ownership, but equally there was no particular reason why they should have been sold back to private enterprise. Of course, nationalisation must be regarded to a considerable extent as an ideological matter, connected with some theories of the decline of capitalism and the growth of socialism. Marx identified the public ownership of capital as the distinguishing mark of socialism. It is not apparent from Marx himself whether a process of nationalisation would in fact represent a method of getting from capitalism to socialism, but certainly other left-wing thinkers, notably democratic socialists in Western Europe and the United Kingdom, did see gradual nationalisation as the procedure by which socialism in some form would be reached. Amongst economists this view was emphasised by Schumpeter (1942).

Ideology apart, a number of reasons have been put forward to justify nationalisation in terms of economics. Firstly, it was seen as a method of dealing with monopoly. In certain industries, largely because of economies of scale, the most successful economic unit gives rise to monopoly, which is regarded as politically undesirable and economically inefficient. Various methods have been suggested to deal with this, notably the introduction of taxes of different kinds of public regulation. The trouble is that the taxes would have to be adjusted to the particular industries, which is likely to be administratively impossible and unfair. Similarly, public utility regulation, as occurs in the United States, may also be seen as administratively extremely difficult and open to corruption. The nationalisation approach, if it is based on laying down general rules of behaviour for the industries within which management may proceed independently, enables the evils of monopoly to be avoided while at the same time allowing sufficient entrepreneurial effort to keep the industries efficient and up-to-date.

A second and related case for nationalisation concerns the problem of industries which are liable to go out of existence in conditions of free enterprise, but which the government wishes to preserve. It could happen that simply as a result of chance forces or miscalculations on the part of private entrepreneurship a concern that is inherently viable becomes bankrupt, but free enterprise and free financial markets are unwilling to provide new finance in order that it may continue. The government may then provide the finance itself, and feel that the best way of doing this, especially when extremely large sums of money are involved, would be by taking the concern under its own wing. The obvious example in recent years is Rolls Royce, but there have been plenty of other examples in many countries over a long period of time. The question then arises of what meaning can be attached to the industry or the firm being economically viable but private enterprise being unwilling to risk its own finance. The answer may lie in a difference of view about the likely risks involved, and also a difference in attitudes to risk. The government can decide quite simply that private enterprise or finance is too cautious. Economic viability is not an objective thing to be determined solely by the estimates of private decision makers in free capital markets. They can be mistaken, and governments can be correct in their estimation of economic prospects. Of course, the reverse is also possible; namely that governments are mistaken and free enterprise correct in their estimates of economic viability.

The cases we are discussing here would not necessarily involve a public interest in the enterprise as such. In others, such as Rolls Royce, there might be national prestige or strategic advantage necessitating that the firm should stay in existence, either by nationalisation or state subsidy.

More generally, what we are discussing are the workings of the economy and the problems of planning. If industries are subject to random shocks of one kind or another, it will happen sometimes that they contract rapidly or go out of existence altogether. Most economists do not believe that free markets always adjust quickly or efficiently enough to be able to cope with this kind of problem. That is why national planning procedures are introduced. The easiest way of introducing planning is via public ownership, especially if the planning structure of the economy is fairly primitive. In the United Kingdom we are still far from being able to cope easily with the decline of individual enterprises and the transfer of the labour force to new enterprises. This process may then be slowed down a little and managed via the public ownership of the declining firm or industry. Advocates of free enterprise argue that this is inefficient compared with letting the declining firms go out of existence and allowing the labour force to become temporarily unemployed. It is difficult to lay down general principles in this area of discourse. The free market solution may be correct in some cases; public ownership will be correct in others. The trouble with the latter is that, setting all ideology apart and concentrating solely on the economic arguments, the subsequent adjustment process may not occur. Nationalisation can become a means simply of keeping particular enterprises in existence for no purpose other than maintaining the labour force in full employment. It is worth emphasising, therefore, that to a large extent this has not been true of public enterprise in recent years in the United Kingdom. In coal mining and the railways, for examples, strong efforts have been made to increase efficiency in the physical sense and reduce the labour force. Under purely free enterprise the industries' labour forces might have declined more rapidly still, but it is not true that they have failed to decline rapidly by national or international standards. Anyway, the pure free enterprise of economic theory exists in few industries in few countries. If the coal industry had remained in private hands it would still have had to be subsidised, and there would have been very strong calls to keep so-called uneconomic pits in existence for social reasons. At the present time, although the Conservative Party is opposed on ideological grounds both to nationalisation and to state subsidy of private enterprise, in specific cases it advocates the use of public funds to preserve particular firms in aerospace, motor vehicle manufacture, and certain enterprises in the defence field.

Other arguments in favour of nationalisation may be mentioned briefly. A curious one popular 50 or more years ago is that employees had a bias on moral grounds against working for private enterprise. They were happier in the public service and in the public sector. It follows that the costs of operation of public enterprises would be lower since they could pay lower salaries than private firms. A second argument concerns industries where inspection is of significance. If they were in private operation, a public inspectorate would have to be set up, adding to their costs; with public operation, the inspection function can be built into the concerns themselves. It is suggested that various sanitation operations come into this category.

At the present time an important argument concerns the role of worker participation in particular enterprises and labour relations generally. It used to be believed 30 years ago that labour relations would be improved enormously if industries were nationalised. Industries such as coal mining were nationalised partly to please the miners. Today, while it is true that nationalised industries take a leading role in improving labour relations, no one could argue that their labour relations are overwhelmingly good or superior to all private enterprise. Similarly, worker participation, while it may be easier in nationalised industries, is not incompatible with private enterprise.

To summarise at this point, there is a need for state interference, for anti-monopoly purposes, to maintain standards, to deal with external economies and diseconomies, to improve the adjustment mechanism of the economic system, to take risks which private enterprise wishes to avoid, and to improve labour relations. These together comprise an explanation of why nationalisation occurs or may be justified. Equally, in almost all cases alternative measures exist, making it a matter of judgement and ideology why a particular solution is or is not adopted.

What is interesting as far as the UK is concerned is that it used to be assumed that public ownership implied public monopoly. The great nationalised industries of Britain are, indeed, as close to being monopolies within their technical field of operation as they could be, but in the economic sense of monopoly – to mean the absence of competition or close substitutes – most are not monopolies at all. The National Coal Board may have a monopoly of the production of coal, but in relevant markets it is not coal that matters but fuels. The coal industry, therefore, is subject to strong competition, frequently from other nationalised industries, namely gas and electricity, but also from private enterprise, i.e. oil. Similarly, the electricity and gas industries and the railways may be technical monopolies, but they are not insulated from real competition.

It is noticeable that the extensions of public ownership in recent years have taken a variety of forms, often quite distinct from the technical monopolies which have been traditionally associated with nationalisation. The National Enterprise Board resulted in a considerable extension of public ownership but without taking over the whole of any industry or, in most cases, the whole of firms. It seems likely that the trend towards greater diversity in public enterprise will continue. The proposals to sell shares in certain nationalised industries to private investors will, if introduced, involve considerable changes in the structure and control of the corporations involved.

The Operation and Efficiency of the Nationalised Industries

I turn now to the problem of the efficient operation of the nationalised industries. Table 1 provides figures of the scale of investment and the gross trading surpluses of the public corporations.

There are two points of interest here. Firstly, the sheer size of the public corporations, of which the nationalised industries comprise by far the largest part, is indicated by the scale of their investment activity. As a share of national investment this has fluctuated somewhat over the decade,

Table 1

	Gross trading surplus £m (a)	*(a)÷ Gross revenue %* (b)	*(a)÷ net capital stock %* (c)	*Gross investment at 1975 prices £m* (d)	*(d)÷ total investment %* (e)	*(d)÷ total public sector investment %* (f)
1967	1,132	19.1	6.8	4,094	22.2	55
1968	1,363	19.8	7.4	3,971	20.6	53
1969	1,451	19.4	7.3	3,292	17.0	48
1970	1,447	17.7	6.4	3,428	17.3	47
1971	1,520	17.1	6.0	3,457	17.1	48
1972	1,681	17.7	5.9	3,023	14.9	45
1973	2,063	19.4	6.1	3,162	14.6	42
1974	2,558	19.2	5.2	3,619	17.1	48
1975	3,093	17.6	5.0	3,983	19.1	55
1976	4,502	20.4	6.3	3,955	19.3	57
1977	5,035	19.4	6.3	3,598	18.2	61

falling from over 22% in 1967 to under 15% in 1973, but it has since risen to over 18%. Within the public sector it has again fluctuated considerably, but as a fraction of gross fixed capital formation excluding dwellings it rose above 60% in 1977. (This large figure was much more due to the cuts in other public sector investment than to the increase in public corporations' investment.)

The industries earn a gross trading surplus equal to just under a fifth of their gross revenues. This trading surplus as a percentage of their net capital stock has fluctuated in the range of 5% to 7%. A comparable figure for industrial and commercial companies in the private sector has fallen from about 18% in 1967 to just over 12% in 1977. In both cases it would be wrong to jump to any simple conclusions on trends in efficiency. The *stagflation* of the 1970s, coupled with a great deal of government intervention in both nationalised and private industry, has significantly distorted the figures, making it impossible to give a definitive view on underlying trends in productivity and financial performance.

One last measure of their relative importance is given in Table 2. This shows employment in the public corporations and compares it with total employment and total employment

Table 2

	Employment in public corporations Th (a)	*(d) ÷ total employed labour force* % (b)	*(a) ÷ total employed in the public sector* % (c)
1967	1,937	7.8	31.4
1968	2,069	8.3	32.3
1969	2,041	8.2	31.8
1970	2,027	8.2	31.2
1971	2,009	8.2	30.4
1972	1,929	7.9	29.3
1973	1,890	7.6	27.9
1974	1,981	7.9	28.7
1975	2,033	8.2	28.0
1976	1,980	8.0	27.1
1977	2,086	8.4	28.2

in the public sector. These show reasonable stability of their share of total employment at about 8%, but a rather declining share of employment in the public sector. It is interesting, considering the attention paid to wage setting in the nationalised industries, what a small fraction of the labour force they employ. Of course, this does not mean that wage bargaining in the nationalised industries is not a significant factor in the overall inflation process, especially in years when those industries are not subject to financial constraints.

In sum, it is clear that, because of their size, their level of investment and their central position in the economy, the operation of the nationalised industries is of primary importance to the performance of the economy as a whole. But the establishment of objectives for nationalised industries or criteria for measuring their performance is no easy matter. While private industry has the relatively unambiguous objective of maximising the return of its owners' capital, the fact that the nationalised industries have been transferred from private into public ownership is indicative of the belief that the profit motive is an unsatisfactory guide for these industries. The simple answer to the question 'How should the nationalised industries conduct their affairs?' is that they should operate in the public interest by seeking to maximise their contribution to social welfare. Such an objective is so vague as to be useless and could be used as a justification for almost any action by a nationalised industry – including gross inefficiency. In a democratic society the direction of the public interest can only be interpreted by our political representatives, yet the detailed control by government over the affairs of the nationalised industries has been implicitly rejected in the organisational structure of public corporations, which is designed to give considerable autonomy to the board of directors.

Up to 1960 government policy showed considerable uncertainty as to the appropriate objectives of public enterprise and the optimal degree of ministerial control. Since then, however, some measure of reconciliation has been achieved between the conflicting objectives of government's need to interpret the meaning of the public interest and the desirability of autonomy for the nationalised industries in their day to day operation, through the laying down by government of general criteria for their conduct. Of considerable importance has been the investment and pricing policies of the nationalised industries and government policy towards these has been expressed most clearly in two White Papers (HMSO 1961, HMSO 1967). Initially, the concern was with the problem of financing the industries' investment, and the desire to meet more of this from the trading surplus rather than from the budget and central government borrowing. Rapidly, however, horizons were widened to include incentives to managerial efficiency and considerations of overall resource allocation. A major publication by the House of Commons Select Committee on Nationalised Industries *Ministerial Control of the Nationalised Industries 1967–68* (1968) stressed the need for explicit rational control by the central government leading to efficient resource allocation. It was in favour of broad ground rules being set by the government, within which the industries would operate, while not being subject to day-to-day *ad hoc* interference from on high.

About the time this report was published, it looked as if the nationalised industries were entering a new era of efficiency and enterprise. Since then there has been a degree of backsliding so that in the early 1970s managerial morale was lower than it might be, and microeconomic considerations were not being given the priority they deserved. In the later 1970s the financial performance of the industries was allowed to improve, and new efforts were made to improve productivity.

Pricing Policy of Nationalised Industries

Let us now turn explicitly to the economics of pricing. Even before the great wave of nationalisation in 1945, there was considerable debate over the correct pricing policies for public enterprises. One point of view was that they should set prices equal to average cost. This objective was supported by the nationalisation acts which required the corporations to break even taking one year with another. An argument in favour of average cost pricing was that, if an industry failed to take in sufficient revenue to balance its books, the deficit would have to be made up by increasing government borrowing or increased taxation. Most economists, however, have regarded average cost pricing as an accountants' criterion and not well-founded in welfare economics. There is also the question of whether average cost pricing policies are to mean simply that the total revenue of the whole organisation should equal its total cost, or whether the rule should be applied to every good and service produced by the particular industry. The legislation threw no light on this, and there was little justification within economics why the organisation should break even. It was perfectly possible for total revenue to equal total cost, but for the industry to earn surpluses on some activities and make deficits on others. One of the early problems that worried students of the nationalised industries, quite apart from the marginal cost controversy, was the justification of the phenomenon of 'cross-subsidisation'. In the case of the railways, for example, what reason was there for profitable lines in certain areas to subsidise unprofitable lines in other areas? In the coal industry certain sorts of coal were easily mined and were much demanded. Did it make sense to earn profits on those in order to subsidise other coal from difficult mines which was not as much demanded?

Another problem that arose in connection with average cost pricing (although it applied equally to marginal cost pricing) concerned the definition of cost. Many of the advocates of average cost pricing assumed that these would be the costs as reported in the accounts of the nationalised industries, but this was not something that economists could make sense of. Much of the capital in the accounts was valued at original cost or purchase price rather than replacement cost. The interest element was at the rate of interest that the industry had contracted to pay at a given date. That particular rate itself could be regarded as arbitrary, not necessarily reflecting the value of capital at the time of the investment decision or at the time that the accounts were being constructed. Even current costs may not be costs in an economic sense. If, for example, some workers would be unemployed if dismissed by the industry, it could be argued that their wages were greater than the true social cost of employing them.

The correct pricing policy is one which maximises welfare.

The problem is then to lay down some welfare criteria and see what pricing policy follows from them. In essence the criteria that the economist has applied in deriving the marginal cost pricing rule assume that, broadly speaking, preferences of individuals as reflected in demand for goods and services and supply of factors of production are a correct basis for the measurement of welfare. He then discusses whether demands for the supplies of goods and services at prices quoted in the market are correct measures of those preferences and, therefore, of welfare. If they are, namely if demand at the market price is a correct measure of marginal benefit received, and if supply at the market price is a correct measure of marginal benefit forgone, then it follows that welfare is maximised when demand equals supply; the supply curve of the firm in competitive conditions being its marginal cost curve. To maximise welfare, therefore, it follows that the nationalised industry should act as though it were a perfectly competitive firm, treating its marginal cost curve as its supply curve and pricing at marginal cost for every level of output. Figure 1 explains the optimality of the marginal cost pricing rule.

The line DD represents the consumers' demand schedule for the output of a nationalised industry. It shows the price

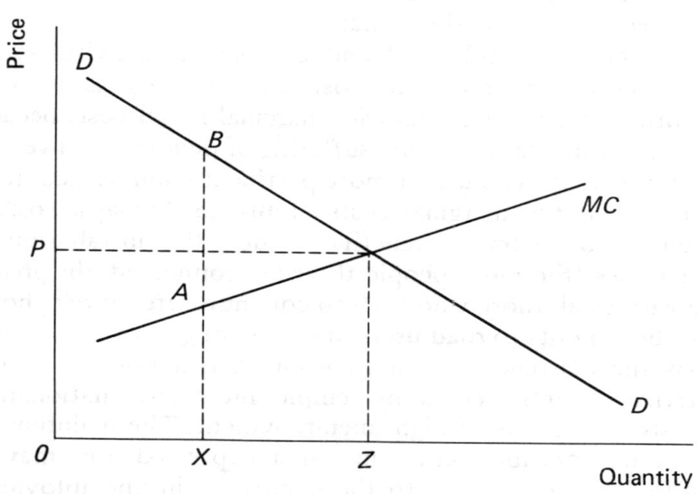

Figure 1

that consumers are willing to pay for different quantities of the product, the price equalling the additional benefit derived from the final unit of the product consumed (the marginal utility). The marginal cost schedule MC shows the addition to total cost of extra units of output. The addition to total welfare resulting from the production of an extra unit of output X is the difference between marginal benefit and marginal cost – the vertical distance AB. The optimal output of the product occurs where, for the last unit of production, marginal cost just equals marginal benefit – an output of Z. If the nationalised industry prices at marginal cost for every level of output, MC is its supply schedule and equilibrium in the market is reached at a price of P and an output of Z – the welfare maximising output.

There are, however, many reasons why neither the demand curve nor the supply curve are correct measures of marginal benefits received or marginal costs forgone. First, there are phenomena of external economies and diseconomies. In the production, sale and consumption of many goods and services benefits may be received by people who do not pay for them, or costs incurred by those who are not compensated for them. The list of possible external economies and diseconomies which are not dealt with through the market is enormous. Included would be the penalties of noise, dirt and other consequences of industrial and commercial activity. It has been argued that the marginal cost of a railway line as measured by British Rail is less than its marginal social cost, because account is not taken of the suffering of people who live near the railway. A similar and more pertinent comment could be made about the marginal costs of British Airways. Possible examples of external benefits include the installation of telephones (the more people there are connected, the greater the gain to all those who wish to communicate by telephone) and the benefits to road users of lower congestion which arise from the existence of rail transport. An important area of external benefit concerns employment by nationalised industries in areas of high unemployment. The maintenance of an unprofitable coal mine in a depressed area may be justified by the savings to the exchequer in unemployment benefit and the benefits of continued employment to the economic and social fabric of the district.

Marginal cost pricing may conflict with the desire of governments to use nationalised industries' prices as instruments of income redistribution. An increase in the price of electricity falls to a disproportionate extent on the poorer sections of the community. This might lead to government wishing to supply electricity at below the marginal cost of production. The modification of the simple rule of marginal cost pricing would depend on whether there were other means of achieving the desired social objective. In the case of subsidising electricity in the interests of poorer people, this could be achieved more directly by special adjustments to their electricity bills or more generally by raising various transfer payments such as old age pensions, social security, etc.

Another modification of simple marginal cost pricing policy arises from so-called second-best considerations. Ignoring both external economies and diseconomies and distributional aspects of the problem, it is still possible that demand does not represent marginal social benefits and supply marginal social costs, because of distortions elsewhere in the economy. The obvious example concerns the existence of monopoly pricing policies. A nationalised industry may use as an input a commodity produced by a monopoly in the private sector. Included in its price would be an element of monopoly profit which was not a true social cost. It could then be argued that public enterprise ought to adjust its own costs downwards to allow for this.

Let us consider what happens if the industry in question increases its output by one marginal unit: the price it charges will measure the resulting increase in benefit. It will require resources to an extent measured by marginal costs, so that some other industry's output contracts by this amount divided by its marginal cost. The value of the contraction in the other industry's output is obtained by multiplying this quantity by its price. There will be an increase in net benefit as long as the price charged by the first industry exceeds the value lost, as given by the formula just described. Thus, the welfare maximising formula would be price equal to marginal cost, divided by marginal cost in the other industry times price in the other industry. It can then easily be seen that if price elsewhere exceeds marginal cost (because, for example, of the exercise of monopoly power), then the correct pricing policy would be for price to exceed marginal cost in the nationalised industry. More generally, it could be stated that price in the nationalised industry should be related to marginal cost by a formula which reflects the extent to which prices in other industries are related to marginal costs. An approximation then would be to allow prices to exceed marginal costs by the average extent to which they exceed marginal costs in the economy at large. A better approximation would be for price to exceed marginal cost to an extent determined by the relationship between price and marginal cost in industries closely related to the nationalised industry.

It is worth remarking that, although all the foregoing discussion modifies the marginal cost pricing rule, it does not make the case for average cost pricing. Rather, what it amounts to is the proposition that price should be related to marginal cost. The second-best procedure also throws some light on the question of public sector surpluses and deficits. If a marginal cost pricing policy were to lead to the industry being in deficit or to producing a smaller surplus than would otherwise be the case, its marginal costs can be adjusted to take into account the way in which other prices and taxes would have to change. If, for example, an industry engaged in a marginal cost pricing policy caused the government to have to raise some indirect taxes, the welfare loss due to those indirect tax changes must itself be included in the marginal cost pricing rule.

Criteria for investment decisions can be similarly derived from basic premises concerning social welfare, the principle being that an investment project is worth doing if it increases the present discounted value of social welfare. A particular problem in establishing investment criteria for nationalised industries is determining the optimal rate of discount to apply to their future returns. As in the case of the marginal cost pricing rule, simple investment rules become much more complex once the issues of externalities, income distribution and second-best are raised.

The 1967 White Paper and the 1968 Select Committee Report had created a framework of control based on a financial target for each nationalised industry together with guidelines for pricing and investment policy which, in principle, should have enabled the industries to pursue the national interest with a minimum of ministerial interference. In practice the system did not work. The difficulty with both the marginal cost rule for pricing and the discounted social welfare rule for investment projects is that they are too far away from the operating practice of the nationalised industries themselves. Their connection with the financial performance of the industry is rather tenuous, and it is extremely hard to use them as rules of regular control and assessment. While such theories are analytically sound *ex ante, ex post* they tend to be some distance from managerial reality.

During the early 1970s ministerial intervention in the decisions of the industries increased while the imposition of price restraint resulted in steadily increasing deficits for some industries. It was recognised that the interrelationships between central government and the nationalised industries were unsatisfactory, that areas of responsibility were blurred, and that rules of behaviour and methods of control were in need of reconsideration and improvement. In 1976 a NEDO report was published based on detailed research. The report made a number of recommendations of an institutional and managerial nature, some of which were accepted by the government. Amongst these were (a) the desirability of appointing civil servants and consumer representatives to the boards, (b) the encouragement of industrial democracy, and (c) the granting of powers to ministers to give specific directives to nationalised industries subject to the approval of Parliament.

Government's response to the NEDO report was in the form of a new White Paper on the operation and control of the nationalised industries (HMSO 1978). The White Paper continued to emphasise the use of financial targets based on the industries' profitability as a method of financial control which would be conducive to economic efficiency. These targets were supposed to reflect the opportunity cost of capital to the economy, sectoral and social objectives relevant to specific industries, together with their economic circumstances. In addition, the publication of performance indicators was recommended to serve as a further inducement to efficiency. Such indicators might include unit costs in real terms and output per employee.

The control of investment was to be based on a new approach, although one which had evolved from the thinking and experience of the previous decade and a half. Its central concept was the *Required Rate of Return on Investment* (RRR). The purpose of the RRR was to give more weight to the investment programme as a whole (as opposed to individual projects). It is suggested that the RRR can be translated into a financial target, thus unifying the *ex ante* and *ex post* appraisal and control of investment. The Treasury has also claimed, therefore, that the RRR would be (and should be) taken into account in setting prices. Having said that, it is not at all obvious what is the economic foundation of the RRR, and in what sense it arises from economic analysis as a method of optimal control.

Nonetheless, it is claimed, and probably correctly, that the new approach will lead to a correct (or more nearly correct) division between the every-day decisions that can be left to the commercial judgement of the industries themselves, and the strategic framework which the individual departments of central government must concern themselves with. The aim has always been to make a distinction between strategy and tactics. Up to now, while the general operating rules have had a reasonable economic basis, they have lacked practical applicability. Equally, it has been too easy for the government to interfere informally on day-to-day matters. The hope is that the rules will now be more applicable and more easily understood. At the same time the government will be allowed to interfere, but in an explicit and (it is to be hoped) rational way.

References

Schumpeter, J.A., *Capitalism, Socialism and Democracy*, Harper & Row 1942.

House of Commons Select Committee on Nationalised Industries, *Capital Investment Procedures 1973–74*, HMSO 1974.

House of Commons Select Committee on Nationalised Industries, *Ministerial Control of the Nationalised Industries*, HMSO 1968.

Nationalised Industries: A Review of Economic and Financial Objectives, Cmnd 3437, HMSO 1967.
The Financial and Economic Obligations of the Nationalised Industries, Cmnd 1337, HMSO 1961.
The Nationalised Industries, Cmnd 7131, HMSO 1978.

4. The economics of agricultural policy

JOHN McINERNEY
Professor of Agricultural Economics & Management
University of Reading
and
DAVID COLMAN
Professor of Agricultural Economics
University of Manchester

Introduction

Farming is often thought to be a rather unique kind of production process. With land as its dominant input, its dependence on biological processes and climatic factors in production, and the variety and widespread geographical distribution of its producing units, agriculture seems to have little in common with what is generally termed 'industry'. However, all industries have their own special characteristics, and from the overall standpoint of national economic policy there is really no fundamental distinction between that sector of the economy which is concerned with food production and those such as the manufacturing, service or other sectors. All consume some proportion of the nation's limited resources, make a particular contribution to GNP, and generate an income for a certain section of the community.[1] With continuing economic growth and development, and changes in incomes, tastes and technology, all sectors are subject over time to a series of economic pressures which demand a continual adjustment in the level and pattern of their outputs and resource inputs, and in their whole structure of production. Agriculture is no exception to this rule, and societies at all stages of economic development have found it desirable to establish specific policies towards the agricultural sector for either (or both) of two reasons: (a) to mould and direct these adjustments along desired lines so that they follow some acceptable equilibrium progression for the economy as a whole, and (b) to correct or modify some of the side effects that result from these changes. It so happens that questions of agricultural policy have come to adopt a particular significance which justifies them as a specific subject of study. This is partly because of the central importance of food supplies to a nation's existence, partly because of a traditional political interest that agriculture retains, and partly because of the special characteristics of agricultural production and the technical and social problems that are created in the adjustment process.

It is the object of this chapter to identify those economic pressures that impinge on the agricultural sectors of developed nations, to examine their effects, and to analyse the various policy objectives that governments assume and the instruments they adopt in response to these pressures. The free market for agricultural products, both nationally and internationally, is usually viewed as closely approximating the classic model of perfect competition and it will be seen that a great deal of understanding of the economics of agriculture can be generated merely by the use of elementary demand–supply analysis.

The Development of UK Agricultural Policies

UK agricultural policy is now set within the wider framework of the Common Agricultural Policy (CAP) of the European Community. Before this, however, there had been a long history of steadily increasing government involvement in the agricultural sector. Following the Repeal of the Corn Laws in 1846, British agriculture developed in an era of free trade and growing industrialisation, which resulted in a steady erosion of its competitive position as the North American and Australasian continents developed as sources of imported food. A collapse of farm prices and incomes after the 1914–18 war resulted in a mild acceptance of government responsibility to subsidise farmers, which gathered strength with the depression of the 1930s. During that period tariffs and quotas were imposed on certain imported commodities, monopsonistic Producer Marketing Boards were established under government sponsorship (of which the Milk Marketing Board is perhaps the now most familiar example) and some specific price subsidies were introduced. The outbreak of war in 1939 saw Britain still heavily dependent on imported food and vulnerable to blockade. Food prices were then brought under the control of the Ministry of Food, and farmers were exhorted to expand domestic food supplies and given assurances about the prices they would receive.

In the post-war situation of severe deficit in world food supplies and the weak position of the pound sterling, the Agriculture Act of 1947 set the scene for agricultural policy for the next 25 years. It formalised the war-time arrangements and made provision for 'promoting and maintaining, by the provision of guaranteed prices and assured markets . . . , a stable and efficient agricultural industry', with due emphasis on domestic food production, proper remuneration for farmers and an adequate return on capital invested. These twin pillars of 'stability' and 'efficiency' were fostered by the provision of free advisory services, production grants for key inputs, and an annual Price Review at which the government and farmers' representatives negotiated guaranteed prices for a wide range of products for the year ahead. Subsequent Agriculture Acts, while still subscribing to the same objectives, saw the emphasis shift gradually away from direct support for farmers' incomes; first towards greater flexibility in domestic price and supply management, and later more towards engendering the kind of desirable technological and structural change that would move the agricultural sector in the direction of adjustment to its long-run equilibrium position in the economy.

Since 1973 Britain's membership of the European Community has required a further and marked change in the style of its agricultural policies. In meeting the diverse needs of the different member countries, the political process has resulted in a CAP which seems at present to be more intent on protecting European farmers from world market forces than on facilitating adjustment to greater technical and economic efficiency. And the resulting shift in Britain from farm income support via Exchequer payments to price support through market intervention has made more evident the essential conflict between producer and consumer interests. We shall return to these issues again later in the chapter.

Particular Characteristics of Agriculture which Shape Agricultural Policy

Secular Decline

Food is one of the main basic necessities for human existence, so the earliest forms of economic activity tend to be centred around agricultural production. In the process of economic growth and development, however, other industries become established and the emphasis in economic life progressively moves away from the agricultural sector towards first the industrial and later the service sectors of the economy.[2] The 'natural' state of agriculture in a growing economy, therefore, is to be declining in importance relative to other sectors.

The essential determinants of this basic pattern of change can be summarised in terms of the income elasticity of demand for agricultural products. At very low levels of income, which can only support biological subsistence, the income elasticity of demand for food is close to unity; any rise in income is largely spent on food to effect an improvement in the diet. As per capita incomes rise above subsistence, enabling a higher level and progressively more varied pattern of consumption, the income elasticity of demand for food inevitably falls, until eventually it approaches zero in the most affluent sections of the community.[3] The reason for this is obvious. There is a limit to consumers' capacity and willingness to consume food, and so the rate of increase in demand for food products in industrial nations falls over time until it approaches the rate of population growth. Once basic food demands have been met, additional income will be increasingly spent on products from the non-agricultural sectors of the economy – clothing, housing, consumer goods and services, and leisure, etc. Thus, in the absence of any direct interference by government, agriculture is steadily being pulled into a new pattern in relation to the rest of the economy, merely by the pressures arising from the continuing process of economic growth.

In the richer societies we must even be careful to distinguish between the demand for 'food' as purchased by the consumer and the demand for the basic output of the farmer. Much of the additional expenditures on food that come with higher incomes represent purchases of an increasing *service* element in the product – frozen, pre-packaged, processed foods, restaurant meals, etc. – which generate income for the food processing and associated service industries, but include no greater component of agricultural output nor income to the farm producer.

This relative decline in the role of agriculture is an inexorable process which has given rise to the so-called 'farm problem' characteristic of the advanced economies such as the USA and the EEC countries, and it provides both a social and an economic basis for establishing policies directed specifically at the agricultural sector. For if agriculture's share of the rising national income declines, then the returns to resources in farming will become progressively lower than those prevailing in the rest of the economy; per capita incomes earned by people working in agriculture will steadily fall below the national average and the agricultural population will show a continuing tendency to form a low income group. Clearly the market signals indicate that resources should move out of agriculture into the more rapidly expanding areas of consumer demand. The obvious remedy, of course, is for labour to move out to these expanding sectors of the economy (for the possibility of land use transfers is limited, while few of the capital inputs can hardly change their use), and to a certain extent this will occur automatically once the earnings differential becomes sufficiently marked to act as a spur.

However, the state may feel it desirable to deliberately intervene in this long-run agricultural adjustment process, rather than leave it to the uncertain hand of free market forces. For one thing, the loss of labour must involve farmers as well as farm workers. In general, it is the smaller farms, which cannot efficiently capture the benefits of capital-intensive technology, which must either gradually disappear for their land to be amalgamated into larger farm units, or their occupiers must find an additional source of income and thereby resort to part-time farming. But since the farm is also the family home and the rural existence a rather traditional and specific 'way of life', the occupational transfer completely out of agriculture is especially difficult for the farm family. In consequence, the adjustment of agricultural labour to the changing needs of the economy is a very slow process, with many farmers hanging on in the face of low incomes and creating a tendency for agriculture to become a depressed sector. The low income situation can become a regional problem of some social importance in those dominantly rural and agriculturally more marginal areas – the poorer farming areas and uplands in Britain for example – where alternative employment opportunities are severely limited.[4] The state often therefore sees a need to involve itself in the agricultural sector for social reasons, much as it does for other disadvantaged groups or depressed regions, in order to cushion the harsh impact of economic forces by supporting the level of farmers' incomes.

Technology Change. If agricultural output is not to decline as a result of losing labour, then some other inputs (specifically capital since the land stock is fixed) must be substituted in its place. But a situation of declining resource returns in agriculture provides neither adequate funds nor economic incentive for remaining farmers to adopt more productive technology and invest in the necessary labour-saving machinery. Given these circumstances, plus a general desire for low food prices, governments often pursue specific policies to encourage the generation, adoption and exploitation of new inputs and new production methods, and to foster changes in the size structure of farms in the search for potential economies of scale. The continual adoption of new technology causes the agricultural supply curve to shift outwards more rapidly than the demand curve – which we have already seen tends to expand slowly over time. In the face of the prevailing economic pressures too many farmers have attempted to remain in agriculture. To maintain their incomes they have struggled to invest in the more productive inputs and methods as they became available, thereby accelerating the rate of supply growth. But while for each individual farmer this type of response is both rational and necessary if his real income is to be maintained (or increased), paradoxically the aggregate effect of all farmers adopting new technology may be a worsening of the farm income problem. For given the approximately perfectly competitive conditions of agricultural production, and the inelastic demand for food products, this merely leads to oversupply and depressed prices. This scenario has been characterised as one in which farmers are on a 'treadmill of technology'. The lower food prices which result are beneficial to consumers (and welcomed by governments), but intensify the pressure on the farmer and the need for agricultural adjustment. Indeed, it is arguable that in countries such as the UK and USA the mass of consumers have benefited greatly at the expense of the farming community, and society appears to accept some responsibility to compensate farmers accordingly.

Instability. There are a variety of other economic and technical characteristics associated with the farm sector that give rise to situations calling for state interference on a more short-run basis. Because there are no technical substitutes for food as a component of consumer expenditures, the demand for agricultural products as a whole is relatively price inelastic. In the face of a demand curve of this nature, prices are extremely sensitive to variations in supply – as the most elementary market analysis makes clear. Yet the supply of agricultural output is inherently unstable because of its dependence on the uncontrollable climatic inputs of rain and sunshine in the biological production process. Despite technological advances in the form of irrigation systems, harvesting and drying equipment, and measures to control pests and diseases which serve to insulate the farmer from some of the vagaries of nature, actual output may still deviate markedly from that which the farmer expected when he made his initial resource allocation plans.

The resulting tendency for agricultural product supply and prices to vary from year to year is disadvantageous both domestically and internationally. For the consumer, fluctuating food prices automatically bring fluctuations in real income and the need for the adjustment of expenditure patterns. For the farmer, especially one who is a specialist producer in one or two products, unstable prices make forward planning of production hazardous, and represent a disincentive for appropriate investment in productive capacity. Furthermore, a price inelastic demand can bring about the somewhat paradoxical situation whereby farmers' revenues and incomes are lower in years of high output than in the seasons of 'unfavourable' production conditions.

As well as random variations in agricultural product prices over time, the relatively long lag between resource commitment and saleable output (one year for cereal crops, over two years for fat cattle, and up to seven years for certain perennial tree crops) can give rise to cyclical price fluctuations as epitomised by the classic 'cobweb' model.[5]

This inherent instability in agricultural product prices, both random and cyclical in character, provides yet another focus for government intervention through policies of price or market stabilisation (though whether these policy goals are primarily designed with the well-being of the consumer or the producer in mind is often a debatable point).[6] For a developing country whose economic fortunes depend on an exported agricultural commodity, the price fluctuations on world markets resulting from variations in world supply can play havoc with attempts to foster a programme of economic advance. Intervention in such cases tends to take the form of multinational (as opposed to domestic) arrangements, such as commodity agreements between producer and consumer countries (e.g. the International Wheat Agreement), or a cartel of producing countries to control supplies.

The Choice of Agricultural Policy Objectives

The package of agricultural policies pursued by any one nation is typically moulded by a set of forces, not always harmonious. Some of these forces originate from the general characteristics of agriculture referred to above (a) that the agricultural sector declines in importance as nations become wealthier; (b) that output prices decline as technology enables supply capabilities to expand faster than demand growth; and (c) that there are inbuilt tendencies for instability in agricultural prices, farm incomes, and the supply of individual commodities. The policies of most countries therefore include some measures to promote the needed 'adjustment' of the agricultural sector, some to enhance production efficiency, and some to improve the stability of agricultural markets.

Agricultural policies are also shaped by the specific characteristics of each country's agricultural sector, particularly its size in relation to the rest of the economy. In the UK and other industrial nations, where agriculture is a relatively small part of the economy, it is feasible to subsidise farm incomes because the cost of such support is relatively minor to the taxpayers or consumers who foot the bill. It is also possible for such countries to pursue agricultural policy to some extent independently of the economic policy directed to other sectors of the economy. The economic justifications for such policies are often unconvincing, and their development owes much to political considerations – as is evident with the CAP.

While the list of special considerations influencing agricultural policy could be extended to a great length it is more instructive to concentrate on a summary of major objectives of agricultural policy and the main types of measures for achieving them. Four principal aims of agricultural policy can be discerned. These are: to secure orderly resource *adjustment;* to *stabilise* farm prices, incomes and supply; to *support* farmers' incomes; and to *tax* away resources from agriculture for national development. (We could also add a fifth objective, that of national agricultural self-sufficiency, which has received powerful political support in such countries as the UK and Japan.)

The separate identification of these objectives does not, however, imply either that they are in practice distinct or mutually compatible. For example, the support and stabilisation objectives cannot be totally separated. During the post-war period developed industrial countries have consistently pursued policies to support farm incomes, in most cases using product market intervention measures. Since all of these measures, as indicated in the next section, involve establishing 'floor' prices in excess of free market prices, producer prices have been largely determined by administrative actions rather then by market forces. Hence pursuit of income support has automatically brought about a degree of price and income stabilisation. Note that there may well be a conflict between price and income stability. Stabilising prices in the face of large year-to-year output fluctuations will actually destabilise incomes; for if prices are fixed and prevented from *counter-acting* changes in supply, incomes will be forced lower in low output years and higher in years of high output. The income support objective also conflicts with that of orderly resource adjustment, inasmuch as it is difficult tc convince farmers they should leave agriculture when their incomes are maintained while they remain in the industry. Because of the inevitability and importance of agricultural adjustment, however, various measures to encourage rational change are present in the policy packages of the EEC, North America and Japan. These include retirement grants for elderly farmers, retraining grants for agricultural workers, small farm amalgamation schemes, and subsidies on certain inputs. The effectiveness of these measures is, however, still restricted by the effect of income support policies which artificially raise all farm incomes, including those of the least efficient, thus diluting the pressures for adjustment at the margin. The fourth objective mentioned above, the heavy taxation of agriculture, is clearly inconsistent with income support policies; it is not, therefore, an element of agricultural policy in industrialised nations, but is in the less developed countries.

Analysis of the Operation of Major Policy Instruments

There are three major classes of agricultural policy instruments: product market intervention measures; factor market intervention measures; and institutional reform. Attention in this section will focus on analysis of the operation of the most important amongst the first two sets of measures, using the procedures of elementary supply and demand analysis. The virtue of this approach is that it readily uncovers important issues about the choice of policy instruments, and it has shed much light on such controversies as the relative welfare effects of alternative mechanisms of farm income support. (See for example Josling 1970 and 1972.)

Product Market Intervention Policies

Deficiency Payments. Deficiency Payment Schemes were the basic method of UK agricultural support prior to its joining the EEC. At an Annual Review the government decided upon *minimum average prices* which farmers should receive for their produce in the following year, these guaranteed prices being almost invariably established at levels in excess of those at which imports were expected to be available. They were therefore designed to increase farmers' incomes above levels which would have occurred in the absence of the policy, and required continuous government subsidies in the form of 'deficiency payments' equal to the difference between guaranteed prices and realised market prices.

The effects of such a policy are indicated by figure 1.

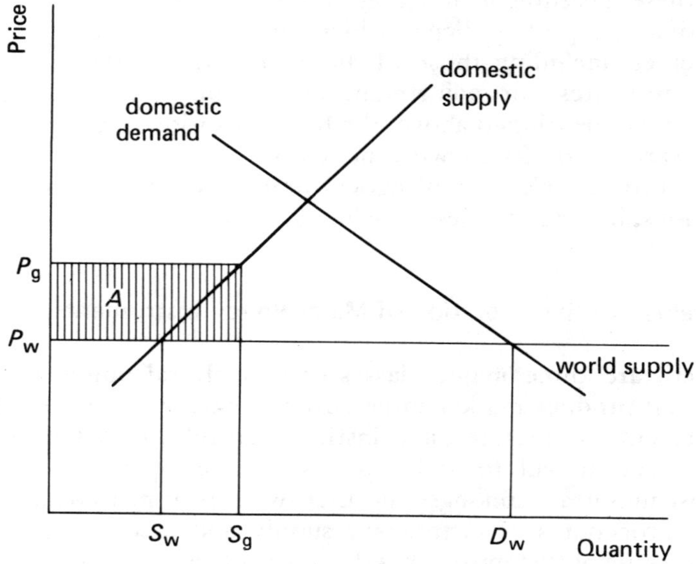

Figure 1

Assuming an infinitely elastic supply of the particular commodity on the world market at price P_w, the establishment of a guaranteed price of P_g would result in domestic supply increasing by an amount $S_g - S_w$. Because domestic supply can only be sold at P_w in competition with imported supplies, the additional domestic production has the effect of reducing imports by the same amount, but leaves unchanged the price paid and quantity consumed by households at P_w and D_w respectively. The shaded area A represents a transfer payment (subsidy) from taxpayers via the Exchequer to domestic producers.

Note that it would be possible to employ deficiency payment schemes in such a way that they played a strong price stabilisation role, but a much weaker income support role than they generally did in the British experience. This could be accomplished by setting guaranteed prices in line with expected average world market prices, so that deficiency payments would not be required in years of average or above average price.

Intervention Buying and Buffer-stock Schemes. These are formally equivalent, although the terms have come to be associated with different objectives for which the same basic instrument can be used. The term 'intervention buying' is associated with the intervention agencies under the CAP and with the Commodity Credit Corporation in the USA – organisations which have acted largely to support farm prices and incomes by removing excess supplies from the domestic market, and so continually needing to be subsidised in their operations. 'Buffer stock schemes' on the other hand are considered in the literature as 'pure' price stabilisation instruments which are self-financed in the long run inasmuch as they return their stocks to the domestic market in periods of low supply (Bateman 1965, Duloy 1966, Massell 1969). The essence of both types of operation is the existence of an agency which is empowered to purchase all supplies of a particular commodity at a pre-announced (*floor*) price. It is clear that in a closed economy produce will only generally be offered to the agency in the event of there being an excess of domestic supply

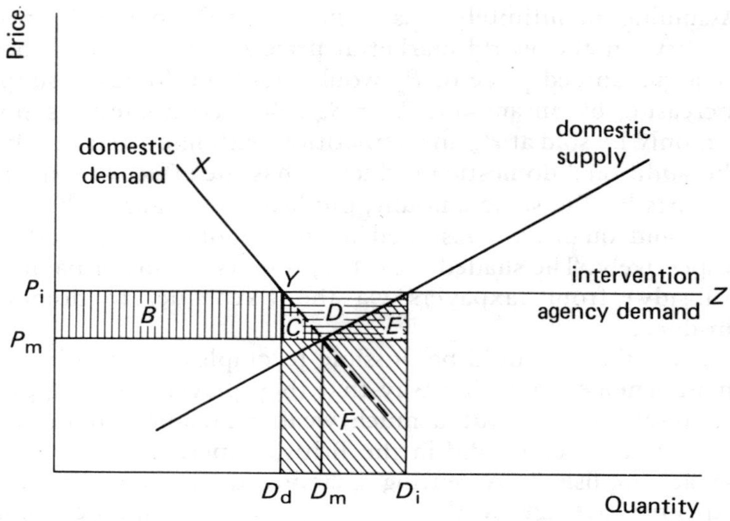

Figure 2

over demand at the intervention price. It is thus from the frequency of intervention buying, the types of produce to which it is applied, and the methods of disposing of the produce, that the distinction between the two types of operation has arisen.

The purchasing operations of this type of organisation are depicted in figure 2, in which a hypothetical agency is empowered to purchase any amount of a commodity at a floor price P_i. The agency thus creates a perfectly elastic demand curve at P_i, so that the total demand curve facing farmers becomes the sum of the normal domestic demand curve and the agency's demand curve; this is shown as the curve *XYZ*. At the intervention price the agency can expect to be offered the quantity $D_i - D_d$. It will be appreciated that, if intervention prices are fixed so that intervention purchases are made in the majority of years, both domestic demand and imports will be less over time than they otherwise would be, while domestic supply and exports will be greater. In figure 2 an export (stored) surplus of $D_i - D_d$ is seen to be created, domestic demand is reduced by $D_m - D_d$, and domestic supply increased by $D_i - D_m$ compared with the free market equilibrium pricing. Farmers' net incomes therefore improve by the amounts represented as the shaded areas $B + C + D$. It will similarly be appreciated that continuous intervention involves a cost to consumers who have to pay the higher price P_i instead of the equilibrium price P_m ; in figure 2 consumers are shown as losing consumer surplus $B + C$. This policy also creates a liability to the Exchequer, since the costs $C + D + E + F$ of purchasing produce into intervention may not be fully recoverable from later sales of the stored commodity.

In practice intervention agencies do not operate in closed economies, and for intervention prices to exceed market prices in an open economy implies that the intervention price exceeds the world market price. In this situation it may be necessary to restrain traders from importing grain at world prices in order to sell it to the intervention agency at the higher price P_i. Under the CAP this is achieved by imposing variable import levies (see below) with threshold prices set above P_i.

The more serious problem of intervention agencies concerns the disposal of the purchased produce. One alternative (as practised by the US during the 1950s and 1960s) is to allocate surpluses as food aid to developing countries. Another alternative is for the agency to sell off the produce at the low prevailing world price, thus incurring trading losses. In the case of perishable commodities this solution is inevitable as the EEC has recently discovered. In 1978 it resorted to selling large quantities of butter to Russia at a price some 20% below that which the European housewife was paying, in order to dispose of the 'butter mountain' that had accumulated through its intervention policy for the dairy sector. In this case it was the obvious transfer of benefits to consumers *outside* the Community that gave rise to a political storm, but other disposal methods are often no less contentious. The average domestic purchaser of food tends to be perplexed by the sheer waste of resources associated with the dumping of excess produce, using it for animal feed, giving it away to selected institutions, or subsidising its availability to selected groups of consumers – all of which are measures proposed to deal with the 'mountains' (or 'lakes') of beef, apples, milk, wine, that the CAP has generated. Trading losses are also inevitable with non-perishable commodities when income support policies are pursued by persistently setting intervention prices above world prices. This situation arose with wheat in the European Community of the Six in the late 1960s, when grain export subsidies (restitutions) were needed to dispose of intervention stocks. The theoretical price-stabilising buffer-stock agency, on the other hand, is not supposed to get caught in this position. It is supposed to set intervention prices equal to the expected average market price, so that stocks bought in low price years can be sold in high price years, with the price gain used to finance storage and administrative costs.

Taxes and Subsidies on Agricultural Trade. Where countries are involved in international agricultural trade the imposition of taxes, or the payment of subsidies, on the traded produce provides a straightforward means of causing domestic and international prices to diverge. Such divergence may be created in pursuit of income support and/or price stabilisation objectives.

Two major instruments of this type are employed under the CAP. One of these instruments is the imposition of *import levies,* which operate to raise domestic prices above international levels for commodities of which the country would be a net importer at the international price. The second is the granting of *export subsidies* which achieves basically the same outcome as import levies or tariffs, but for commodities of which the country is a net exporter at the protected domestic price.

Under CAP import levy schemes, as shown in figure 3, a threshold price is fixed below which no imported produce is allowed to enter the country. This threshold price P_t is enforced by charging levies to importers, the amount of the levy being varied depending upon the desired level of price support.[7] Because importers cannot afford to charge consumers less than P_t for their product, this becomes the domestic market price in net importing situations. As with the guaranteed price and intervention buying policies, pushing the price above P_w increases domestic supply from S_w to S_t

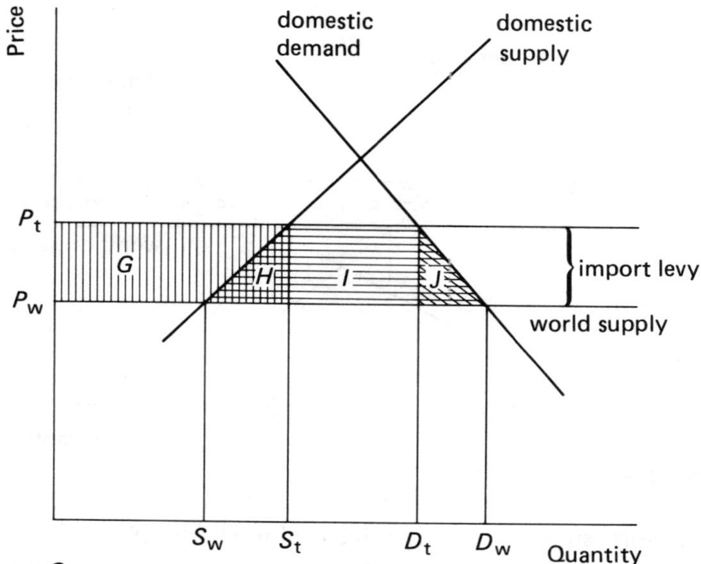

Figure 3

and thereby reduces import demand by a similar amount. There are, however, a number of effects which import levy policies share with intervention buying and export subsidy policies, but not with guaranteed prices for producers. These are that consumers are forced to pay P_t rather than the lower free market price P_w, which results in a cut-back in demand from D_w to D_t and an equivalent reduction in imports. It also causes a reduction in consumer surplus, represented by shaded areas $G + H + I + J$ in figure 3. It is because of these various effects that import levy and intervention buying schemes for supporting agricultural prices are considered more damaging to the interests of domestic consumers and overseas producers than guaranteed price policies through deficiency payments. To domestic producers the choice of policy is not so important, as under each they can obtain the same net income transfer shown for the import levy scheme as shaded area G in figure 3. The one group who in abstract clearly benefit from import levy or tariff schemes are taxpayers, for as shown in figure 3 the government receives revenues equal to shaded area I for the levy on imports $D_t - S_t$.

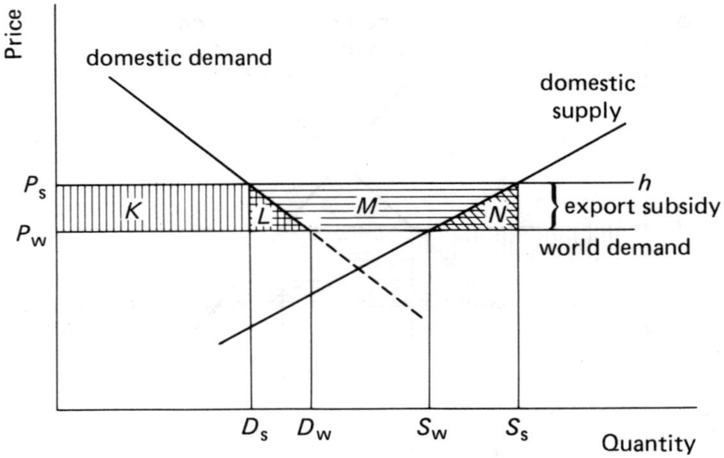

Figure 4

Export subsidy schemes have almost identical effects to import levies, except from the point of view of the taxpayer, who has to bear a subsidy cost (represented by the shaded areas $L + M + N$) of maintaining the higher product price P_s, as shown in figure 4. The effect of paying this subsidy is that exporters continue to export home-produced output until the domestic price rises to the level of the world price plus unit subsidy. Thus as with import levies, domestic prices are forced upwards, stimulating additional output (with a consequent increase in net farm incomes of $K + L + M$), domestic demand is reduced and the volume of exports increased. Hence domestic consumers again suffer higher prices with a loss of consumer surplus (shown as shaded areas $K + L$), and foreign producers are made to face additional (subsidised) competition in international markets.[8]

Crop Taxation Policies. This type of policy is of interest as a classic illustration of the exercise of monopsony power. The usual pattern, as found mainly in developing countries, is for a statutory organisation to be established to which all farmers have to sell their produce. For simplicity let us call such monopsonies Marketing Boards (although in practice not all so-called Marketing Boards have such power). Monopsony Marketing Boards can then employ their power to raise tax revenues for governments by paying farmers lower prices than are received by the Boards. This type of policy has been extensively pursued by African Marketing Boards in relation primarily to export crops (Helleiner 1966, Bauer 1971); because of the ease with which Boards can be circumvented in the marketing of food crops consumed domestically, monopsony power is difficult (and perhaps undesirable) to enforce for domestic food crops.

Marketing Boards acting as sole purchasers of farm produce were also established in Britain in the form of the Milk and the Hops Marketing Boards. These organisations, however, used their monopsony position at the farm-gate to establish monopoly power at the wholesale level, which they exploited via discriminatory pricing in different markets (for example the liquid and manufacturing milk markets) to raise producer revenues. The essential characteristic of these Boards is that they used their monopsony powers to exploit monopoly power at a higher stage in the market.

Factor Market Intervention Policies

Input Subsidies. Input price subsidisation is a widespread agricultural support measure, and is also employed in the form of direct grants and concessionary taxation allowances on capital investments. Unlike intervention in product markets which requires a scheme for each commodity, the subsidisation of, say, fertilizer reduces the production costs of all products which rely directly or indirectly upon fertilizer. It thus makes more sense to analyse the effects of such a policy using the aggregate agricultural supply and demand functions, rather than those for individual commodities.

The main effect of an input subsidy is to shift 'outwards' the agricultural supply curve; that is, to lower the marginal cost of production curve. If the agricultural land area is fixed, each additional increment in output will require successively larger applications of fertilizer and non-land inputs per acre, with the consequence that the subsidy per unit of output rises with the level of output. This is represented in figure 5 by a non-parallel shift of the supply curve. As can be seen, the effect of the subsidy is to increase domestic supply from S_0 to S_s and to reduce imports by the same amount. In the

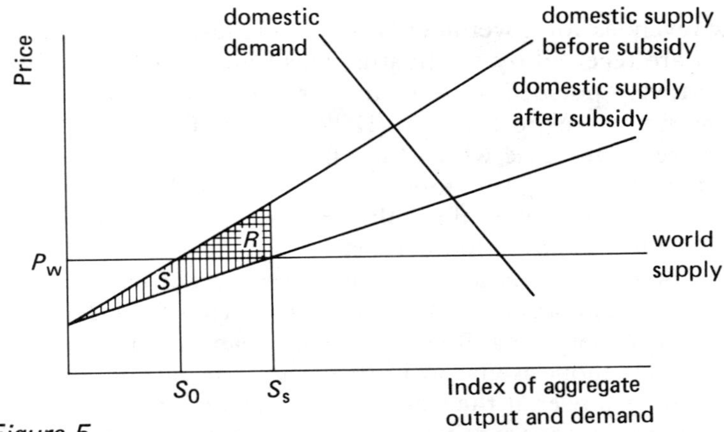

Figure 5

open economy depicted, the subsidy has no effect on consumers since the aggregate product price is unchanged at P_w. Producers, however, gain to the extent of an addition to net incomes equivalent to the shaded area S, and this is at the expense of taxpayers who have to bear a subsidy cost of $S + R$.

This static analysis of the benefits of the input subsidisation policy perhaps does it less than justice. One of the characteristic outcomes of subsidising the inputs associated with new technology is that it induces a permanent change in established production methods and a shift in the supply function which is not necessarily eliminated by terminating the subsidy. Product price support policies are not usually considered to exhibit this property, cessation of price support being assumed to cause supply to fall back to near its pre-support position.

Acreage Diversion. This unusual, but well-known, policy was instituted in the USA after intervention buying schemes to support farm prices during the early 1950s had resulted in the accumulation of large surpluses of grain and cotton which were costly to store. Moreover the grain stocks had continued to grow despite large-scale exports at subsidised prices. To combat the increasing public costs associated with the disposal or continuous holding of such stocks, the novel policy was introduced of paying farmers a subsidy for diverting some of their land to 'non-productive' use. Effectively this caused the agricultural supply curve to shift to the left, causing a reduction in the excess of domestic production over commercial demand at the intervention price, and hence reducing the amount of produce offered to the Commodity Credit Corporation. Broadly speaking the policy can be considered to have been neutral from the standpoint of domestic consumers, taxpayers and producers; obviously so in the case of consumers. For producers the diversionary payments compensated for the loss of net income from the sale of produce. From the taxpayers' point of view the costs of handling excess stocks were exchanged for the costs of the diversion subsidy.

General Remarks

The limitations of partial, comparative static supply–demand analysis should be borne in mind in the foregoing discussions. First, partial analysis may tend to overstate the magnitude of the effects of policy. For example, while a rise in the guaranteed price of wheat will cause expanded domestic supply and increased net farm income, the resources to produce the extra wheat may be drawn away from the production of other commodities such as barley or potatoes, whose supply is thereby reduced. In an open economy this will cause some decline in net farm income from these other sources. Second, static analysis takes no account of the long-run implications of these market intervention policies and their impact on the continuous process of adjustment that agriculture is undergoing. Furthermore, the effects of market intervention policies depend upon the institutional structure of agricultural marketing. Pricing policies are clearly only fully effective where well-functioning markets exist. Where efficient markets do not exist, chiefly in underdeveloped countries, policy action is often required to correct this by the setting up of state marketing organisations, small-farmers credit schemes and by the building of physical infra-structure. Conversely, the types of institutions are often a product of the policy measures implemented – witness the bureaucracy and complex administrative arrangements that have grown up around the CAP.

The CAP and Possible Future Directions

Each of the original six countries that joined to form the EEC under the Treaty of Rome in 1958 had evolved intervention measures suited to the characteristics and objectives of its own agricultural sector. To develop a European agricultural policy that was to operate uniformly across the diverse circumstances of all countries, therefore, required a great deal of political horse-trading and negotiation of competing interests; and, inevitably perhaps, the structure that finally emerged to become the CAP represented the kind of inflexible compromise that few would expect to serve as the ideal framework for fostering balanced adjustment towards a dynamic and efficient Community agriculture. Added to this the UK, only 50% self-sufficient in food and with its own distinctive and well established system of agricultural support, represented an obvious alternative viewpoint and competing interest, so that Britain's accession in 1973 placed further strain on an already creaking structure. Subsequent economic and political developments have required various *ad hoc* policy adjustments, and the CAP continues to provide an arena for dispute in the Community. It appears that various devices will enable the common policy to be patched up for a little longer, but there are suggestions from all sides – administrators, national politicians, academic commentators, producers and consumer groups – that the whole basis of the CAP must ultimately be restructured.[9] This is not to say, however, that any obvious alternative and feasible common policy suggests itself, and so modification will probably come more by adjustment than by wholesale reform.

Despite the fact that, in practice, it operates as a stunningly complex structure of administrative arrangements, in concept the CAP seems quite simple. A common wholesale price (the *target price*) is established across all member countries for each of a defined list of agricultural products.[10] For commodities available more cheaply on world markets, this necessitates imposition of a *threshold* price below which no supplies are permitted to enter the Community. Imposition of an import levy equal to the difference between the threshold price and the (lower) world price serves to ensure this minimum level of internal price. In the case of commodities in local over-supply the 'floor' or *intervention price* at which the Community's agencies will purchase any production offered by domestic farmers is then set below the target price. Because of the high support price levels many commodities tend to be in over-supply year after year and give rise to ever accumulating surpluses. To help reduce such surpluses restitutions (export subsidies) are paid by the CAP equal to the difference between the world price and the higher target price.[11]

The common levels for all these institutional support prices are specified in *units of account* (ua) and determined at farm price review negotiations held between December and March annually.[12] Farmers cannot be paid in ua, however, for it is not a currency but merely an accounting device. The translation of prices set in ua to prices in national currencies has become the source of many of the complexities, anomalies and distortions that now surround the application of the common pricing system across member countries, as we shall see.

Setting community prices in terms of national currencies was comparatively simple at the outset of the EEC in the era of fixed exchange rates. The breakdown in the fixed exchange rate system, first in the late 1960s with the devaluations of weaker currencies, and then with the move to floating exchange rates during the early 1970s brought the system of common agricultural prices under strain.

The maintenance of common agricultural prices requires that the conversion of prices set in ua to prices set in national currencies is at the prevailing exchange rates between member countries. Under a system of fixed exchange rates (as existed until the early 1970s) this poses few problems, but flexible exchange rates mean that farm prices in each country fluctuate with daily movements in exchange rates. Apart from making it impossible to administer a scheme of intervention buying at pre-specified intervention prices, such price fluctuations destroy the whole concept of farm income support and stability through the establishment of fixed target prices to guide farmer decisions. In consequence, for the purpose of expressing CAP prices in terms of member countries' currencies, the EEC has maintained fixed exchange rates in the form of *representative rates of exchange* (green currency rates).

Maintaining fixed green currency rates leads to further problems. Depreciation in a country's currency on the foreign exchange markets reduces all its prices in terms of other countries' currencies, thereby making its produce more competitive in trade; conversely, appreciation in its currency leads to higher, less competitive, prices in trade. To counter these effects on competitiveness between member countries and thus preserve a common price, a system of border taxes and subsidies known as Monetary Compensatory Amounts (MCAs) was introduced. These were intended as a temporary expedient but, with the accession of the UK, Ireland and Denmark to the EEC in 1973 and the progressive move to floating exchange rates, the MCA system was expanded and became increasingly complex.

The breakdown of the international monetary system based on fixed rates of exchange also prompted a redefinition of the ua, which from 1973 was linked to the value of the currencies in the European 'snake' and became effectively the *joint float unit of account*. Community agricultural prices were set in terms of this unit and as the currencies of the snake appreciated/depreciated on world currency markets so Community farm prices rose/fell in relation to world prices. Since the snake included only the stronger European currencies, CAP prices rose against world prices as the snake appreciated against other currencies; as a result the typical European wheat farmer is now protected by as much as a 60% import levy from wheat imports from the USA.

Following the creation of the European Monetary System in March 1979 the ua was again redefined. The inclusion of most of the EEC currencies in the EMS allowed some simplification of the MCA system, since there were fewer exchange rate changes to adjust for. Because sterling is outside the EMS, it attracts *variable* MCAs as the market rate of sterling varies with the ua. The German mark, on the other hand, is inside the EMS and attracts a *fixed* MCA.

The level of the farm prices in member countries therefore depends not only on the agreed common CAP prices, but also on the green currency rates of the individual countries. Annual farm price reviews are concerned not only with common prices, but also with revaluations and devaluations of the seven green currencies.[13] The negotiations have tended to become exercises in *national* price fixing, with the net effect of progressively weakening the reality of common prices. The artificial green rates have been set more to reflect individual national food and farm price preferences than the market rate of exchanges of the countries' currencies. The level of farm prices in Germany is fully one third higher than those in the UK, with those in Benelux, Denmark and Ireland (in that order) not far behind. In this sense the value of the ua, and even the ua prices themselves, are largely irrelevant; the CAP is 'common' only in the institutional arrangements by which it interferes in agricultural markets.

The UK's interest in any future developments in the CAP is high. As a major food importer its concern lies with enjoying low food prices – with due attention being given to the well-being of farmers as an interest group. Prior to joining the Community the British consumer could reap the advantage of purchasing basic food commodities at relatively low world prices, while income support to farmers came in the form of deficiency payments through the Exchequer. In the EEC system of farm income support via market prices, Britain's general interest would seem to be in maintaining a high exchange rate for the green pound to keep her own domestic food prices as low as possible in relation to whatever level the 'common' prices may be set in the CAP (although this would clearly not be in the interest of British producers). The higher sterling's green rate relative to its market rate of exchange, the higher the MCA's on food imports into Britain – which are effectively subsidies paid from Community funds to the British consumer.

On the other hand, the present structure of high maintained farm prices and the associated administrative arrangements to satisfy different member countries' competing requirements, comes at some real cost to both Britain and other EEC members. The budget costs, for one thing, are exceptional; three-quarters of the total Community budget is absorbed by the CAP, 70% being income support and only 5% being directed to fostering structural adjustment in the agricultural sector. In terms of resource allocation efficiency, the long term costs to the Community of distorting price signals and impeding the 'natural' adjustments of agriculture are probably very high. These costs come in the artificially induced domestic production (and persistent over-production) at the expense of potentially cheaper supplies from third countries; in the loss of benefits from regional specialisation and rational allocation of agricultural resources that an effective common pricing system would (theoretically) encourage; in the undiscriminating (and unnecessary) transfer of more benefits to the larger and wealthier producers than to the smaller and more vulnerable farmers for whom income support objectives are relevant; and ultimately in the leakage of these benefits away from farmers anyway as the support policy raises the demand for non-farm inputs, encourages inappropriate investment and bids up the price of agricultural land – possibly leaving the farmer no better off than before. Many of these costs are clearly perceived by those who must bear them; by the consumers who must pay higher prices for food; by efficient foreign producers denied access to EEC agricultural markets and whose markets in third countries are threatened by subsidised EEC exports; and by EEC taxpayers who are increasingly called upon to bear the rising costs of the CAP (since import levies provide a progressively smaller share of the necessary revenue).[14] These groups constitute a strong force with a common interest in reducing the high price support levels of the CAP and in its reform. Although they have not had any major impact yet, partly because there are such major political difficulties in changing the system, support price increases have been modest in the last two price reviews.

Many suggestions have been made to modify the CAP and reduce both its cost and its anomalies. One of these is for budgetary restrictions to be imposed on the intervention purchases and export restrictions, thus effectively either establishing a quota on the amount of product eligible for support or limiting the unit level of support offered. Another proposal is that the former British system of deficiency payments should be adopted as the farm support mechanism, but this is probably unacceptable, even under a different name, to the original Community members. More realistically, Marsh (1977) has suggested a modification of existing arrangements based on a different concept of the ('common') price which the Council of Ministers negotiates each year. Instead of attempting to fix a price appropriate for consumers and producers, the Council would negotiate a *trading* price at which agricultural commodities would change hands between member countries. Having settled this, member states would then be entirely free to fix their own internal prices – possibly separating consumer and producer prices by means of subsidies if they chose, or perhaps raising prices to both groups by levies and intervention buying. Whatever internal price policy were followed, the cost of diverging from the common price levels of the Community would be borne by the individual member country. Such a policy of common trading prices but differing domestic prices has the advantage of allowing national interests to be expressed while still maintaining a collective policy structure. The trading price would represent a degree of preference for Community goods over third country produce. It would afford a secure outlet for agricultural exporting member countries and secure access to the Community market for importing member countries. The extent of the preference given to Community producers could take into account such issues as stability in supplies and prices, food aid commitments the Community wished to service, as well as a protective element similar to that accorded to other industries through the Common External Tariff. The price-enforcing mechanism could continue to employ variable import levies, intervention purchase and export restitution.

Whatever particular mechanisms are adopted, however, there would always seem to be an essential paradox involved in a policy which, although framed in terms of a recognition that the secular economic pressures on agriculture imply a need for continuing structural adjustment in the sector, acts to nullify these pressures and impede the progressive transformation of agricultural production. Seen in this light, measures to support low farm incomes seem to be a classic example of treating the symptoms of the disease rather than its cause. Added to this, the enlargement of the EEC to embrace the larger consumer market of Britain, and the subsequent inclusion of the Mediterranean agricultures of Greece, Spain and Portugal (as proposed), represents a fundamental realignment of the forces of food demand and supply and signals an array of economic forces for agricultural readjustment that probably cannot be handled with a policy framework originally devised as a compromise to enable six countries slowly to harmonize their agricultures along common lines. Even more than before, the contemporary EEC is faced with the difficult choice between the potential economic benefits of resource use rationalisation over a wide geographical area, and the political and social consequences that the inevitable redistribution of benefits amongst previously separate and competing nations must imply.

Notes

1. Indeed, even though employing less than 3% of the working population, agriculture ranks as one of the largest single industries in the UK, having an annual gross output of some £7,250 million.
2. Not all national economies follow an identical route in this direction though, and there are some exceptions to the general pattern: Denmark and New Zealand for instance are 'developed' economies which are also heavily dependent in international trade on their highly productive agricultural sectors.
3. In the UK the income elasticity for all food products taken together is now in the region of 0.2.
4. Such regions are specifically identified as 'less favoured areas' and singled out for special support under the provisions of the CAP.
5. See for example Lipsey (1971, Chapter 12). The price of beef in the EEC seems currently to be suffering from just such a phenomenon.
6. For a review of agricultural stabilisation policies, see Colman (1978).
7. With this method the levy varies inversely with movements in the world price level, and is known as a *variable levy*. More common in

international trade are constant absolute or proportionate value tariffs or levies. The basic analysis in figure 3 is applicable to all types of tariffs or levies.

8. The impact of the CAP on third countries who find themselves squeezed out of the European market in various ways has received much attention recently. Austria, Yugoslavia, New Zealand and Botswana have all been cited as cases in point.
9. In particular it is argued that emphasis must be placed on *structural* policy for agriculture, which was originally one of the CAP's twin aims, but over time has become swamped by *support* policy.
10. These are: cereals, sugar, dairy products, beef and veal, pigmeat, poultry and eggs, vegetable oils and fats, and various fruits and vegetables. The main exclusions from the British point of view are sheep products and potatoes.
11. Many other prices are referred to in the CAP, especially in connection with livestock products, e.g. guide prices, basic prices, reference prices, etc. Their operation is not substantially different from those described above, though the policy for each commodity does have its distinctive features.
12. See Harris and Swinbank (1978) for a useful account of this system of essentially political negotiations between the Commission, the Council of Ministers and other interested parties. The flavour of the whole process is indicated by their conclusion that 'a mechanism which relies on the exhaustion of the main negotiators in order to produce agreement is inherently suspect'!
13. Thus throughout the Spring of 1979 the British Minister of Agriculture fought against any general rise in CAP prices (which would disadvantage British consumers) but did support a 5% devaluation of the green pound (which would raise the prices received only by the farmers of Britain and no other member country).
14. The high budgetary costs of the CAP, and Britain's major share in contributing to them, became a hot political topic in early 1979 when it was suggested that membership of the EEC cost the UK population £20 per head annually. (Such gross calculations, however, have very little real meaning.)

References

Colman, D.R., 'Some aspects of the economics of stabilisation', *Journal of Agricultural Economics*, Volume 29, September 1978, pp. 243–256.

Harris, S. and Swinbank, A., 'Price fixing under the CAP – proposition and decision', *Food Policy*, Volume 3, November 1978, pp. 256–271.

Josling, T.E., *Agriculture and Britain's Policy Dilemma*, Thames Essay Number 2, Trade Policy Research Centre, London 1970.

Josling, T.E. *et al.*, *Burdens and Benefits of Farm Support Policies*, Agricultural Trade Paper Number 1, Trade Policy Research Centre, London, 1972.

Lipsey, R.G., *An Introduction to Positive Economics* (4th edn), Weidenfeld and Nicolson, 1975.

Marsh, J.S., *UK Agricultural Policy within the European Community*, CAS Paper Number 1, Centre for Agricultural Strategy, University of Reading, November 1977.

Swinbank, A., *The British Interest and the Green Pound*, CAS Paper Number 6, Centre for Agricultural Strategy, University of Reading, June 1978.

5. The economics of energy policy

CHARLES K. ROWLEY*
Professor of Economics,
University of Newcastle upon Tyne

Introduction

The voices of those who forecast an approaching world energy apocalypse as a direct consequence of the excessive depletion of finite and irreplaceable energy resources have become much more muted with the passage of time since the upward adjustment of world oil prices following the 1973 Yom Kippur War. For, with the notable and serious exception of the United States of America, the Western world for the most part has responded to market forces, however reluctantly, and has set in process a chain reaction of energy conservation adjustments. The short-term oil market disruption triggered by the religious revolution in Iran yet may induce a similar response within the USA which, for understandable reasons, has been slow to adjust to its unaccustomed position as an energy-importing economy.

* Although I am a member of The United Kingdom Radioactive Waste Management Advisory Council, the views expressed in this chapter are entirely my own, and not necessarily those of the Council itself. This chapter was written whilst I was on leave from The University of Newcastle upon Tyne as a visiting research associate at The Center for Study of Public Choice, Virginia Polytechnic Institute and State University, Blacksburg, Virginia, USA. I am indebted to members of the Center, most especially James M. Buchanan and Gordon Tullock, for their support, encouragement and critical comment.

Yet, the notion that energy resources in some sense are special persists throughout the Western world, and remains a notable feature even of newly-Conservative Britain, despite the apparent success of market forces in equilibrating the changing forces of supply and demand when unfettered by government and bureaucratic interventions. In order to understand just why such a situation persists and the extent, if at all, to which it is justified, an excursion is required into the relatively new economic theory of public policy at the interface between the disciplines of economics and political science. For the energy study, in reality, is an excellent example of just how far the mixed economies of the West have slipped from the sound principles of market economies first formally outlined in 1776 by Adam Smith in *The Wealth of Nations*. That such slippage has indeed occurred would disturb but not surprise a freshly-reincarnated Smith, for the wily sage is known to have remarked with penetrating perspicacity that 'there is a great deal of Ruin in a Nation'.

The World Energy Situation

The Planet Earth is endowed with an accumulated stock of energy resources, mainly, though not exclusively, in the form of fossil fuels and of uranium, together with a continuing flow of additional energy resources mainly, though not exclusively, from the sun. In neither case are these resources easily quantified nor are they the subject of precise definition. Indeed, the principal problem of measuring known energy resources is that such resources in no sense are a physical constant but are dependent upon future time-paths of recovery costs and of energy prices. For whether or not a source of potential energy is indeed a resource is an economic and not a physical issue – a fact that too often is ignored by doomsday scientists. Furthermore, materials which appear to offer no potential as an energy resource may have much to contribute to some future society as a consequence of scientific advance (uranium, for example).

Estimates of world mineral energy reserves are given in table 1, defined in terms of millions of tons of oil equivalence (MTOEs).

Table 1. *Total world fossil fuel and uranium reserves and consumption*

Fossil fuels	*Proved reserves (thousand MTOE)*	*Estimated ultimately recoverable reserves (thousand MTOE)*	*1975 consumption (thousand MTOE per annum)*	*Proved reserves ÷ 1975 consumption (years)*	*Ultimate reserves ÷ 1975 consumption (years)*	*Duration ultimate reserves at 4% exponential growth consumption (years)*
Oil	80.4	233	2.7	30	90	37
Gas	56.5	171	1.1	50	155	51
Coal	329.0	645	1.9	175	340[1] – 1700[2]	71[1] – 110[2]
Total	465.9	3225	5.7	—	—	—
Uranium[3]	*Proved reserves (thousand MTOE)*	*Proved and provable reserves (thousand MTOE)*				
Up to $15/lb[4]	19	37				
Up to $30/lb[4]	32	59				
Up to $30/lb in fast reactors	1590	2932				

1 and 2. 10% and 50% recovery rates respectively. There are no published estimates of recoverability factors applicable to ultimate reserves of coal. There is a wide range of possible recovery rates, depending on economic and other factors.

3. Excluding Communist countries

4. Use in current design of thermal reactors

(Source: Cmnd 7101, *Energy Policy: A Consultative Document*, HMSO 1978)

The estimates of ultimately recoverable reserves of fossil fuels are subject to very considerable uncertainty, for reasons outlined above. Even the calculations of proved reserves are prone to error, since they are based upon recovery rates which almost certainly are conservative in that they were based on forecasts of energy prices that have already been greatly exceeded. The estimates of ultimately recoverable uranium reserves are subject to yet greater uncertainty. Exploration of uranium has not been as extensive or comprehensive as that for fossil fuels and additional reserves may turn out to be large. However, some reserves will not easily be recovered and the issue of economic attractiveness is difficult to forecast. In the absence of further information, it was not considered to be meaningful to present statistics for the duration of reserves as was done for fossil fuels.

Table 1 suggests that oil is the energy resource which is closest to exhaustion, whether attention is centred upon proved or upon ultimately recoverable reserves. Proved reserves are sufficient to support only 30 years consumption at current rate and indeed, if further discoveries do not occur, consumption would become severely constrained in the very near future since, for technical reasons, only a small proportion of remaining reserves can be produced at any point in time. Major uncertainties exist as to the level of undiscovered reserves and the rate at which they will be located and exploited. But even the most optimistic forecasts envisage oil supplies levelling off and then declining before the year 2000, whilst forecasts based upon a 4% exponential growth rate in consumption would eliminate all 'ultimate reserves' by the year 2015.

Natural gas supplies appear to be less close to exhaustion than oil supplies, although the future role of gas must be constrained by the fact that it is more difficult and expensive to transport over long distances. The most significant consumers of natural gas are the USA, Europe and Japan, whilst over 50% of the world's gas reserves are located in the USSR and the Middle East. It cannot be assumed that the bulk of such latter reserves will be available for would-be Western consumers.

Evidently, the level of world coal reserves will not act as a constraint on world coal production through the year 2000.

Like gas, however, coal is relatively difficult and costly to transport. Moreover, some 63% of proved and probable world coal reserves are believed to be located in Communist countries, mainly China and the USSR. Of the remainder, some 78% is located in North America. The availability of coal through the Western world, therefore, will depend upon the export position adopted by the USA.

The level of uranium reserves, from the viewpoint of energy consumption, depends crucially upon the prospects for the widespread adoption of the fast reactor. For, without the fast reactor, the limited availability of uranium might constrain the commission rate of nuclear power stations even during the early 1990s. Since fast breeder reactors offer up to 70 times as much energy output as the equivalent volume of uranium utilised in light water reactors, the acceptance of the fast breeder reactor would greatly increase the importance of uranium as an energy resource.

A number of other energy resources make small additional contributions to world energy supplies, most notably such non-depletable inputs as hydro, geothermal, tidal, wind and solar power. Of these, it is unlikely that any other than solar power will make major *additional* contributions to world energy supply in the foreseeable future. The immense potential for solar energy awaits future technical progress, but constitutes the single most likely solution to the energy depletion problem in the very long term. In the interim, the prospect remains of obtaining energy from atomic fusion – a process in which light atoms (e.g. hydrogen) are joined together and release energy via hydrogen-bomb-type reactions – and the resources most likely to be utilised in such a process, namely deuterium and lithium, appear to be available in large quantities in the sea. Even the more conservative of scientists predict that fusion will be technically possible within 45 years, whilst optimists predict its introduction by the turn of the century. If the 1979 attitudes within the USA to the energy depletion problem are sustained, the optimists will be proved correct.

Although forecasts of the non-Communist world fossil supply situation in the year 2000 are beset by extreme uncertainty, even when rendered conditional explicitly upon specific nuclear scenarios, table 2 sets out three alternatives,

Table 2. *Non-Communist world fossil fuel supply in 2000 AD (billion tons of oil equivalent)*

Source	*1975 actual*	*Department of Energy*	*WAES High-growth high-coal scenario*	*WAES Low-growth high-nuclear scenario*
Oil (including shale oil and tar sands)	2.2	3.0–3.5	3.6	3.0
Natural gas	0.8	1.0	1.2	1.0
Solid fuels	0.9	1.5–2.0	1.7	1.1
Total	3.9	5.5–6.5	6.5	5.1

(Source: Cmnd 7101, *Energy Policy: A Consultative Document*, HMSO 1978.)

as outlined by the Department of Energy in the United Kingdom. Although the Department of Energy presents no conditional statements underpinning its own forecasts, it appears to be taking an intermediate position between the two alternatives presented by the 'Workshop on Alternative Energy Strategies' (WAES) in its analysis of 'Energy Global Prospects 1985– 2000'.

The long-term rate of world energy consumption is no less difficult to forecast than is the ultimate supply situation and the rate at which it will be released. Naive demand models, such as those espoused by the Club of Rome during the early 1970s simply express energy consumption as a linear function of real income and then proceed on the basis of exponential extrapolations of world output growth to the doomsday conclusion. However well such econometric models may appear to fit past data over a time-period when energy resources were relatively plentiful and cheap, it cannot be expected that they will predict at all effectively a future situation in which the increasing scarcity of energy resources is reflected in sharply rising real market prices, which themselves feed back negatively upon the rate of growth of world output. Clearly, in such circumstances more sophisticated econometric modelling is required, with some attempt at least to estimate the price and income elasticities of demand for energy resources and the nature of the relationship between energy resource depletion as reflected in real energy prices and the rate of world economic growth. Nor should any such conditional forecasts be treated with anything but acute scepticism, given the very considerable uncertainty which surrounds all aspects of the exercise.

A number of forecasts of energy demand exist for the non-Communist world for the year 1985 and table 3 outlines four recent examples, all of which were prepared prior to the disruption of Iranian oil supplies in 1979. The fact that all the forecasts assumed that oil prices would remain roughly constant in 1977 real terms indicates the limited validity of exercises of this kind.

Forecasting world demand for energy in the year 2000 is an altogether more treacherous exercise, since the future rate of economic growth is very difficult to forecast over such a lengthy time-period. It is generally accepted, however, that the achieved growth rate of 5% per annum from 1960 to 1973 will not be maintained. Estimates range between 3 to 4% per annum at the present time. Moreover, although over the period 1960 to 1973 energy demand increased *pari passu* with economic growth, the former is expected to increase at a relatively slower rate in the future as a consequence of rising real energy prices. On such assumptions, non-Communist world energy demand in the year 2000 will lie between 7.5 and 10 billion tons of oil equivalent. It is clear that fossil fuels will be insufficient to satisfy such a scale of world energy demand at the turn of the century.

The implications of this are fairly obvious. Countries increasingly will have to rely upon some combination of energy conservation and of developing alternative non-fossil-based energy resources. At best hydro-electricity can be expected to provide only 0.5 billion tons of oil equivalent energy by the year 2000. The only alternative is nuclear electricity. If the expected shortfall in energy consumption is to be closed, nuclear capacity will have to increase in the non-Communist world at the rate of 80 gigawatts per annum between now and the turn of the century. Such a rate of expansion is feasible only if fast breeder reactors are utilised.

Table 3. *Non-Communist energy supply and demand 1985 and demand for OPEC oil (million tons of oil equivalent)*

	Department of Energy	*OECD*[1]	*CIA*[2]	*WAES*[3] *(scenario D low growth)*
Assumed economic growth in OECD area (1975–85)	4.3%	4.8%	4.2%[4]	3.1%
Non-Communist world:				
Energy consumption	5935	6128		5475
Energy supply (excluding OPEC oil)	4356	4356		3795
Net oil imports	1579	1772	1925–2125	1680
Net Communist oil imports	–40	–40	175–225	–
OPEC oil exports	1539	1732	2100–2350	1680
OPEC oil consumption	208	208	250–200	140
Residual and increase in stocks	42	25	–	–
Demand for OPEC oil	1789 (35.8%)	1965 (39.3%)	2350–2550 (47.51%)	1820 (36.4%)

1. OECD 'World Energy Outlook' January 1977, reference case, (economic growth rate adjusted from base year 1974 to base year 1975).
2. Central Intelligence Agency 'International Energy Situation' April 1977.
3. Workshop on Alternative Energy Strategies, 'Energy Global Prospects 1985–2000'.
4. Excludes Australia and New Zealand.

(*Source:* Cmnd 7101, *'Energy Policy: A Consultative Document'*, HMSO 1978.)

There is a sense, therefore, in which the nuclear battle already almost is won. Certainly, those countries which fall foul of the anti-nuclear lobbies condemn themselves, in gross national product per capita terms, to relative poverty during the early part of the 21st century.

The Relative Importance of OPEC Oil

Reference has already been made in this chapter to the particular advantages of oil as an energy resource as a consequence of its relative cheapness in transportation and its adaptability as a resource input, especially in premium markets such as liquid fuel for automotive purposes. Between 1950 and 1973, oil accounted for a very substantial proportion of the growth in world primary energy consumption of 4.6% per annum, together with natural gas and primary electricity. Coal consumption barely changed during this period.

The rapid expansion in oil consumption was induced in large part by the availability of very low cost oil during the 1950s and 1960s from the Middle East and North Africa. During this period, imported oil was cheap in the consuming countries compared with indigenously produced energy. The increasing reliance of the energy consuming nations upon the oil exporting countries for low-cost energy supplies encouraged, in 1960, the formation of the Organisation of Petroleum Exporting Countries (OPEC) and, in 1971–73, in the assumption by producing governments of control over oil production and prices. Such controls were exercised in the autumn and winter of 1973–74 when OPEC imposed a limited oil embargo following the Yom Kippur War and doubled and then redoubled oil prices in October and December 1973. Thus OPEC oil prices rose from around $3 per barrel in mid-1973 to some $11.65 per barrel in January 1974. Following the disruption of Iranian oil supplies during 1978–79, OPEC oil prices have jumped once again, though less uniformly than in the past, with prices in mid-1979 ranging from $20 to $25 per barrel for regular contracted supplies and peaking at around $30 per barrel for emergency supplies in certain European 'spot' markets. There are signs that OPEC, or certain of its member states, will raise prices once again to compensate for the decline in the value of the US dollar which their most recent price increases have helped to accelerate.

Although great play is made both in the popular press and in the more professional literature about the alleged cartel powers of OPEC, too much should not be made of this phenomenon. From the outset OPEC has appeared to be a highly unstable cartel, unlikely to survive effectively even in the medium term. For, although it controls some 50% of world oil output, some 66% of world proved oil reserves and over 90% of world crude oil exports, OPEC nevertheless is made up of eleven independent nation states spanning several continents. The market share of individual members is widely dispersed, offering high incentives for individual members to increase their market share through undetected price shading. In addition, the political philosophies of member states vary widely, giving rise to very different attitudes (for example, as between Saudi-Arabia and the Gulf States on the one hand and Iraq on the other) concerning the impact of oil prices on the economic well-being of the non-Communist world. In such circumstances the present difficulties within OPEC, with the emergence of a two-tier pricing system and conflict between members over output decisions, was predictable from 1974 onwards (indeed was predicted in the predecessor to this chapter). To all intents and purposes OPEC is now defunct as a cartel organisation.

Indeed, even if OPEC should re-establish its monopoly position in the wake of some further international event (for example, the downfall of the Khomeini regime and subsequent Soviet penetration into the Gulf) there are limits to the price increases that a self-seeking cartel will try to impose. Once prices have risen to the monopoly level, only by assuming continuously increasing monopoly power is it possible to envisage further and continuous monopoly-induced price increases for OPEC oil. Of course if OPEC itself were to fall into Soviet hands – as the Shah of Iran has predicted will occur – self-seeking by the monopoly supplier might take on political rather than economic characteristics with very serious implications for the non-Communist world. In such circumstances, the failure of the Western world to support the Shah's position may come to be viewed as one of the most serious political errors of the postwar period. But that, let us hope, is another story.

Future trends in oil prices will be strongly influenced by the expansion of production capacity by the producing countries. Prior to the disruption of Iranian supplies, OPEC appears to have been operating significantly below its estimated production capacity of 1950 million tons annually and current plans indicate an expansion to 2250–2350 million tons by 1985. This should be adequate to satisfy all the forecasts of consumption growth outlined in table 3, although a failure of such capacity to emerge would undoubtedly necessitate the curtailment of consumption by further increases in OPEC real prices.

The United Kingdom Energy Situation

Energy plays an important role in the United Kingdom economy, within the context both of production and of consumption. If the energy industries are confined by definition to coal mining, petroleum and natural gas production, coke ovens and manufacture of fuel, mineral oil refining, gas, electricity and wholesale distribution of petroleum products, they employ some 3% of the working population and contribute about 4½% of gross domestic product at factor cost. In 1976 their customers expended £13½ billion on energy, including over £2 billion in taxes. In 1976 the net visible trade deficit on fuels stood at about £4 billion, though it is now disappearing as North Sea oil output increases.

Between 1950 and 1973/4, the United Kingdom had diversified from an essentially two-fuel economy based on coal and imported oil into an economy based on four primary fuels, namely oil, coal, natural gas and nuclear electricity. Oil, the dominant fuel, then was wholly imported, although oil reserves already had been located in the North Sea. Coal remained an important fuel, accounting for some 38% of primary energy supplies, but had been contracting throughout the period in question largely as a consequence of the relative cheapness of oil. The gas industry, stimulated first by the switch from coal to oil as a primary energy input, and subsequently by the discovery of natural gas, was expanding in response to market growth. Nuclear electricity accounted for only some 3% of energy supplies.

Since 1973 the overall impression of the UK as a four-fuel economy has not changed, although the previous continuing increase in oil's share of the market has been reversed; indeed it has declined from 46% in 1973 to 40% in 1977. North Sea oil is contributing significantly and increasingly to UK energy supplies and the first two Advanced Gas Reactor stations have now come on stream. Total energy consumption has been constrained at a level below that achieved in 1973.

By comparison with most industrial countries the UK appears to be well-endowed with primary energy resources. Although as yet there are no proven reserves of uranium ore, there are substantial reserves of oil and gas and very large reserves of coal. The depleted uranium available from past operations of nuclear programmes constitutes an energy reserve which, if used in fast reactors, would be equivalent to some 40 billion tons of coal. In such circumstances, the UK is expected at least to be self-sufficient and possibly to be a net exporter of energy for some years from 1980 onwards. Such a situation is unlikely to insulate the UK from longer-term constraints, however, as the 20th century draws to a close. For, at present, the UK consumes some 3% of the world's annual output of oil and gas, whilst estimates of total recoverable reserves of these resources suggest that they will account only for some 1–2% of the world total. In such circumstances important decisions will be required (and undoubtedly will be forthcoming) concerning the nature of UK energy supplies through the turn of the century.

The Nature of Government Intervention in the United Kingdom Energy Market

Much of the United Kingdom energy industry has been in public ownership for the major part of the postwar period, with all that this implies for the attenuation of strictly market pressures.

Coal

The coal industry assets, which were nationalised immediately after the war, are vested in a public corporation, The National Coal Board, which possesses a statutory monopoly in coal production and is responsible to Parliament and to the Secretary of State for Energy. Since nationalisation, government intervention directly to influence the policies of the Board has been frequent.

Despite very large underlying reserves of coal in the UK, some 45 billion tons of recoverable coal which would last 300 years at present rates of extraction, the coal industry has been in decline with the loss of many of its traditional markets, as a result of technological developments and competition from cheap oil. Between 1950 and 1972 output declined from 220 million tons to 140 million tons and the industry had become highly dependent on sales to the (nationalised) Electricity Boards, which, in 1976, took over 60% of an annual output of only 122 million tons (and some of that under government duress). Closure of less efficient pits and increased mechanisation resulted in productivity rising from 24.9 cwt per man shift in 1957 to 44.1 cwt per man shift in 1971. Subsequently, however, productivity actually has declined, largely as a consequence of the growing influence of the National Union of Mineworkers within the quasi-political system of coal production.

In March 1974 the Labour Government established a Tripartite Group, comprising itself, the National Coal Board and the labour-unions, to 'chart the way ahead'. In the event, this Group merely endorsed the Board's own 1973 'Plan for Coal' which aimed at a total output of about 135 million tons by 1985 (the same as in 1972/73), with some 42 million tons of output arising from new investment, balancing the tonnage which would be lost through exhaustion. It is now estimated that the 'Plan for Coal' will involve an overall investment outlay of some £3,000 million at March 1976 prices, and the increased borrowing limits in the Coal Industry Act 1977 are designed to make this feasible (and to buy off the union militants).

For the period beyond 1985, the Board expects exhaustion of existing capacity to average 2 million tons per annum and proposes that for purposes of strategic planning the industry should set an output target for the year 2000 of 170 million tons per annum. Such a programme would cost some £400 million per annum at March 1976 prices. It is assumed that markets will be available for such a volume of output and will offer an adequate financial return. Albeit, this expectation is dependent upon coal remaining a less expensive resource input than oil, an outcome which is far from certain given the recent high real wage increases driven through against a backcloth of falling productivity by the National Union of Mineworkers.

Oil

The United Kingdom North Sea oil industry also is riddled both with public ownership and with a complex of regulations controlling the behaviour of private licensed producers. These arrangements were implemented by the Labour Government through the *Petroleum and Submarine Pipelines Act* 1975, through negotiations which secured majority participation by the state, and through the *Oil Taxation Act* 1975.

The *Petroleum and Submarine Pipelines Act* enables the Secretary of State to control exploration, development and production. Under this and earlier legislation, he may regulate the rate at which fresh territory is licensed for exploration, control the establishment and effecting of development and production programmes, delay development of a field and require that production should be cut back or expanded. One of the main purposes of this legislation was to establish the British National Oil Corporation (BNOC) as the principal agent of majority State participation offshore. The Corporation commenced its activities in January 1976 and has consolidated the North Sea assets acquired from the National Coal Board with those purchased from Burmah. By end 1977 the government had reached agreement with 42 oil companies on terms for majority State participation in those companies' interests in producing fields. These agreements provide BNOC with options to purchase oil. In subsequent 'licensing rounds' BNOC was to be the majority equity shareholder in each licence. With government consent, BNOC may also enter into refining, marketing and other related activities.

The extensive powers of BNOC have been criticised both by existing licensed companies and by others who have argued that BNOC has retarded the process of oil supply from the North Sea. The new Conservative Government has announced measures designed to clip the power of BNOC, to divest it of some of its holdings and to de-regulate somewhat the oil supply industry. It is yet too soon to assess the effectiveness of such policy proposals. If successfully implemented, such policy changes are unlikely to slow down the process of oil reclamation.

The *Oil Taxation Act* 1975 was designed to increase Exchequer receipts from oil (and gas) production. Under this Act, for fields on blocks licensed under the first four rounds, the government is expected to take 70% of net reserves whilst, for fields discovered and developed under the fifth round, BNOC will receive profits from its 51% share, and the total 'take' of net revenue will rise perhaps to 85%.

Although the magnitude of UK oil reserves yet is uncertain, estimates suggest that the total recoverable reserves are in the range 3,000–4,500 million tons (equivalent to some 5,000-7,000 million tons of coal). Output is expected to expand from 80–95 million tons in 1979 to a 'self-sufficiency' level of 90–110 million tons in 1980, with production thereafter lying within the range 100–150 million tons per annum. Present predictions are that the rate of output will peak in the mid-to-late 1980s and will decline through the 1990s, offering perhaps 80 million tons per annum by the year 2000.

In 1974 the government stated that up to two-thirds of North Sea oil would be utilised for refining in the UK. Since North Sea oil is a low-sulphur, light crude, it is suitable for premium markets and exports will be allowed, whilst the UK imports cheaper crude where satisfactory for consumption purposes. In the event of a serious disruption of supplies, internationally agreed special arrangements will apply.

Gas

Gas supply in the United Kingdom is vested in a public corporation, the British Gas Corporation (BGC), which is responsible for its activities to Parliament and to the Secretary of State for Energy. With the discovery and exploitation of natural gas in the UK Continental Shelf, gas rapidly expanded its share of the UK energy market and currently supplies almost 25% of UK final energy consumption and over 40% of the domestic market. At present some 3,600 million cubic feet of gas per day is drawn from the North Sea and this is expected to rise to around 6,000 million cubic feet early in the 1980s. Proven reserves stand at 28.6 trillion cubic feet, additional probable reserves at 12.8 trillion cubic feet. In addition, there is the possibility of purchasing further supplies from the Norwegian shelf. It is possible, therefore, that gas supplies may be sustained at least until the year 2000 at rates expected in the early 1980s.

Ultimately of course, gas supplies from offshore sources will decline and the gas industry then will decline unless it successfully locates other sources – possibly oil, but more likely coal. Techniques for manufacturing substitute natural gas from both sources now exist, but coal-based methods require improvement to extend the range of acceptable coal inputs. At present, depletion policy is designed to match supplies closely to the premium markets (both domestic, commercial and industrial), with a minimal level of non-premium sales required for balancing the load. Concern exists currently that gas supplies are under-priced by reference to competing energy sources, thereby stimulating over-consumption possibly to the long-term detriment of the economy. Certainly, successive British governments (Conservative more frequently than Labour) have meddled with UK gas prices, more in pursuit of inflation control than of optimal rate of depletion objectives.

Electricity

The Electricity Supply Industry is entirely publicly-owned in the United Kingdom with the responsibility for supply and distribution resting with Area Boards, co-ordinated through a central Council and with the process of electricity generation under the control of the Central Electricity Generating Board. Electricity accounted for some 4.5% of UK primary energy in 1978 (mainly with nuclear power but with a small amount of hydro-electricity). This proportion will rise substantially as commissioned nuclear plants come on stream. The industry is the largest UK consumer of fossil fuels, burning in 1977 some 30% of total UK fossil fuel consumption to produce electricity. It has become (in part as a consequence of direct pressure by the government) a crucial outlet for coal, consuming some 65% of the coal industry's output in 1977, and increasing its coalburn from 66 million tons per annum in 1973 to 78 million tons in 1977, whilst reducing its oilburn from 29 million tons of coal equivalent to some 18 million tons of coal equivalent over the same period. Table 4 outlines the composition of UK generating capacity in January 1978.

Since electricity at the present time is a relatively high-cost energy source, its expanding role in the future economy is dependent upon forecasts of the relative increases in the prices of fossil fuels as depletion becomes a serious problem, as well as on forecasts of the long-term rate of growth of gross domestic product. On the (relatively optimistic) assumption that the UK economy will grow at an average rate of just under 3% per annum to the year 2000, the Department of Energy has estimated that electricity sales in the UK could grow from 217 TWH (terrawatt hours) in 1975 to about 470 TWH by the year 2000, also an annual growth rate of 3%.

Such an expansion in electricity supply would require some 83 GW (gigawatts) of new plant (including replacements)

Table 4. *UK Electricity Generating Capacity, January 1978*

Source	*Total (gigawatts)*
Coal	41.6
Oil	12.0
Nuclear	5.1
Dual oil/coal and mixed coal/gas	3.5
Other (natural hydro, pumped storage, gas turbine, diesel)	5.0
Total	67.2

(Note: In addition, nominal capacity of about 4.5 gigawats (GW) of nuclear plant, about 9 GW of oil-fired plus 1.3 GW of dual oil/gas fired plant, 1.8 GW of pumped storage plant, and about 1 GW of gas turbines were then under construction in the UK.)

(*Source*: Cmnd 7101, *Energy Policy, A Consultative Document*, HMSO 1978.)

over the period in question, of which 15½ GW has already been commissioned by 1978. The maximum 'prudent' nuclear contribution (excluding the already commissioned programme) was judged to be some 35 GW. The remainder would be fossil-fired, some by gas turbine plant and some by coal. Department of Energy estimates suggest that there would be a shortfall in indigenous fuel for such power stations by the year 2000 of some 50 million tons of coal equivalent. Such a shortfall might be satisfied by additional nuclear plant, by expanded coal production or by energy imports. However, if electricity sales were to grow more slowly (realistically, say at 2% per annum), producing sales of 360 TWH by the year 2000, the urgency of the requirement to develop renewable sources would be much reduced. Research already is well advanced in the UK with respect to fast-breeder technology, which can efficiently utilise the plutonium produced as a by-product in thermal reactors and which can breed fresh finite material from the bulk of uranium which cannot be used in conventional reactors. It seems inevitable that such reactors will be utilised before the turn of the century, almost irrespective of the resistance of the environmental lobby.

A Libertarian Energy Market Alternative

The United Kingdom energy market, as outlined above, bears little if any resemblance to the unregulated, competitive, free enterprise markets which take centre stage in the textbook economics literature. Instead of a range of competitive suppliers, subject themselves to further free entry competition, we find government monopolies protected by statute from any potential of new entry. Instead of entrepreneurs with an equity stake in their business which will rise or fall in value according to the efficiency or otherwise with which they cater for consumer preferences, we find politicians catering for the preferences of their particular electorates and responding to the wishes of the more dominant of pressure groups. Whitehall bureaucrats, concerned not a little with expanding the size of their bureaux, and state-appointed corporation officials whose principal income is determined by the political system whence they were appointed, make long-term decisions for which they will not be accountable. Instead of the pattern of resource allocation to energy being the outcome of the demand and supply interactions of consumers and suppliers, with prices serving the dual role of market equilibration and resource adjustment signals, we find the composition of UK energy supply to be *predetermined through the turn of the century* by bureaucrats, with energy prices subjugated to the limited role of market-clearing as in Communist Russia – and with little more than a passing reference to consumer tastes and preferences. Fortunately, there is still time to halt such a development, especially with the recent change in government and in consequence a more attractive environment for capitalism.

Let us then imagine a 'greenfield site' situation in which the United Kingdom energy market was to be reconstructed following its complete institutional destruction, say as a consequence of civil war, in which libertarian forces defeated the supporters of bureaucratic socialism. Further allow that the victorious libertarians were concerned to avoid significant efficiency losses (in the Paretian sense), but sensitive to the impossibility of establishing perfectly competitive energy markets and in any event fully aware of the second-best nature of any solution which might be attained.

Let us turn, then, to the reorganisation of production. The coal industry, with its restricted scale economies, would present no problem whatsoever. Coal assets would be returned to private ownership in sufficiently decentralised units as to ensure competitive markets (perhaps 10 independent companies). The government would retain within the public domain all undiscovered reserves of coal but would license exploration and development rights in competitive auctions open to all applicants. The industry would be policed via an effective policy of antitrust, but otherwise would operate without governmental regulations of any kind.

The oil industry also would lend itself easily to substantial deregulation. All exploration and development licences would be renegotiated via competitive auctions without the presence of BNOC or of taxation impositions other than those which normally apply to the corporate sector. Clearly, in such circumstances, the licence bids would be enormously in excess of bids which reflect a closely regulated and penally-taxed environment. It would be for the government to determine whether or not a particular licence bid was sufficiently high to reflect the present value of the potentially discoverable reserves within a specific tranche. If not, the licence need not be granted. If would also be the responsibility of the government so to arrange its licences as to maintain effective competition in oil supply, although in this respect international competition would also exercise a powerful policing influence over potential production inefficiencies. Otherwise successful oil producers would be free to sell their produce in international markets, without further government regulation.

The gas industry presents a more difficult problem as a consequence of the scale economies which undoubtedly exist at the regional level in the distribution process. No such scale problems exist, however, in the process of gas discovery and supply, which in all essential respects mirrors the situation with oil. For gas discovery and supply, therefore, the oil solution would hold, with companies unfettered with respect to markets and to pricing policy. The distribution of gas would be organised on a regional or a local basis, initially with private 'monopolies', but without statutory protection from potential new entrants. To obtain such distribution rights, companies would have to place bids in periodic auctions, rather like the independent television arrangements at the present time. By careful specification of the nature of the bid, which would include a detailed contingent investment programme together with a contingent price/output scheme, the government could simulate one important aspect of competition, namely that the distributor would earn only a normal return upon efficient distribution costs. Given the highly specific nature of gas distribution capital, and the lengthy lead time for much such investment, the auction intervals necessarily would be lengthy, perhaps as long as 15 years.

In the electricity industry production by private enterprise similarly raises few problems, an exception being nuclear generation where the seriousness of the environmental issues might initially justify the restriction of generation to public corporations. The main difficulties again lie with distribution, where it is frequently argued that the natural monopoly characteristics of the national grid necessitate a state monopoly. In reality this is not so; the additional costs of maintaining two competitive national grids might be more than offset by the saving in bureaucracy costs of a state-run monopoly, and in any event national grids can be provided by private enterprise (e.g. as in the USA). A libertarian solution might be to auction off to private enterprise the right to operate the existing national grid (either for a period or indefinitely), then to allow the successful bidder to charge electricity producers and distributors to use the grid. It might also be argued that, even at local level, monopoly is not essential to electricity distribution. As with gas distribution, scale economies are important, but it is notable that in 17 localities in the USA competitive electricity distribution exists, apparently with low distribution costs and relatively well-satisfied customers.

Some Problems with the Libertarian Solution?

The prospect of such a radical reform of the UK energy market is bound to raise a number of questions in the mind of the inquisitive reader. In this section, a number of extremely important problems are outlined and an attempt is made to assess the robustness of the libertarian approach in their resolution.

Problems Associated With Uncertainty

The world energy market generally, and the United Kingdom energy market specifically, is characterised by very considerable uncertainty, particularly with respect to conditions of supply but also, in the longer term, with respect to conditions of demand. In such circumstances, economists not infrequently argue that the efficiency of the free enterprise solution depends on the provision of a comprehensive network of futures markets (e.g. for the provision of a specified volume of oil to a specified customer at a specified price in the year 2000) and a comprehensive range of insurance facilities to cover participants against various contingencies (such as, for example, the failure of the nuclear fusion process as an economic proposition in the year 2050). For, it is argued, only thus will all the costs and benefits of a particular activity be internalised to the decision makers. In the absence of such a network, it is argued, private enterprise must fail and government intervention is justified.

The absence of futures markets may result in myopic decision-making, with energy suppliers, for example, pursuing short-term speculative policies of purchasing and selling resource titles with an eye more to capital gains than to the ongoing process of resource supply; the result being a failure to optimise long-run depletion of energy resources and a tendency towards instability in energy resource markets. The absence of enforced insurance arrangements designed to internalise the risk that technical progress may not supplement energy resources in the future encourages capitalistic energy markets to over-deplete resources. This will enhance the natural tendency of the present generation to under-regard the preferences of future generations.

The seriousness of the problem of uncertainty-based externality for the libertarian solution is difficult to assess, but in evaluating it, it is necessary to confront three fallacies which permeate the conventional literature on 'market failure'. First, the *fallacy of the free lunch* arises when resources are treated as costless when judging the efficiency of markets. With respect to energy, futures markets are not free resources; hence their absence does not necessarily indicate market failure. Secondly, the *fallacy of nirvana government* involves the recommendation of government intervention wherever private markets are identified as imperfect. Yet in the context of the UK energy market, it is the failure of government and its bureaucracies, rather than the failure of capitalist markets, which is most apparent. Thirdly, there is the *fallacy that people can be different*. If participants in the UK energy market under-rate the preferences of future generations or take up gamblers' positions regarding the future success of technical progress, does this really constitute market failure?

For if the individual preferences of existing society should not decide the issue, then who should? Is it really any better to trust the judgement of a government minister or bureaucrat, who will not bear any personal responsibility for the decision that he imposes?

Problems Associated With the Environment

The potential environmental problems associated with unregulated free enterprise capitalism very frequently are cited as compelling reasons for the regulation, indeed the public ownership, of energy production in the United Kingdom. In particular, environmental issues are considered by many commentators (and of course pressure groups) to be of overwhelming importance with respect to the composition and rate of development of electricity supply. For large power stations inevitably intrude substantially upon the landscape, their construction and sometimes their operation cause noise, dust and disturbance. Overhead transmission lines have a significant visual impact and yet the additional cost of transmitting underground appears to be unjustifiably expensive. The potential air pollution from gases – in particular sulphur dioxide – is a major problem with fossil-fuelled power stations. The possibility of radioactive emissions from nuclear-fuelled power stations is a matter of current public hysteria.

Public concern over the environmental problems arising from the production of energy is often misdirected or based on incorrect information. An interesting case in point is the argument put forward by the anti-nuclear lobby that the nuclear generation of electricity is so unsafe as to deny itself any significant role in resolving the long term energy depletion problem. Over two decades of experience with nuclear power has provided evidence that the environmental costs and risks to human life arising from nuclear energy are *less* than those associated with other sources of energy. Firstly, it is to be noted that a nuclear power plant cannot undergo a nuclear explosion; the only danger is in a significant release of radioactivity and that danger is localised in a few cubic metres of space, where it can be surrounded by a multi-layered in-depth defence. Secondly, the time scale of a possible accident is so lengthy – melting of the fuel, melting through the pressure vessel, possible failure of the containment building – that there is time to bolster the threatened defences, and/or indeed to evacuate the endangered area. Thirdly, the radiation threat from nuclear energy plants is small: the radioactivity of coal smoke (due to radionuclides in coal) is up to 50 times higher than routine emissions from a nuclear plant. Futhermore, there is little evidence that the high rates of natural radioactivity in certain localities (e.g. Colorado) are seriously detrimental to health. Even if some significant loss of life were to occur from a nuclear accident, it would be likely to be far below the deaths tolerated in the production of other sources of energy. For example, it is estimated that some 20,000 US citizens die premature deaths (many from carcinoma) each year as a direct consequence of the effluent of coal-fired power plants. Throughout the world, it is estimated that coal-fired power takes a toll of between 40 and 200 lives per annum per 1,000 MW (megawatts), mostly via air pollution, but also in transportation and in the mines. Further casualties arise as a result of oil fires, gas explosions and hydro-electric dam bursts.

Of course, the fact that the representations of the anti-nuclear lobby are inaccurate, does not justify ignoring the relevance of *an environmental case* for some intervention to curtail the rate of growth of energy supply in the otherwise libertarian solution. For a continuing case can be made out that libertarian rates of energy resource depletion would be excessive, if environmental pollution and conservation externalities were not by some means internalised to the decision-makers. The same argument applies equally to the bureaucratic socialist solution. Indeed, the main thrust of the environmental lobby in the UK, with regard to energy resources, is directed against government and its bureaucracy and not against capitalism.

A number of interventions, therefore, might be justified in the libertarian solution as a consequence of externalities. Firstly, if overall energy output is to be reduced, a number of alternative instruments of intervention bear consideration. One solution simply would be to define property rights securely in the resources at risk (energy or environmental) and allow bargains to be struck between their owners and those who wished to utilise the resources. To the libertarian this is an optimal solution, where transaction costs do not rule out the bargaining outcome, since the continuing role of the state is reduced to that of the provision and enforcement of the rule of law. Where transaction costs appear excessive, however, the tax-price solution is worthy of libertarian consideration since it allows those affected by its imposition to reveal changes in their preferences for the resources in question by varying their utilisation rates. With limited information, which is typical of externality situations, suitable tax-price vectors usually are favoured also by economists on general efficiency grounds. A third method of intervention, where fixed solutions are rejected, is that of direct regulation by some organ of government to control the rate of use of energy and environmental resources. To libertarians this solution is anathema, a last-ditch approach subject to all the potential abuses that discretionary power offers to regulatory bodies. To economists, with a few notable exceptions, it is viewed as inferior on efficiency grounds to the tax-price solution in that it tends to abate resource-utilisation rates at a relatively high cost to society.

Of course, any of the three interventions outlined above are costly to apply (those who pretend otherwise have succumbed to the fallacy of the free lunch) and are potential sources of abuse and/or of mistaken application (remember the fallacy of nirvana government). Unless, therefore, the externalities at issue are seen to be unambiguous and significant, it is better that they are ignored entirely in the free market solution.

Secondly, if the composition of energy output is to be influenced by externality considerations, it is nuclear energy which should be advanced at the relative expense of coal, gas and oil, by reference both to environmental depletion and to conservation arguments. For nuclear electricity is the relatively safe fuel and it is the least subject to depletion problems if fast breeder reactors are endorsed and commissioned as quickly as the evidence suggests is justified. Whether this is to be achieved by property right definitions (e.g. as to where waste is to be disposed) or by tax-price interventions or by some combination of both must be a matter for immediate research.

Thirdly, the location of energy processing plant clearly must be influenced by environmental considerations. In this case, property rights usually lie with regional and municipal bodies and bargaining solutions are the typical outcome. Libertarians would stress the advantages of the maximum possible decentralisation of such bargaining procedures. For if central government becomes involved in locational issues, it may well impose a monolithic judgement on the spatial location of energy suppliers without adequate appreciation of the underlying market considerations.

Fourthly, the public good characteristics of research and development in the energy field (fossil as well as nuclear-based) justify continued government intervention both directly and via subsidised programmes to offset the potential underprovision of research and development that a free market might well provide. Once again, libertarians would stress the advantages of diversifying such provisions over a wide range of institutions to maintain competitive pressures and to avoid the emergence of a single, perhaps narrow-visioned research body which might ignore avenues of fruitful research.

Finally, the government will wish to intervene directly to supervise the safety characteristics of the energy industry and perhaps to ensure that energy suppliers are made directly responsible for the full social costs of all environmental damage for which they are responsible. For it is by internalising such potential costs that the self-seeking of individual entrepreneurs is most appropriately harnessed to the achievement of environmental objectives. In contrast, the bureaucrats in a public enterprise solution are much more difficult to motivate from the environmental viewpoint.

Problems Associated With Supply Monopolies

Readers may well be concerned about the establishment of limited supply monopolies in the libertarian energy market solution, notably if gas and electricity rights are auctioned on a regional basis and if the right to operate a national electricity grid is auctioned centrally. The free enterprise solution does, however, provide restraints upon the ability of producers to profiteer at the expense of the consumers. First, the monopolies established are far less powerful than the bureaucratic alternatives which presently exist (which for the most part are both national and permanent). Second, the auction process, if fully competitive, ensures that any potential monopoly rents are extracted by government. Third, the libertarian solution by providing greater decentralisation and allowing consumers greater choice means that the private supply 'monopolies' are much less susceptible to supply 'shocks' (particularly strikes) than their bureaucratic counterparts.

Conclusion

Energy policy in the UK has been associated with the rejection of the libertarian market solution and reliance upon central planning operating primarily through state-owned monopolies. While, as we have seen, free markets in energy are unlikely to operate perfectly because of problems such as the environment, scale economies and optimal rates of long-term depletion, this does not imply that the bureaucratic solution is necessarily any better. In recent years the naive view of an omniscient and impartial government has been seriously challenged by recognition that political parties, politicians and bureaucrats pursue their own utility maximising objectives.

The course of UK energy policy since the war clearly reflects the various motivations within, and imperfections of, the political system. The strong preference for intervention over market solutions can be attributed to the desires of civil servants and ministers to maximise their influence and the size of their bureaus. Once adopted, the interventionist approach is subject to the vote-maximising (usually short-term) objectives of government and the influence of pressure groups (the most effective of which are producer orientated). The pressure for a rational energy policy which operates in the national interest is limited by the generally ill-informed state of the public and politicians on energy matters. The inefficiency of the interventionist approach is revealed in the unsatisfactory performance of the UK energy industries – despite heavy investment over the past three decades, productivity by international standards has been low, standards of consumer service poor and serious errors of long-term planning have occurred.

'Put not your trust in Princes,' called out Stratford to Archbishop Laud as he made his way to execution sanctioned by his sovereign, Charles I. How much safer are we to entrust our future energy policies to politicians and bureaucrats from the Department of Energy, under pressure from militants within the trade unions and environmental extremists in the Friends of the Earth and other groups? Past and present performance of the UK energy sector suggests the need to question that trust.

By comparison, the libertarian solution has much to commend it.

References and Bibliography

Adelman, M.A., 'Politics, economics and world oil', *American Economic Review*, May 1974.

Beckerman, W., 'Economists, scientists and environmental catastrophe', *Oxford Economic Papers*, November 1972.

Beckmann, P., 'Nuclear is the safe fuel', *Daily Telegraph*, August 7th 1979, p. 14.

Buchanan, J.M., 'From private preferences to public philosophy: the development of public choice' in *The Economics of Politics*, Institute of Economic Affairs, Readings 18, 1978.

Gordon, S., 'Today's apocalypses and yesterday's', *American Economic Review*, May 1973.

Energy Policy: A Consultative Document, Cmnd 7101, HMSO 1978.

Rampton, Sir J., *National Energy Policy*, Annual Convention Lecture, The City University, May 1979.

Rowley, C.K., 'Market failure and government failure' in *The Economics of Politics*, Institute of Economic Affairs, Readings 18, 1978.

Tullock, G., *The Vote Motive*, Institute of Economic Affairs 1976.

6. The economics of educational policy

ADRIAN ZIDERMAN
Professor of Economics,
Bar-Ilan University, Israel

The Education Industry

The economics of the nationalised industries was the subject of an earlier chapter; yet *education*, in fact, is Britain's largest nationalised industry. Looked at as an industry, the educational sector is vast indeed. Although we do not have readily available measures of the outputs of the industry, total public expenditure on education (in its wider sense, including spending on libraries and the arts) now exceeds £7,500 million annually. Relating total public expenditure on education to GDP provides a broad measure of its relative importance – but a rough and ready yardstick only, because educational expenditure includes such items as transfer payments which are not part of GDP. These apart, UK educational expenditure in 1976 was some 6.8% of GDP, compared with 5.6% in 1967 and only some 3% 25 years earlier. Public expenditure on education as a percentage of GDP in 1976 exceeded that on the national health service (5.7%), defence (5.5%) and housing (4.8%).

Looking at current expenditure on nursery, primary and secondary schooling by central and local government, this totalled £3,881 millions in 1976/7, with capital expenditure on schools adding a further £397 millions. The universities spent £647 million, including £88 million in capital grants;

further education and teacher training together accounted for expenditures of £1,044 million (including £77 million on capital account).

A further indication of the sheer size of the education sector is its total employment of over 1.8 million people; second only to retail distribution, it has the largest labour force of any industry (Annual Census of Employment), and includes over half a million of the nation's most qualified workers. This compares with total employment in other major industries of some 457,000 workers in motor vehicle manufacture, 377,000 in agriculture and 303,000 in coal mining. However, the most interesting economic issues in educational policy stem not from the magnitude of the industry but, as we have already hinted, from the fact that it is predominantly operated by the state and, in common with most nationalised industries, its services are provided below cost (in this case, virtually free).

The role of the state is dominant at all levels of educational provision, particularly so in the schools. As shown in table 1, well over 90% of schools in England and Wales, accounting for 94% of all full-time pupils, are maintained by the local educational authorities (LEAs). The vast majority of these schools are virtually nationalised institutions, run directly by the LEAs and financed out of central and local government funds. Although those maintained schools that are voluntarily controlled or aided do have a slight margin of autonomy and, in the case of aided schools, meet a very small part of their expenditure out of their own resources – most of which can be reimbursed by the Department of Education and Science (DES) – these schools too are essentially state-run. The direct-grant schools, officially described as schools whose governing bodies are 'assisted' by grants from the DES, in fact obtain three-quarters of their income from government funds. The private sector thus now accounts for about 7% of schools and, because of smaller average class size, only 4.3% of all pupils. Moreover, the size of the private school sector has been falling over time, both in absolute and relative terms; ten years ago 6% of all pupils were in the independent sector. A similar picture emerges from an examination of the official statistics relating to other parts of the education system, whether technical college, teacher training college or polytechnic.

Table 1. *Distribution of schools and pupils between private and state education in England and Wales, 1976*

	Schools (No.)	*Schools* (%)	*Pupils* (No.)	*Pupils* (%)
Schools maintained by local education authorities	30,471	92.0	9,123,925	94.4
Direct grant schools	293	0.9	130,558	1.3
Independent schools	2,336	7.1	414,756	4.3
	33,100	100.0	9,669,239	100.0

Source: Department of Education and Science, *Statistics of Education, 1976*, HMSO Volume 1, Table 3.

Although the 46 UK university institutions are, in a formal sense, private institutions, some 85% of their income comes from public provision via the Universities Grants Committee which exerts a powerful influence on the scope of their activities.

Education provision in Britain, then, is dominated by the state; and it is also highly subsidised. No fees are charged at the local education authority schools, of course, except for a small part of the cost of school meals and milk; yet, even at the 170 direct grant grammar schools in England and Wales, fees account for less than a quarter of total expenditure. Only 7.3% of LEA current expenditure at all institutions of further education is covered by fees; at LEA maintained teacher training colleges fees account for only 3.3%. Finally, whilst 5% of university current expenditure in 1974/5 was covered formally by fees, in fact the bulk of this fee income was paid directly by LEAs rather than by the student consumers themselves or by their parents.

Why State Provision?

We may well ask: why is education provided in this way in Britain? Does it stem simply from the interplay of historical factors, with the pattern once set, maintained, even strengthened, over time mainly by institutional inertia? Or, as was briefly suggested in Chapter 1, does education constitute such a clear case of market failure that the present well-established system of state intervention in education remains as necessary now as in its formative years? Put another way, why do we not rely upon the inter-play of market forces, in the form of the private educational choices of parents and students as consumers, and of the profit-maximising activities of privately-run schools and colleges, co-ordinated by the price mechanism, to ensure the provision of a socially optimal amount of schooling? Could education not be produced by private enterprise and purchased by consumers on the free market? In short, does the state have to educate?

To help answer these questions, consider an education system contrastingly different from that existing at the present time. Assume that schools, colleges and so on are operated by the private sector rather than the state, on profit-maximising lines; parents (or students) purchase amounts of education according to their preferences, at non-subsidised prices on the free market.

This hypothetical situation is illustrated in figure 1(a), which shows, at varying prices, the supply and demand of schooling, here assumed to be a homogeneous good. The supply curve S is the long-run marginal cost curve of educational services and assumed to be upward sloping. The demand curve D_p represents the quantities of education that would be purchased, other factors being equal, at various levels of tuition fees. The amount of education provided in such a free market would be Q_1 at price P_1. Is this situation socially (i.e. Pareto) optimal? This would be so, as with most goods provided by markets, if the marginal valuations of the benefits of the good by the consumers (as measured by demand curve D_p) were coincident with the benefits at the margin to society as a whole, and if the marginal costs incurred by private producers equal marginal social costs. Whilst we may assume that the latter condition does hold, there are good reasons for believing that the private demand for education substantially understates the value of education derived by society as a whole. Hence too little education is demanded (and so provided). Although the proposition that the private market would underprovide education can be supported by a wide range of arguments, most of which can

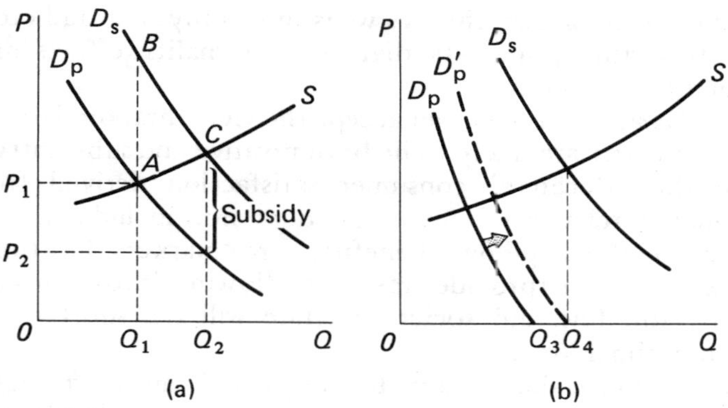

Figure 1

be traced back to the writings of the major classical economists, E.G. West (1965), in one of the most thought-provoking books written on education in recent years, subsumes these arguments under two main headings. Essentially, it is argued that a strong case can be made for state intervention in education (but not, as we shall see, for direct state *provision* of education) on two counts, namely, the externality effects of education and the alleged incompetence or ignorance of parents. We now discuss these arguments in turn.

Externalities

Education is widely believed to provide benefits to society over and above the benefits enjoyed by the direct recipients, the 'educatees'. These positive externality, or spillover, effects are both multiple and far-ranging. They include *inter alia* raising the earnings of certain complementary factors of production (e.g. less educated workers working alongside the educated), the creation and dissemination of new knowledge through research and invention, a more flexible labour force, and so on. They may also lead to such intangible benefits — which Blaug (1972) prefers to call 'atmospheric effects' — as a more enlightened, literate and cultured society. However, one should not overstate the extent of these beneficial spillovers. For example, it is often asserted that they include a reduction in crime and greater political stability. Yet the evidence supporting this view is not only contradictory but, if anything, suggests that the externality effects may frequently be negative.

Be that as it may, we can accept the view that, on balance, these spillovers are likely to be both positive and substantial.[1] Since the educatees' consumer satisfaction derived from marginal purchases of education does not include or take account of these spillover benefits, a free market educational system will underprovide; resources flowing into education will be too few and societal welfare will fall short of the Pareto optimal level.

These conclusions may be presented more formally. Returning to figure 1(a), we may conceive of a societal demand curve D_s which includes both private consumers' valuations of benefits (measured by curve D_p) and the spillover benefits, over and above these, that accrue to society generally (as measured by the vertical distance between D_p and D_s). If only the benefits of the direct purchasers of education are considered, then the free market equilibrium level of educational provision will be Q_1, at which quantity the direct benefit of education, measured in terms of willingness to pay are, at the margin, equal to costs. However, at Q_1 the amount of education provided by the free market is too small, because no account has been taken of the externality benefits: marginal social benefits of education exceed marginal private benefits, which in turn are equal to marginal private (and social) costs. Marginal benefits to society as a whole exceed marginal social costs by the vertical distance AB. The correct level of educational provision is at that quantity Q_2 where society's valuation of education corresponds to the costs (i.e. the equilibrium point C). Here there is no divergence between the social benefits of education (measured along D_s) and the social–private costs (measured along S).

However, at Q_2 the private valuation by the purchasers of education is only P_2, considerably below the costs. Fortunately, state intervention can bring about an optimal situation by providing a subsidy to the education producing firms, as shown in the diagram, so that education is made available to purchasers at the low tuition fee P_2; at this price quantity Q_2 will be purchased. The cost of the education subsidy may be legitimately met out of general taxation on the grounds that society as a whole does benefit (via its spillover effects) from the extra education provided.

A situation could well arise in which education must be made available at zero (even negative) tuition fees, in order to secure a socially optimal level of provision. This possibility is illustrated in figure 1(b): curves D_p, D_s and S have the same interpretation as before. The socially optimal level of output (where curves D_s and S intersect) is now at Q_4. However, even with zero fees and taxpayers meeting the full costs of education, no education will be purchased in excess of Q_3 (at which point D_p touches the quantity axis). In this case, the state may induce individuals to purchase extra education up to the socially optimal level Q_4, by the offer of monetary bribes (in the guise of student maintenance grants?), thus effectively raising the private demand curve for education to D'_p.

Summarising the argument so far: market failure, in the form of externalities associated with the private demand for education, does make out a case for state intervention, but only through state *finance* of education. Nothing in the externality argument warrants either state *provision* or *compulsory consumption* of education, two of the most characteristic features of Britain's school system.

Parental Incompetence

There is, however, a second, more forceful argument popularly advanced in support of state intervention in education (though at the school level, rather than in further or higher education). The argument runs along the following lines: in privately functioning markets for education, some parents – particularly the less well-off – will demand too little education in the sense that they are generally unaware of the benefits to be derived from education or, if they are so aware, are so irresponsible or negligent that they prefer to 'misspend' their income on goods (from which they enjoy more immediate benefits) rather than spending on the education of their children. Alternatively, poor parents may lack the means to purchase sufficient amounts of education in the free market.

In these cases, since some consumers would purchase less education than the state (i.e. the majority) thinks they require, state intervention is necessary to correct the 'inadequacies' of parental choice. In other words, education is seen as a *merit want,* a class of goods defined by Musgrave (1959) as those 'considered so meritorious that their satisfaction is provided through the public budget, over and above what is provided for through the market and paid for by private buyers'. Here we have deliberate state interference with consumer sovereignty, justified on the grounds that the basic assumptions on which it rests – market knowledge and rational appraisal – do not hold. The state intervenes to ensure that at least a certain minimum amount of education is consumed by all.

Whilst both parental incompetence and externalities, in the absence of state intervention, result in too low a level of total market demand for education, the sense in which demand is inadequate differs in the two cases, with consequent differences in their policy implications. In the externalities case, the state subsidises education in an attempt to secure a socially-adequate *total* level of educational provision; the fact that some individuals, with high demand elasticities for education, will purchase considerably more education whilst others may not respond positively at all, is not relevant to the issue. In the parental incompetence case, however, state intervention is focused primarily on those particular consumers (perhaps a minority) who would otherwise purchase inadequate amounts of education, rather than on the adequacy of total market demand for education *per se*. In this case educational subsidies may produce a satisfactory *total* quantity of educational provision, but its distribution may well be suboptimal since some individuals are not thereby induced to increase their purchases of education to a level generally regarded as necessary for their personal wellbeing (or that of their children). Therefore compulsory education, up to a certain minimal quantity, is required; since this may place a heavy financial burden on some families (particularly the poor), compulsory education may have to be subsidised, offered free or even with maintenance grants to offset family earnings forgone during the period of study.

Yet all this is a far cry from general state provision of education. Indeed, it has to be conceded that publicly provided education cannot be justified on purely economic grounds; rather it is in non-economic terms that the issue is usually argued. Advocates of state education in the past have usually rested their case predominately on the two extra economic considerations of equality of opportunity and social cohesion which, according to Blaug (1972), 'have become literally everyone's argument for publicly provided education'.

Social Cohesion

The relevance of the social cohesion argument, which sees in the uniform, universal provision of education by the state a powerful tool for creating and promoting social cohesion through common values and national unity, differs both over time and geographically. It carries more force in less homogeneous societies, such as in the USA with its large immigrant and racial minorities or in poor countries that are rent by linguistic and tribal divisions, than in Great Britain at the present time. Even given the view that provision by the state is the most effective form through which education can contribute to the achievement of these social goals, these are likely to be secured only at the cost of a school system that is highly uniform in structure and affords limited scope for the exercise of parental discretion over the type of education (particularly in relation to their ethnic background or religious adherence) that their children should receive. Indeed, in more highly developed societies such as ours, one sees perverse effects: not only is the conflict between social uniformity and freedom of the individual likely to become more marked, but the educational system itself, in stressing social conformity and accepted ideas, may produce the very opposite of the result intended in the form of student protest, alienation and opting out.

Equality of Opportunity

Turning now to the equality of educational opportunity argument, we come to the very centre of contemporary debate on educational policy. For many, egalitarianism in education is seen as a powerful force for the achievement of a just, more equitable society, through its contribution to greater social mobility, the 'breaking of any connexion between the distribution of education and the distribution of personal income' (Blaug), and the erosion of class divisions and privilege. Yet the equality of education concept can be given a variety of interpretations, each leading to different policy outcomes; in particular, equality of education may concern equality of *access* to education, equality of educational *treatment* or equity of ultimate educational *performance*.

Such diverse policies as compulsory schooling up to a certain age, tax allowances for children receiving full-time education and maintenance allowances for students in higher education can be seen partially as attempts (usually less than successful) to make education, at the various levels, more equally accessible to all social groups.[2] The 1944 Education Act, which made free secondary schooling universally available, was heralded as a major step in this direction, since equality of opportunity in education was then seen as something relating primarily to secondary education. Yet subsequent research has shown that in many areas working class representation in the grammar schools was smaller than previously (when a quota of places had been available for children from poor families). The methods of selection to the grammar schools militated against working-class children whose physical and cultural backgrounds are not conducive to successful performance in such seemingly objective tests of ability as the 11 plus examinations. The growing evidence, in Douglas (1964) and others, that educational selection inevitably involves some social-class bias (and an enormous waste of talent), underpins the massive shift in recent years towards comprehensive schooling, replacing separate grammar and secondary modern schools. Comprehensive schooling fits in well with what Torsten Husen (1972) has called the 'liberal' conception of equality of educational opportunity: equality of educational treatment whereby all children regardless of social class have the opportunity to be educated up to (but not exceeding) a level commensurate with their ability. This objective of uniformity of educational provision, in which education is available not in accordance with parental willingness to pay but rather in relation to capacity to learn, underlies Labour Party policy for the merging of the partially autonomous direct grant grammar schools into the state comprehensive system as well as, ultimately, the abolition of the independent sector (the 'public schools') which, it is argued, exhibits a pronounced class-based ethos and inculcates socially divisive values.

The private purchase of extra education, outside the state system, would be disallowed, since education is to be provided on purely meritocratic grounds. In sum, the case for state provision of education here rests on the view that this is the most secure method of ensuring a socially acceptable degree of uniformity of the standard and type of education provided at each level of schooling, with the ultimate aim of achieving a more just, open society.

The underlying premise of the 'liberal' policy approach to educational equality has been called very much into question by recent sociological research into enrolment rates and educational achievement in relation to social class. This has shown that the massive expansion of educational provision in recent years, involving the increased formal accessibility to free secondary and higher education of all children of a given age, has not succeeded in changing the social structure of the post-compulsory school age enrolment to any marked extent. Further, at all levels of schooling, children from poorer homes going to the same or similar schools as the better-off did less well: education not only seems to fail to offset the disadvantages of deprived home backgrounds but even reinforce, rather than diminish, existing social inequalities.

Two contrasting policy conclusions may be drawn from this accumulating sociological research. Firstly, those who adopt what Husen (1973) calls the 'radical' approach to educational equality, would see here strong arguments for extending even further the state's role in educational provision. They argue that the 'liberal' goal of providing education according to each individual's capacity or aptitude (rather than his socio-economic background) is unhelpful because the criteria used for identifying aptitudes, or 'intelligence', are themselves correlated with social background. Hence society must adopt special methods to compensate for the deficiencies of the environment in which children grow up and which account largely for their unequal educational performance; this would take the form of a national policy of 'positive discrimination' in education in favour of the under-privileged. This approach was first given official recognition in 1967 in the Plowden Report on primary schools, which led to the designation of educational priority areas (EPAs), i.e. neighbourhoods where children were most severely handicapped in their educational performance by their environment. Special provision of extra educational resources was made for schools in EPAs. The recent expansion of nursery education is to be seen as an attempt to compensate, at an even earlier age, for the disadvantages of home backgrounds. Basically, this approach calls for equality of educational treatment (i.e. equal schools) 'but equally effective schools, whose influences will overcome the differences in the starting point of children from different social groups' (Coleman 1966), so that each child 'is equipped at the end of school to compete on an equal basis with others, whatever his social origins.' Whether or not the widely adopted policy of positive educational discrimination can, in fact, succeed in adequately compensating for the inequalities arising from differences in parental backgroups in the pre-schooling years is a hotly debated issue.

A counter-reaction, however, comes from those adopting a so-called 'conservative' approach to educational policy (Husen), typified, for example, in the views held by the authors of the recent Educational Black Papers (e.g. Cox and Dyson 1969 and 1970). They see some vindication of their opposition to current egalitarianism in educational policy in the doubts raised about its efficacy by the recent sociological research referred to earlier. Fundamentally, their opposition towards a more uniform, increasingly state-run educational system is ideological. The grammar schools and the independent sector should be preserved and private markets in education protected, even extended, with the aim of encouraging educational variety, elitism, a more economically efficient schooling system and, above all, broader scope for the exercise of parental choice over the type and amount of education that their children should receive (Wiseman 1959, Peacock and Wiseman 1964). The advocates of this approach are untroubled by the implied concomitant reversal of trends towards greater educational equality, the over-enthusiastic pursuit of which, they argue, has brought about a marked decline in educational standards.

The widely canvassed proposal for *educational vouchers* is associated with those who adopt this generally 'conservative' approach to educational policy. The voucher idea is not new and variants of the scheme have been propounded on a number of occasions this century, not always with the same objectives in view. The revival of the educational voucher proposal in Britain in recent years has come largely from economists basically interested in widening the extent of educational choice open to parents. Although differing in detail, the essential characteristic of the various schemes is the cessation of the direct state financial support of schools; instead, all parents of school-age children would receive a non-transferable voucher (or coupon) of a certain value which would be used to pay for education in any school of their choice, provided only that it meets the general standards set by the state. It is usually envisaged that vouchers would have a monetary value equal to the average costs of schooling; state and private schools would co-exist, the former providing education at the price (and cost) of the nominal value of the voucher, whilst private schools would be free to provide a more expensive education, the difference being paid as a fee by parents who wished to send their children to these higher-cost schools.

Vouchers could be made into a more flexible instrument of social policy in a number of ways: they could be made subject to a means test with their value falling as parental income rose. Alternatively, vouchers of the same nominal value could be issued to all parents but, as with family allowances be subject to income tax; in addition, vouchers issued to parents with schoolchildren over minimum school leaving age could be supplemented by cash grants, in relation to parental income, to help offset family income forgone.

The advocates of the voucher proposal see many advantages of its implementation: competition between educational suppliers would lead to a more efficient school system; a greater variety of educational institutions would develop, in response to the diversity of parents' interests, values and beliefs; more resources, it is asserted, would be brought into education; above all, parents would be able to enjoy a real choice (rather than being faced by a virtual state monopoly) and thereby basic educational decisions would no longer be made by civil servants but by parents themselves. Against the voucher proposal, it is argued that the scheme would be cumbersome and costly to administer; that it would not necessarily bring extra resources into education and yet, if it did so, these would be spent on better-off children; the state schools, offering a basic minimum provision only, would gradually decline into a type of second-class institution, catering generally for poor and problem children, in disadvantaged neighbourhoods – it would thus be divisive, exasperate social tensions and above all reverse the trend towards greater equality of educational provision. Fundamentally, the debate over educational vouchers is one of political and ideological objectives and centres on the policy conflict of parental free-choice versus educational equality, on the resolution of which economic theory, as such, has little to offer.

Educational Planning and Efficiency

Whatever balance is finally struck between private and state provision of education, we now turn to a more immediate policy issue. Given the state dominance in educational expenditure in Britain, how socially optimal are expenditures on education at the various levels? The problem essentially arises from the absence of freely functioning private markets and decentralised decision-making in education by consumers and suppliers; there is no mechanism whereby consumer valuations of extra amounts of education can be signalled to the producers nor, in turn, are producers constrained by consumer sovereignty to supply amounts and types of education that are socially desirable. How then does the state decide on the amounts and types of education at the various levels and how optimal is the resultant educational mix?

Until recently there has been very little serious planning of education in Britain. If anything, the major attempts at planning over the last two decades have taken the form of a series of major reports by specially designated external committees (usually named after their chairman), on various areas of education; these include Crowther on 15–18 year olds, Newsom on secondary modern children, Robbins on higher education, Plowden on the primary schools and James on teacher training. Only in the past few years have more serious planning attempts been made by the DES and the role of the external committee has waned.

The dominating factors in planning educational provision are demographic; demographic trends determine the school population size up to age 16; estimates of its rate of voluntary staying-on beyond the school-leaving age applied to population trends give forecasts of the number of schoolchildren above 16. The number of students in teacher training is based on future teacher requirements, as forecast from the estimated size of the future school population and desired pupil-teacher ratio norms. For higher education the DES has adopted similar mechanical procedures involving estimates of the number of school leavers together with estimates of 'A' level attainment and assumptions regarding the proportion of qualified school leavers who will apply for higher education. It should be noted, however, that the demand for education by students depends upon a large number of factors, including the costs of education in terms of earnings forgone (minus maintenance grants) and the returns from education in terms of expected higher future earnings.

Total expenditure at each educational level depends not only on the number of places provided, but also upon the costs of provision per person. The sharply rising real costs of education in recent years have been differentially interpreted as evidence either of rising educational quality or of declining productivity of educational institutions. Blaug and Woodhall, on the basis of estimates of total educational inputs (including student time) and educational output (adjusted for quality change), have shown a steady decline in productivity over time in secondary and higher education. For example, average secondary school productivity over the period 1950–63, fell annually by between 4½ and 1% (depending on the particular measures of input and output used). Whilst these results imply a decline in efficiency and wasteful expenditure in education, the difficulties of correcting educational output measures for quality changes invite a cautious interpretation. On the other hand, there are no grounds for adopting the opposing viewpoint taken by so many educational administrators – who seem to welcome almost any increase in educational inputs on the grounds that an improvement in the quality of education must necessarily, almost automatically, follow.

Whatever the implications of rising unit costs of education in terms of the efficiency of educational institutions, the question concerning the breakdown of *total* educational expenditures, to which we have already referred, remains as yet unanswered: how optimally are these total educational expenditures spread between the various levels and types of education? The rate of return on educational investment is a device that is broadly favoured by economists for probing this issue (but whose use is far from generally accepted either by educationalists or educational administrators). It arises out of the recent rekindling of interest in the concept of human capital and its application to policy issues of planning the provision of education. Since expenditures on education raise the productivity and earning power of the individual and thence the levels of output available to society, questions concerning the profitability of these investments in human capital become relevant. Rates of return on educational investment (i.e. cost–benefit analysis applied to education) may then provide guidelines to governments on how appropriate current expenditures are on different levels and types of education.

Educational cost–benefit analysis involves the systematic comparison of the resource costs to the community of educational provision with the resulting increase in resource benefits to society as a whole. The investment costs are measured by the monetary value of goods and services that must be withdrawn from other uses to make possible the educational provision. Although, in fact, externality benefits should be included in the measure of the resource benefits, in practice the benefits measure is confined to the increase in national production resulting from the educational expenditures and as reflected (on the basis of marginal productivity theory) in the earnings differentials of those individuals benefiting from this extra education.

But whilst the positive connection between educational attainment and higher earnings has been clearly demonstrated in a now wide-ranging literature, alternative explanations have been advanced to account for this relationship. The majority view (held by the so-called 'human capital school' and reflected in the line of argument taken in this chapter) sees the measured correlation between educational qualifications and earnings, as the result of educational spending, raising the productivity of the workers concerned. This approach is strongly opposed by a minority of economists including, however, some of the most distinguished in the profession. This latter view (the 'screening hypothesis') denies the productivity-augmenting rate of educational investment and lays stress rather on the relationship between formal educational qualifications and those worker personality traits which characterise trainability and promotability within the organisation. Thus firms treat educational attainment as a screening device for identifying and selecting those job applicants which are the most promising candidates for training and internal promotion. A recent attempt to test the validity of the screening hypothesis is given in Katz and Ziderman (1981).

In the policy context rates-of-return results can only point to general directions of educational change (e.g. expansion or contraction), but not by how much. Clearly, very high rates of return will indicate greater expansion than lower rates of return, but whether or not the overall size and composition of the educational sector remains more or less correct from the economic point of view, can be decided only on the basis of the continuous monitoring of the benefits and costs of education at its various levels (and recalculation of rates of return) over time. Such an exercise was not possible in this country in the past, because the necessary data have not been forthcoming until recently. The results of a first attempt to calculate educational rates of return for Britain are described in the final section that follows.

Educational Rates of Return for Britain

Estimates of educational rates of return for Britain have been computed by the author together with researchers at the DES. The procedures and assumptions used are discussed in Morris and Ziderman (1971), which provided a range of results based on alternative assumptions. One set of results, which the authors regard as the most realistic, is given in table 2.[3] The outstanding features of the table are the low rates of return on postgraduate qualifications (the high resource costs of which are not sufficiently offset by extra earnings) and the very high rates of return on the Higher National Certificate (both along or supplemented by extra qualifications to gain membership of the major technical professional institutions).

What implications do the results in table 2 carry for questions concerning the adequacy of educational investment at various levels in Britain? Using as a rough standard for comparison the 10% test discount set by the Treasury for appraising public sector investment projects, it appears that the British education system is turning out the wrong mix of educationally qualified persons (or at least was doing so in the late 1960s). Societal investments in education for the GCE 'A' level, the Ordinary National Certificate and first degrees seem to have been at roughly the right order of magnitude. However, whilst postgraduate education is not very profitable, part-time technical education at the higher level is extremely so, indicating that a relative expansion of the latter and a relative decline of the former would result in a more efficient use of resources within the educational sector. The validity of this conclusion, however, would depend on the weight to be given to the (unestimated) externality effects of education, at each level.

Yet the failure to include a measure of the externality effects of education, in the results given in table 2, may not be as serious a problem for policy purposes as some of the critics of educational rates of return suggest. In principle, educational rates of return are useful, in a policy context, in two regards: as a means of achieving an overall balance *between* the educational sector and the rest of the economy and as a guide for resource allocation *within* the educational sector itself. In practice, however, (and second-best problems apart), the inherent difficulties involved in measuring spillover in both education and the other sectors would effectively

Table 2. *Alternative Estimates of Rates of Return to Society on Male Educational Investment, England and Wales 1966/67*

Full-time courses:	% †
'A' Levels (from 'no qualification')	9.0
First degree (from 'A' levels)	12.5
Masters degree (from first degree)	3.0
Doctorate (from first degree)	2.5
Part-time technical courses:	
ONC (from 'no qualification')	9.0
HNC (from ONC)	21.5
HNC/PQ* (from HNC)	18.0

Source: Ziderman (1973a)

† Rounded to the nearest 0.5%
* HNC with additional qualifications, giving membership of professional institutions.

preclude the use of educational rates of return in the first role. In any case, however, the well established practice in Britain is for the overall allocation of resources between the private and public sector and between the broad divisions of the public sector – defence, education, roads and so on – to be settled not by reference to rates of return but by the political-cum-administrative processes of government. In fact, resource allocation within the public sector may best be seen as one of capital rationing (in which the capital rations are negotiated), and each public sector branch is then faced with the task of optimally allocating its resources within a budget constraint. This, however, is precisely the second possible role for educational rates of return, noted above: that of making the best use of available resources engaged in the educational sector.

If this then is our focus, we need be less concerned with precise estimates of social rates of return (including spillovers) at each educational level than with their broad rankings. In this case, our inability to measure educational externalities need not trouble us; all we need to consider is their relative importance at the margin, for different educational levels. If external effects of education are roughly proportional to the direct measured benefits (or even broadly equal for each level of education), then no problems of misallocation will arise, since the rankings of educational investments would remain unchanged whether or not spillovers had been included. There is, however, the possibility that externalities may exert a disproportionately large effect at certain levels and types of education. Relatively fewer spillover effects may be expected from part-time technical qualifications (e.g. HNC) than from full-time, more academic ones (PhDs for example). The important issue is whether differences in spillovers are sizable enough to change the relative order of magnitude of the results shown in table 2. Is it *likely*, for example, that the inclusion of externalities would raise the PhD rates of return towards those of the first degree? When it is recalled that we are concerned not with the *total* value of spillovers for each level of education but only with the *additional* spillover benefits attached to changes in education at the margin, then we may feel that the results shown in table 2 may not be too far off the mark after all.

Notes

1. But see Peacock and Wiseman (1964) and West (1965) for a dissenting view.
2. However, even nominally free, openly accessible education does not provide equality of educational opportunity beyond the minimum school leaving age because of the inability of many working class homes to forgo the wages that their children contribute to family income; the high drop-out rate of poorer children from full-time schooling between the ages of 16–18 stems largely from the dearth of student maintenance support for this age group.
3. These results relate to educational rates of return accruing to society as a whole; these should not be confused with somewhat similar calculations relating to the individual students themselves (private rates of return). For some recent estimates see Ziderman 1973b.

References

Blaug, M., *An Introduction to the Economics of Education*, Penguin 1972.

Coleman, J.S., 'Equal schools or equal students?', *The Public Interest*, Summer 1966.

Cox, C.B. and Dyson, A.E., *Fight for Education: A Black Paper*, London 1969.
Cox, C.B. and Dyson, A.E., *Black Paper Two: The Crisis in Education*, London 1970.
Douglas, J.W.B., *The Home and the School*, Macgibbon & Kee 1964.
Husen, T., *Social Background and Educational Career*, OECD, Paris 1972.
Katz, E. and Ziderman, A., 'On education, screening and human capital', *Economics Letters*, 6, 1980.
Morris, V. and Ziderman, A., 'The economic return on investment in higher education in England and Wales', *Economic Trends*, May 1971.
Musgrave, R.A., *The Theory of Public Finance*, McGraw-Hill 1959.
Peacock, A.T., and Wiseman, J., *Education for Democrats*, Institute for Economic Affairs 1964.
West, E.G., *Education and the State*, Institute for Economic Affairs 1965.
Ziderman, A., 'Rates of return on investment in education: recent results for Britain', *Journal of Human Resources*, Winter 1973a.
Ziderman, A., 'Does it pay to take a degree?', *Oxford Economic Papers*, July 1973b.

Suggestions for Further Reading

In addition to references indicated in the chapter, a fuller discussion of all the issues raised is given *inter alia* in the standard work on the economics of education:
Blaug (1972).
A shorter, general introduction to the subject, is provided by:
Sheehan, J., *The Economics of Education*, George Allen & Unwin 1973.
Perlman, R., *The Economics of Education*, McGraw-Hill 1973.
A good review of empirical (mainly American) studies is given in:
Cohn, E., *The Economics of Education*, Ballinger 1979.

7. Economics and the health services

A.J. CULYER
Professor of Economics, University of York

In Britain, formal medical care is mainly provided by the state[1] and decisions are taken by politicians, professional administrators and members of the medical professions. In many ways there is a lack of explicit consideration of the economic issues underlying these decisions, yet the problem of efficient allocation of life-saving and life-enhancing resources subject to a severe budget constraint falls plainly within the economic field. Much of the disquiet that exists about the National Health Service (NHS), both amongst those who work in it and those who are its reluctant customers, stems from a failure to face up to these issues: the doctors always want more resources but resolutely resist the invasion of 'clinical freedom' required to ensure that resources are put to the best use; the administrators find themselves in a relatively weak position because of the difficulty of quantitative comparison between frequently (but not invariably) obvious costs with usually elusive benefits.

This chapter emphasises the problem of choice within the NHS. It is divided into four sections. In the first the general nature of health care technology and the supply of health care is examined in a historical context. In the second we discuss the principal features of the National Health Service and the demand for health care. Section three discusses the role of pricing in health care. Section four examines investment decisions in the NHS.

Health Care Technology

The benefits of medicine may be hard to quantify, but they are obviously enormous. Are they? For the greater part of man's history, the relatively crude information provided by population and mortality data is sufficient to chart the story of the social impact of medicine. The remarkable fact appears to be that only after the 20th century was well into its majority is it possible to produce any evidence that the clinical procedures of medicine had any substantial impact on health.

Causes of death were first registered in Britain in 1838 and there is little doubt that the principal factor contributing to population increase since and before that time was a decline in mortality rates due to a reduction in the number of deaths from communicable diseases. Since mortality was falling and life expectancy rising before the causes of death were properly understood, the reduction cannot be attributed to medical science. But could it be attributed to medicine? Knowledge of smallpox was an exception to the relative ignorance prevailing in the 18th and 19th centuries and, since smallpox accounted for about 30% of all deaths, inoculation against it in the 18th century has been held by economic historians to be the principal explanation for the dramatic population rise after 1750. But despite the plausibility of this thesis, it is unlikely that smallpox inoculation, even had it been done with the most effective of modern vaccines, could have had such an impact. A more important cause of the fall in the mortality rate and the rise in population was the improvement in general living standards over the period. Better nutrition enables people the better to withstand disease – especially tuberculosis, rickets and other then prevalent chronic diseases, which also accounted for a large proportion of all deaths. Nutrition improved enormously at this time, partly because of greatly increased agricultural productivity and also – despite its squalor – because of increasing urbanisation as the industrial revolution got under way; for agricultural life was far from Arcadian. The sanitary reforms of the 19th century, improved drainage and water supplies and refuse disposal away from publicly frequented places, had an undisputed impact on mortality. The decline in mortality from intestinal infections such as cholera is alone an adequate indicator of their effectiveness.

Until this century, then, it would appear that, apart from any spontaneous declines in the virulence of disease that may have occurred, the chief agents improving the health of the British people were improved nutrition and hygienic measures. The activities of the medics, whether the humble apothecary or the Fellows of the hugely prestigious Royal College of Physicians,[2] were relatively insignificant.

During the 20th century entirely new developments in medical technology and, especially, in pharmacology made it possible for the first time for medical intervention to have a marked and indisputable impact on the natural history of disease. The principal causes of death today are cancers, heart disease, cerebrovascular disease, pneumonia and bronchitis; all of which strike primarily at older persons. Mortality rarely occurs before the age of 45 and is even then unlikely to be caused by infection or contagion from another diseased person. Such a death is more likely to have been caused by a road accident. There has also been a remarkable reduction in the severity of spells of morbidity. But the wonders of modern surgery have become effectively applicable only in the last two decades with the development of anaesthesiology, which has made long and complicated operations on the vital organs both safer for the patient and easier for the surgeon.

The great killers of previous centuries – the infectious diseases – are, with the possible exception of influenza, almost entirely vanquished. The great decline in mortality from pneumonia began only, however, in the 1940s, as did death rates from diphtheria and tuberculosis. Today, the diseases from which men die in Britain are chronic and their onset insidious. Once again the biggest contributors to further reductions in morbidity are probably environmental. But while once it was an environment of poverty that killed, today it is an environment of wealth. Traffic accidents, smoking, obesity and the emotional stress of urban living are among the principal causes of mortality and morbidity.

This, then, appears to have been the broad pattern. Until the 1930s the chief causes of improvements in health were improvements in the environment. From the 1930s to the 1950s the chief contributors to better health were drugs and new surgical techniques. In the 1960s the revolution in psychotropic drugs took place and really effective treatment of mental illness became possible for the first time. Today, the major sources of further improvement appear once more to be environmental. The wheel has come full circle.

Diagnosis and treatment are, today, highly technical procedures. But the mystique and prestige of modern medical science can serve to give a false picture of its precision. It is now increasingly difficult to distinguish unambiguously between a healthy and a diseased state using technological measurements. For haemoglobin levels, blood pressure, blood sugar levels, and several other testable indicators, a decision has to be taken as to how far above or below average a measure must read before action is warranted. Observer error exists, notably in the reading of X-ray photographs, but also in the measurement of blood pressure. Even among the most experienced hospital doctors, diagnoses can vary quite markedly. One study compared the diagnoses made by consultants in a major hospital with the final diagnosis reached, usually after surgery had taken place. For one common condition, appendicitis, only 75 of the 85 cases were correctly diagnosed by the most experienced men in the hospital. Overall, they were 80% correct in their diagnoses.

Appropriate treatment is likewise far from being as easy and unambiguous to identify as may be popularly thought. There is generally a choice of treatment. In an appendix to the Sainsbury Committee's report on the pharmaceutical industry it was reported that 455 general practitioners prescribed over 30 different prescriptions for each of five common illnesses. Only 8 out of a total of 2,275 prescriptions were found to be unacceptably toxic or ineffectual, but the cost variation was substantial. For painful osteo-arthritis, for example, 11% of GPs recommended Indocid at a prescription cost of 75p, while 10% recommended Asprin at a cost of 1p.

Hospital practices can also vary widely. For example, despite strong evidence that bed rest is unimportant in the treatment of pulmonary tuberculosis, the mean length of stay in hospital is falling only slowly and is very variable from specialist to specialist. (In one case nearly 20% of male patients were discharged in under a month and all within 3 months. In another 10% were discharged in under a month and over 20% were still in hospital after a year).

Hospitalisation is, of course, extremely costly. Some costly treatments in hospital may actually do patients harm. There is evidence that surgery for small-celled cancer of the bronchus reduces life expectancy compared with radiotherapy without surgery. Intensive care in hospital coronary care units has the effect, it appears, of reducing life expectancy for coronary patients compared with bed rest at home. When death approaches a relatively young patient, dramatic and costly interventions may be undertaken, of little or no therapeutic value in terms of improving the prognosis, whose major value seems to be to provide evidence that 'all possible is being done'.

The effects of several standard treatments on the normal course of disease are unknown or in dispute. Tonsillectomy, for example, is the commonest cause for the admission of children to hospital and the operation has a positive (if small) mortality. Yet there is evidence to suggest that the best medical treatment may be superior, or not inferior, to surgery. Certainly, admissions for tonsillectomy vary enormously per head of population from region to region in Britain (from 234 per 100,000 population in Sheffield to 410 in Oxford in 1971, of which 81% of the cases were aged 14 or less). The treatment of mature diabetes is in doubt, as compared with diabetes in the young for whom insulin appears effective. Modern psychiatry is replete with therapies whose theoretical foundations are in dispute and whose effectiveness remains very largely untested in any systematic way.

Finally, modern techniques have introduced new considerations into the choice of therapy. Detection of abnormalities in foetuses still in the womb raises the question of abortion as a probably increasingly common surgical operation done on clinical grounds; and contraception, spare-part surgery (including blood transfusion), euthanasia in an increasingly ageing population, all these raise major ethical problems of choice for patients, doctors and society.

The NHS is big business, employing about a million people

and spending approaching £10,000 million a year. For most of its services, patients pay nothing or very little. Our brief historical review naturally invites questions about the marginal effectiveness of these resources, how they are best allocated, why they should be available free, and so on. Many of the most important questions relate to the production functions in health: how is health best promoted, what contributions do specific treatments or preventive measures make? But we shall focus on the more obvious economic questions: what is the demand for health? Why are prices so conspicuously absent (is this a good thing)? What can economics contribute to greater efficiency?

The Demand for Health

One of the basic beliefs of the founding fathers of the NHS was that the provision of medical care free of charge would enable the 'backlog' of sickness to be worked off. With the removal of the price barrier, the health service bill would, after an initial period, tend to decline as a healthy nation became yet healthier. Instead the utilisation of health services has, on almost every indicator, increased continuously since the Second World War.

How could they all have been so wrong? The major error lay in supposing that there was a fixed stock of sickness in society which, once treated, would eventually lead to a reduction in the incidence and prevalence of sickness. Rather, as we have seen, the clinical distinction between a 'sick' and a 'well' person is sometimes rather an arbitrary one. There is also doubt about what 'needs' to be done in some cases. As Shaw spitefully wrote in the Preface to *The Doctor's Dilemma* (1906) 'the distinction between a quack doctor and a qualified one is mainly that only the qualified one is authorised to sign death certificates, for which both sorts seem to have about equal occasion'! Since Shaw's day, and especially since the Second World War, both the definition and the scope for treatment have changed a great deal and there can be no doubt that there is more *effectively treatable* disease today. But the language of 'need' can be as misleading today as it was then.

Second, there was an error about what determines people's

behaviour in going to the doctor. Just as clinical distinctions between sickness and health are sometimes ambiguous, neither do people behave as though there were a clear-cut division between them. In fact, feeling unwell is a perfectly normal thing. A recent survey in London revealed that 95% of those interviewed had some symptoms of ill-health during the preceding two weeks. But only 20% had consulted a doctor; the rest either ignored their symptoms or treated them themselves. The patient normally makes the first and all-important general judgement about seeing a doctor, and here economic, social and cultural factors, as well as clinical ones, come into play. Some demand reassurance. Job satisfaction is an important determinant of 'sickness' absence from work.

On purely clinical criteria, there is a vast potential yet for new demands on the health service. An early attempt to identify the magnitude of the so-called 'iceberg of sickness' found in the late 1930s that over 90% of more than 3,000 people examined had some identifiable sickness, but only 26% were aware of being sick and only 8% had been receiving medical attention. Similar studies at intervals since the war have come up with similar findings.

Social class, income, education, the price of health care, all are known to affect the demand for health care by the patient. It is tempting to treat the demand for health services in an *ad hoc* fashion by just listing the factors that seem to be relevant. And yet there is no need for *ad hoc* theorising about these phenomena. There is a general theory to account for them, a theory based on the proposition that individuals to a large extent *choose* the state of their health: a theory based on the familiar propositions of general demand theory in economics. Note that a theory that will account for these phenomena cannot be merely a theory of the demand for health care. It must be a theory of the demand for *health itself.* It may seem obvious that a fall in an individual's health status will (*ceteris paribus*) increase demand for health care, but why has his health status changed? If we cannot predict this, then we cannot predict the demand for health care; nor can we predict what the future trends of mortality and morbidity will be.

The demand for good health is the demand for an investment good – one that yields services over a period of time. The services yielded by a person's 'stock' of health are basically two: the direct 'utility' of feeling well and the indirect benefits derived from the increased amount of healthy time available for productivity use both in work and non-work activities. At any point of time, an individual 'owns' a particular stock of health which is subject to depreciation as time passes and which, if depreciation goes far enough, falls low enough to result in death. Like other capital stocks, the stock of health can usually be increased by investment. The key inputs into the individual's investment production function are diet, exercise, housing, consumption habits, environmental factors such as public health provision and education; health education affects the efficiency with which other inputs in the production function are combined. Finally, an important input is, of course, consumption of medical care.

Since many of these variables are under the control of the individual, he may be regarded as *choosing* his preferred stock of health, or rate of investment, subject to constraints which are principally the amount of time available to him and the value of his time in work (i.e. his wage).

Some of the implications of this approach to the demand for health are relatively straightforward implications of the law of demand. If, beyond a certain age, the rate of depreciation of the capital stock is positively correlated with age, the cost of health capital rises as age increases and a lower stock will, *ceteris paribus*, be chosen as optimal: as a person becomes older, he will become less healthy. Rising wages influence both the cost of health (via the cost of time in the production function) and the demand for health (via the value placed upon future healthy days). If X is the proportion of the cost of investment accounted for by time, then a 1% rise in the wage would increase marginal cost of investment by X% and the proportional (net) increase in the return on one unit of health capital (marginal efficiency of capital) would be $1 - X$, assuming no change in the cost of capital. So long as time is not the only input in the production of health ($X \neq 1$), the net effect is an increase in the demand for health, *ceteris paribus*. Richer persons (earned incomes only), according to this analysis, would also be healthier if other factors are held constant. Mortality and real wage rates should be inversely related. If consumption goods that are harmful to health, such as tobacco, alcohol and motor cars, have high income elasticities, it may also be the case that health and *income* are inversely related: implying a positive relation between mortality and income. Thus, in cross-section analysis comparing different countries, it is not inconsistent with theory to find that mortality and income may be positively correlated, while at the same time rising earnings in one country are associated with reduced mortality.

If education improves the efficiency of health production, it reduces the amount of inputs required to produce a given amount of investment and thus increases the marginal efficiency of health investment, causing the demand for health to shift to the right. To the extent that education also increases the productivity of working time, the effect on the demand for health would be intensified. Note that increases in the demand for health need not always be associated with increases in the demand for health services. For example, improved education raises the productivity of inputs in the health production function *other than* medical care and can thus induce some substitution *away from* medical care consumption.

Some empirical results for the USA that are consistent with the analysis are shown in table 1. The signs of the relationship between mortality rates and income and education are particularly striking.

More speculatively, we might conceive the demand for health as being complementary to other dimensions of the 'good life'. It has been widely noted that *age-adjusted* mortality rates are much higher for widowed and divorced men rather than for married men. It is surely not implausible to suppose that this is because they lack some other dimensions of life that make good health valuable. Some evidence in support of the hypothesis is that death rates for the widowed and divorced men are much higher from suicide, motor car accidents, cirrhosis of the liver and lung cancer, where

Table 1. *Percentage changes in US age-specific mortality rates resulting from a 10% change in several variables.*

	Variables (10% change in): *Income*	*Education*	*Cigarette consumption*	*Per capita health expenditure*
% change in mortality	+2.0	−2.2	+1.0	−0.65

Source: R. Auster *et al.*, The production of health, an exploratory study, in V. Fuchs (ed), *Essays in the Economics of Health and Medical Care*, NBER, Columbia University Press 1972, table 8.3, p. 145.

'choice' is more possible, than from vascular lesions, diabetes or cancer of the digestive organs, where it is less possible or, at least, where the relationship between life-style and health status is somewhat obscure. Married persons, generally, have better health and live longer.

It is thus clear that both the demand for health and the demand for health care services depend upon a complexity of factors, only one of which is, of course, the monetary price of purchasing inputs (including the price of medical care). The hopes of the founding fathers of the NHS to abolish sickness were, with hindsight, extremely naive.

Pricing and Health Services

One of the great policy questions of the political economy of health has concerned the appropriate role of prices in the allocation of health services to patients. We will begin by examining the traditional economic model of markets and then see what modifications have to be made to it in order to understand the special nature of the problems arising in the health context.

Figure 1 shows the demand for health care (note: the demand for *services* not, as we discussed above, the demand for health itself) and its supply, for a prevailing pattern of disease in the community.

The standard argument would run as follows: if D represents

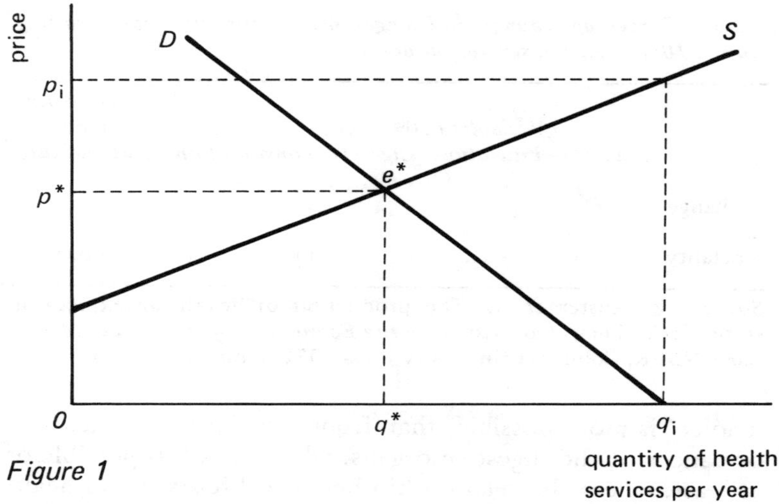

Figure 1

the true marginal values of the community for health care and *S* the true marginal costs of provision, then the optimal quantity consumed per year is *Oq** since this maximises the sum of consumers' (patients') and producers' surpluses. Via a market mechanism, the price *Op** would enable this optimum to be attained.

Not a single developed economy, however, allows the demand and supply of medical care to be determined in this way and it is instructive to ask why. There are basically three reasons:

(a) The actual supply curves in the health sector are unlikely to reflect marginal costs accurately because of elements of monopoly in the organisation of medical manpower and in the distribution of facilities, especially hospitals, and because the majority of hospitals and medical practices are not profit-seeking organisations. Instead, they pursue a complex set of goals, mostly professionally determined, which make it unlikely that any level of service is provided at the minimum feasible cost.

(b) Because many health expenses can be a sizeable proportion of an individual's income, individuals prefer to insure against such costs, which tends to drive the effective price of care when sick well below Op^*, creating excess demand in the process. Thus, who actually gets what care depends very much on how the excess demand is choked off.

(c) Because there are widespread feelings of empathy among members of society, the demand curve understates the social value of medical care. The true value at the margin must include these externalities.

We cannot go into each of these in any great detail. The question of productivity efficiency is taken up in the next section concerning cost-effectiveness in the health services. In the remainder of this section we focus on the demand factors: insurance and externality.

Insurance

Individuals typically prefer to be insured against the possibility of large financial losses. The economic rationale for insurance is the diminishing marginal utility of income that individuals are generally assumed to experience. If the marginal utility of income increases as income is reduced, then individuals will prefer the certain but small reduction in income that medical insurance involves, to some finite probability of incurring a large reduction in income due to costly medical care.

The effect of insurance on the market for health services is shown in figure 1. In the absence of insurance, price and quantity equilibrium is at Op^* and Oq^* and expenditure on the health services is $Op^* \times Oq^*$. If open-ended insurance is taken out, the price to the consumer falls to zero (since the insurance company picks up the bill) and his demand increases to Oq_i. At this level of demand the supply price (to the insurance company) rises to Op_i and expenditure on the health service rises to $Op_i \times Oq_i$.

Now, we have admittedly simplified in several respects already mentioned. In addition, note that we have not allowed for the income effect on the demand curve of the premium payment. This is unlikely, anyway, to be very substantial, even though the income elasticity of the demand for health care is positive. Also, we have assumed that the *only* price paid is a money price. In practice the patient has travel costs, time costs, etc. But none of these potentially complicating factors really affects the basic point that insurance destroys the usefulness of the price mechanism as a means of allocating health care, although we need them to explain some observed phenomena: for example why, when price at the point of consumption is zero, people living distant from the hospital more frequently fail to turn up to appointments, or why salaried people are more responsive to the introduction of additional charges.[3]

A further effect of insurance can be to alter the *probability* itself of sickness occurring: knowledge that one is insured against financial loss may make one less careful in avoiding activities that are harmful to health (in terms of the discussion of the previous section, they reduce the demand for *health* by making rich diets, etc. *relatively cheaper*). Thus, in addition to the movement *along* the demand curve from e^* to q_i, the curve itself may shift outwards.

The combined effects of insurance in terms of movements along the demand curve and of shifts of the whole curve are termed 'moral hazard' in the insurance field. The former can be combated to some extent by introducing *coinsurance* (whereby the insured person pays some proportion of the price) and by setting limits to the benefits receivable. But coinsurance obviously reduces the utility of insurance, while limits on the benefit implies non-price rationing of health services, which is a substantial departure from the free-market philosophy so often used to justify insurance-based systems of finance.

Externalities

In the NHS health care is available at a money price which is effectively zero. One reason for this is undoubtedly because of a widespread feeling that the risks of having to bear substantial costs of medical care should be pooled across the whole community and paid for by 'premiums' (taxes and national insurance contributions) that are related to ability to pay rather than the probability and cost of sickness. But a further reason is also that individuals manifestly care about the health of others in the community and it is widely felt that inability to pay directly for care, or for insurance, should not be allowed to deter consultation for medical care.

Again, therefore, the logic of these arguments suggests a low or zero price at the point of utilisation. In addition, however, the externality argument suggests that, if the feeling is widespread that people care about the health of others, the appropriate kind of non-price rationing to use in eliminating excess demand (by, on the one hand, rationing existing resources to patients and, on the other, by deciding what resources to make available in the first place) would be *not* to provide care of dubious or no effectiveness in its impact on health status.

Thus, while in Britain today one can still occasionally hear arguments for the imposition of consultation charges or hotel charges (in hospital), policy has mostly focused on (a) establishing which procedures are of demonstrable effectiveness, (b) identifying the least-cost method of providing effective services and (c) in allocating resources by area so far as possible in proportion to the professionally judged need for effective care in each area.

Prices are thus not of great help. There is a danger that money prices on top of time (etc.) prices will tend to discourage consultation and hence the early detection of dangerous disease, while the likely exceptions for special categories (children, maternity cases, pensioners, those in receipt of supplementary benefit, etc.) are likely to cause substantial administrative costs as well as to stigmatise those exempted and to lock the poor even more solidly into the 'poverty trap'. Nor do prices offer much in the way of an additional source of revenue: whatever is raised over and above administrative costs can easily be offset by a reduction in public expenditure out of taxation by governments committed both to controlling its rate of growth and to a balance of resources as between health, education, housing, etc.

In short, both private insurance-based systems and the British NHS system tend to destroy the efficiency role of pricing in medical care. Instead, the focus falls upon the development of non-price methods of allocation.

Cost–Benefit Analysis and Health Service Policy

Outcome Measurement

Health Service planning is in practice largely dependent upon a multitude of political, administrative and professional pressure groups and other influences. It is often conceptualised in terms of the institutional features of the system and the language in which they are rationalised, such as norms of provision and finance, and the health 'needs' of the population. It is a major task to separate out value judgements from purely positive analysis; to identify clear objectives, methods of treatment, outcomes, costs and priorities.

The analysis of the preceding section suggested that the market mechanism is largely self-destructive in the allocation of health services: at the very least it requires a non-price mechanism for coping with the excess demand that insurance generates. If, as externality considerations seem to suggest, we can suppose that the most general objective of the health services is to maintain and improve *health* (rather than consumer satisfaction alone), then the measurement of health outcome, as the *output* of the NHS, becomes of central importance. And here we run into severe practical difficulties.

An explicitly rational system of resource allocation in the health field, as in any other, would ideally be based upon knowledge of (a) the technology (the means of attaining ends), (b) the values placed on those ends and (c) the costs of attaining them. Again ideally, the latter two dimensions would be measured in units comparable with those used in other resource-using areas, from private consumption to public investment in, say, education. In practice, however, as we have seen, technologies are sometimes uncertainly successful and many are in dispute. Certainly practice varies widely. Outcomes are barely known. The hospital statistics characteristically measure inputs, throughputs and utilisation rates only. Valuation is held in profound suspicion. Costs tend to be identified with public expenditures, with rather little thought being given to the wider concept of *social* cost, familiar to economists, and of key importance in the health field which is highly labour-intensive and where wages and salaries are administratively fixed or the outcome of bilateral bargaining, and where patients' time, and often that of friends and relations, is a significant input in many therapeutic processes. A consistent treatment of the dating of costs and benefits and their reduction to comparable units, by discounting, is generally required. There has been and, one suspects, still is a widespread resistance, particularly in the medical profession, to techniques that explicitly expose the key issues and question publicly the traditional theoretical assumptions that life and good health are priceless (i.e. either of infinite value or inherently incapable of being reasonably valued); that doctors are the only conceivable arbiters of what needs to be done; and that clinical freedom is in the best interests of both society in general and patients in particular.

The absence of a really satisfactory measure of outcome is the most fundamental difficulty facing national planners. Ideally, this would measure individuals' states of health, and changes in their states of health, in response to at least some of the multiplicity of variables which affect them. At one level, some people are seeking an aggregate measure of more subtlety than the current morbidity and mortality data – a social indicator of health – which might ultimately be placed among similar indicators in other social areas to qualify and complement the conventional, but narrowly economic, measures of the progress of human societies (such as national income). While such an indicator may be of interest in calling attention to broad 'problem areas', it is unlikely to be of great value in planning health, or any other, services. On the other hand, a satisfactory and reliable indicator at the micro level could be of inestimable value in decisions concerning the deployment of specific sums of money (will *X* thousand pounds spent here yield a greater increase in 'health' than the *X* thousand spent there?), in the assessment of the effectiveness of alternative methods of treatment and in the development of a science of prognosis – especially long-term prognoses for patients with chronic conditions (such as elderly persons tend to suffer), and for conditions whose cure or amelioration needs to be monitored over long periods (such as head injury victims). Many of these areas are, of course, those where measurement is very complicated and, at least in the first instance, multi-dimensional. (Geriatric cases, for example, are complex because they are multi-symptomatic and because sickness and disability in the old tends to interfere with the entire life-style in a drastic way and over long periods of time.)

Any such index of health (or ill-health) will normally be derived from a set of 'characteristics' measuring (i.e. assigning numbers to) particular dimensions of a condition that are considered (by whom? surely not doctors alone) to be relevant. Pain, both physical and emotional, mobility, sensory perception, emotional stability, ability to care for oneself, are some illustrative dimensions that would probably figure in anyone's list of potentially relevant characteristics. A number of studies have proved the feasibility and reliability of such measurement, provided that each dimension is not measured too finely (e.g. Wright 1978).

The next stage is to combine the characteristics into a single indicator. This involves value judgements about which levels of which characteristics are regarded as equally good or bad. It also involves value judgements that identify how much worse (or better) one combination of characteristics is than another. Thus, if the dimensions are such that 'more' means 'worse health state' (e.g. pain, disability, mental confusion), it becomes possible to locate those combinations regarded as equally bad in an 'indifference surface' with higher planes corresponding to lower health states. The basic economic model of individual choice, with its familiar curves, provides the guidelines for evolving a consistent methodology of the health indicator and has the advantages of distinguishing those elements in its construction that involve social value judgements and those that are technical or scientific. The final index will be a variable measured in pure numbers – any set of numbers will do, provided that they are linearly related.[4] The final tasks then become to assign values to the index (monetarily expressed ones would be the most convenient but should not be confused with market prices), to define production functions relating inputs of medical and other resources to the output index, and to compare the social costs of the inputs with the social value of the output. Alternatively, if the problem is of establishing the most cost-effective means of achieving an objective, defined in terms of the output indicator, *that has been predetermined,* the difficult step of placing values on the indicator becomes unnecessary.

Cost–Benefit and Cost-Effectiveness

The basis of cost–benefit analysis is to compare the full costs and full benefits of a procedure and only to adopt it or to continue with it if benefits exceed costs *and* if no alternative procedure would achieve the same end with a greater differential of benefit over cost. Cost-effectiveness analysis focuses on alternative procedures by which a pre-selected objective may be fulfilled and seeks to identify the least-cost procedure. Cost-effectiveness cannot establish whether or not the objective is worth pursuing; it may be that even for the least costly procedure, the costs exceed the benefits and to this extent cost-effectiveness analysis is more limited than cost–benefit. In this section the analytical techniques are illustrated by reference to two empirical studies in the health field: one of the cost-effectiveness variety; the other a more ambitious cost–benefit study.

In the cost-effectiveness study by Piachaud and Weddell (1972) two alternative procedures for treating varicose veins were examined. Since the medical outcome of each procedure was taken to be the same, the thorny problem of output valuation was avoided. The method of treating varicose veins is to remove them either by injection-compression sclerotherapy in an outpatient clinic or by surgery as an inpatient.

Since injection-compression treatment takes place in special clinics, the costs of an outpatient session were relatively unambiguously identifiable and amounted to £41.50. It was assumed that money outlays measured the relevant dimensions of cost accurately. The average number of patients treated per session was 31 and the average number of attendances per patient was 7.3. The total cost of the procedure per treated patient was thus, on average £9.77. The estimation of surgical costs was complicated by the substantial amount of resources shared by veins patients with other surgical and medical inpatients (e.g. catering, laundry, administration, nursing). These costs were divided up according to estimates (some of which are at variance with those used in other studies) of the relative intensity of their utilisation by veins patients. The estimated total cost per case (which was probably, if anything, an underestimate) was £44.22. The institutional costs of surgery thus substantially exceeded those of injection-compression.

Two further dimensions of cost were also considered in this study: time off work and patient time used up in treatment. The average number of days off work due to treatment and convalescence for surgery was 31.3 days compared with 6.4 days for injection-compression treatment. As for patient time, allowing for post-operative outpatient attendances and travelling time, surgery cost about 100 hours and injection-compression sclerotherapy about 30 hours. Since these results reinforced the institutional cost results, there was no necessity to express them in monetary units: the cost-effective solution is rather unambiguous. Even with substantial reductions in the inpatient length of stay, surgery appears not to be cost-effective. Cost differentials of this magnitude occur with surprising frequency amongst those cost-effectiveness studies that have been undertaken in the health service field and suggest that even had some refinements of analysis been utilised, the results would not be substantially altered: the conceptual difficulties that may intimidate at the *a priori* stage sometimes vanish in the context of practical application of the basic analytical apparatus.

The existence of the submerged 'clinical iceberg', discussed above, as well as other more general humanistic concerns and technological developments has led to an increasing demand for mass screening of the relevant populations at risk to identify pre-symptomatic disease and to cure patients in the early stages. Cervical smear programmes, amniocentesis with abortion for women carrying mongol foetuses, testing for high blood pressure, are much talked about screening procedures. But perhaps the best known screening programme in Britain was the mass miniature radiography (MMR) programme for detection of pulmonary tuberculosis – now, of course, being abandoned on a large scale.

At the end of the 1960s this programme was costing around £1m per annum – not a large sum by comparison with other expenditure categories; but was it money well spent? The objects of MMR were basically threefold: to identify cases at a stage when they could be 'nipped in the bud', to tackle part of the submerged clinical iceberg, and to prevent the infection of others by those with pre-symptomatic tuberculosis (TB). The cost of finding an active case of pulmonary TB was around £500. The benefits depend upon the probability of secondary infection from primary cases, the time lags involved (time discounting becomes important here), the differential cost of treatment earlier rather than later, and the reduction in output resulting from reducing or eliminating disability, prolonged hospitalisation or death.

Technological developments in pharmacology imply today that drug therapy is almost completely effective, irrespective of the stage of TB. Disease activity ceases within a few days of the start of treatment. There is little or no cost differential in identifying cases picked up by MMR or symptomatically – and many of those positive cases picked up by MMR would have cured themselves anyway. In recent years there has been an annual rate of decrease in notifications of TB of about 9% per year. The principal potential gain from MMR clearly has to lie in the prevention of secondary cases, if the programme is to be regarded as worthwhile in today's conditions.

Pole (1971), using a 10% discount rate, found the range of potential benefits from finding a case of TB indicated in table 2, assuming that MMR works with maximum effectiveness by completely eliminating the infectious phase of the disease. On the assumptions that are thus most favourable to MMR, the costs are almost twice the benefits. In a social sense, prevention need not be better than cure, and here is a case in which it appears not to be. The decision to abandon mass

Table 2. *Maximum average present value of finding a tuberculosis case by MMR (£)*

		Case avoided after:		
		10 years	*20 years*	*30 years*
Assumed annual rate of decline of new cases notified	5%	285	75	26
	10%	181	34	7

screening for pulmonary tuberculosis was, it would appear, amply justified.

Conclusions

The health service problems to which economic analysis has been applied are much more numerous than those that we have been able to illustrate here and include, for example, the optimal size of hospitals, the control of waiting lists, investment in medical education and area allocation of resources to achieve equity. In addition there is a substantial literature on the welfare economics of the NHS dealing, among other issues, with the vexed question of the appropriate roles of the market and the government in health care provision. Finally, there are macro descriptive studies dealing with international comparisons, the role of health service expenditure in macro stabilisation policy and so on. For the reader whose appetite has been whetted, the further reading will help to guide him into these and related areas. We have had to be severe in what has not been covered in the present chapter.

One of the fascinations of health economics lies in the twin facts that the organisation of health care systems has been a traditional political battleground, and in the difficulty of overcoming the contemporary awe of doctors and fear of illness sufficiently to clarify issues and get conceptual approaches straight. Yet, clearly, the potential pay-off to improved decision making and clearer thought about organisational forms is enormous. In an age of wealth and expectations unthinkable before the therapeutic revolution, and at a time when we are witnessing an ever-increasing aged population, there are few fields more worthy of thoughtful economic attention; or, given its importance, less thoroughly tilled.

Notes

1. But much also takes place outside the National Health Service. Besides the small private medical market there is much amateur diagnosis and treatment. About 30% of drug spending is outside the NHS.
2. As late as 1834 membership of the College (established in 1518)

could be obtained (provided you were an Oxbridge graduate and, of course, Church of England) for 50 guineas and by passing three twenty-minute examinations. Sir David Barry, in 1834, remarked that the exams could be passed by a man 'who is a good classical scholar but knows nothing of chemistry, nothing of medical jurisprudence, nothing of surgery, little or nothing of anatomy, nothing of the diseases of women in child-bed, and nothing of delivering them'. The College of Surgeons (far from 'Royal' at the time) was a mean affair and the social status of surgeons was low – and probably deservedly so. (See Abel-Smith 1964).

3. Salaried people do not usually lose income when they attend (say) outpatient hospital departments. Thus, if a charge is imposed, this represents to them a higher proportion of the total price than it is to a wage earner with the same annual income when well. Therefore salaried people have a higher price elasticity of demand for health care. The same differential effect will apply to low wage earners relative to higher wage earners: perhaps a more important consequence given current social values.
4. Thus, if X is one vector of such numbers and Y is another, they should be related by the linear equation $X = a + b\ Y$, where a and b are any constants. This differs from the usual indifference curve analysis. (How?)

References

Abel-Smith, B., *The Hospitals 1800–1948,* Heinemann 1964.

Auster, R., *et al.*, 'The production of health, an exploratory study', in V. Fuchs (ed.), *Essays in the Economics of Health and Medical Care,* Columbia University Press 1972.

Cochrane, A.L., *Effectiveness and Efficiency. Random Reflections on Health Services,* Nuffield Provincial Hospitals Trust 1972.

Piachaud, D. and Weddell, J.M., 'The economics of treating varicose veins', *International Journal of Epidemiology,* vol. 1, 1972.

Pole, D., 'Mass radiography: A cost–benefit approach', in G. McLachlan (ed.), *Problems and Progress in Medical Care 5,* Oxford University Press 1971.

Shaw, G.B., *The Doctor's Dilemma,* Longman 1906.

Wright, K.G., 'Output measurement in practice' in A.J. Culyer and K.G. Wright (eds), *Economic Aspects of Health Services,* Martin Robertson 1978.

Suggestions for Further Reading

Cochrane, A.L., *Effectiveness and Efficiency: Random Reflections on Health Services,* The Nuffield Provincial Hospitals Trust 1972.

Cooper, M.H., and Culyer, A.J., *Health Economics*, Penguin Books 1973.
Culyer, A.J., 'On the relative efficiency of the NHS', *Kyklos*, vol. 25, 1972.
Culyer, A.J., 'Need, values and health status measurement' in A.J. Culyer and K.G. Wright (eds), *Economic Aspects of Health Services*, Martin Robertson 1978.
Culyer, A.J., *Need and the National Health Service*, Martin Robertson 1976.
Culyer, A.J., Lavers, R.J. and Williams, A., 'Social indicators: health,' *Social Trends*, No. 2, 1971.
Feldstein, M.S., *Economic Analysis for Health Service Efficiency*, North Holland 1967.
Fuchs, V. (ed.), *Essays in the Economics of Health and Medical Care*, NBER, Columbia University Press 1972.
Grossman, M., *The Demand for Health: A Theoretical and Empirical Analysis*, NBER, Columbia University Press 1972.
Miller, H., *Medicine and Society*, Oxford University Press 1973.
Newhouse, J.P., *The Economics of Medical Care*, Addison–Wesley 1978.
Williams, A., 'The cost–benefit approach,' *British Medical Bulletin*, vol. 30, 1974.
Wiseman, J., 'Cost–benefit analysis and health service policy,' in A.T. Peacock and D.J. Robertson (eds), *Public Expenditure: Appraisal and Control*, Oliver and Boyd 1963.

8. Policy on income redistribution

C.T. SANDFORD
Professor of Economics,
University of Bath

Introduction

Almost any government policy has some effect on income distribution. With some policies the link is direct and obvious as with a policy of a national minimum wage – although the outcome may be far from obvious and may differ from what was expected. With other policies the link is indirect, as say with policy on education, which affects the relative supply of workers of different skills and hence their remuneration; or housing, where subsidies, tax concessions and rent control constitute a complex web of income redistributing threads. It is impossible for us to deal with all such policies and, indeed, some are covered in other chapters. Our concentration will be on tax policy.

Within the field of taxation we shall look particularly at personal income tax. Income tax is the largest source of government revenue (yielding 46% of central government tax revenue in 1978/9) and is the most powerful tax instrument currently available to the government for redistributing income. But the effect of the other taxes should not be ignored. Taxes which influence the distribution of wealth, like death duties, gift taxes, capital gains taxes and an annual wealth tax (to which the Labour Party remains committed) affect the distribution of investment income; whilst taxes on the consumption of goods and services affect the distribution of real income.

Clearly, too, we cannot examine redistributive policies without looking at the social security system – measures designed to support the poor, or keep people out of poverty when they are threatened by misfortunes like unemployment and sickness. In practice, in the United Kingdom, the overlap between tax and social security is so marked that taxation policy and social security policy must be considered together; and a major issue of policy is how far taxation and social security provisions can be either integrated or coordinated so that they are complementary rather than overlapping. Rationalisation is urgently needed in this policy area.

But let us begin by examining the latest data on the distribution of income.

Distribution of Personal Income in the United Kingdom

We must start by recognising the limitations of the data. The underlying fact is that, almost invariably, the primary statistics which the social scientist uses are collected as a by-product of administration; they are not devised and derived expressly to meet the needs of the economist. The figures on income distribution are certainly no exception to this rule and suffer accordingly. But even if we could produce perfect statistics we should still face conceptual problems to which no wholly satisfactory solution can be found. Let us briefly look at some of the main problems.

What Should Count as Income?

On the conceptual plane this has been a subject of debate amongst economists for generations, some economists arguing that we should include receipts of gifts and inheritances within a comprehensive concept which defined income as any addition to purchasing power over a period of time. Even if we ignore such uncommon interpretations, there are still difficult borderline cases in defining income. All economists would agree that we ought to include income in kind (such as a rent-free house or the use of a company car) as part of income, though there might be dispute about what value to put on such income. Most, if not all, economists would take the view that the person who owns, rather than rents, a house should have a rental value 'imputed' to the house, which should count as part of his income (for he could have let it to someone else at this value and rented accommodation himself, as some people do). More controversial is the treatment of capital gains, which many economists consider should be classed as income. Capital gains are the appreciation of assets over a period of time.

In practice the main source of our income statistics are data collected by the Inland Revenue for income tax purposes. The Inland Revenue data exclude all income which does not come within the taxing statutes, e.g. sickness benefits, unemployment pay and student grants for educational purposes, and they tend to be deficient on very low incomes. Income in kind is generally subject to tax, but the value put on such income often fails to reflect the full value to the recipient. Currently there is no tax on the imputed rental of housing accommodation; and capital gains are not taxed as income, so that they do not figure in the income statistics. Clearly, also, any income which evades tax, e.g. from moonlighting, fails to find its way into the figures. The Inland Revenue data can be supplemented by income and expenditure data collected by the Family Expenditure Survey (FES), an annual sample survey of some 7,000 families, which is particularly useful in making good the deficiencies of the Inland Revenue data in relation to social security incomes and low incomes.

Whose Income Do We Want?

Another difficult conceptual problem is to decide what unit should be used for analysing income distribution. Do we want individual incomes, family incomes or household incomes — defining a household as those engaged in common housekeeping? There is no wholly satisfactory answer. Where individuals live together there is a degree of sharing and economies in living such that to treat their incomes on an individual basis might be misleading. On the other hand if the household is taken as the unit, meaningful comparisons are only obtainable within defined categories, because households vary so much in composition. In practice we are constrained by our data. The Inland Revenue figures are compiled on the basis of the tax unit, under which the non-married are generally treated individually whilst married couples are generally treated as one unit. The FES is conducted on a household basis.

How Do We Measure the Pattern of Income Distribution?

The typical way is to look at income distribution in relation to single years (which can, of course, be compared to other years) and to express the distribution amongst persons in terms of the proportion of total personal income received by particular 'quantiles' of the population, e.g. the top 1% received 4% of income, the top 10% received 25% of the income, and so on. The distribution of income by quantile shares may be expressed graphically by means of the Lorenz curve (see figure 1). But comparison of different years using quantile measurements does not always give an unambiguous answer to whether income distribution has become more or less unequal; inequalities may have been reduced at one end of the distribution but increased at the other. When this happens Lorenz curves will cross.

The use of a single year in this way, however, has its disadvantages; it represents a snapshot relating to a very limited period of time. Most people's incomes vary considerably during the course of a lifetime and in some ways a comparison of the lifetime distribution of income for particular cohorts of the population would be more meaningful than looking at single years. For example, university students might be amongst today's poor, but they are nearly all likely to finish up in the top 10% of the income distribution.

However, we have no regular data on lifetime income distribution. It would be a major exercise to collect it and such data would always be very much out of date, so we have little choice but to use the single year figures.

The final judgement on the deficiencies of the statistical material can be left to the *Royal Commission on the Distribution of Income and Wealth* from whose Seventh Report (HMSO 1979) our subsequent figures are largely drawn. Having listed the limitations of the statistics they conclude:

'What we present, therefore, are particular distributions which, while not as comprehensive as we would wish, provide worthwhile indicators of inequality and trends in inequality.'

Distribution of Income by Factor Share

We can examine the distribution of personal income both by broad division into earned income, investment income and transfer income; and by quantile shares. Table 1 shows the former for three years covering the most recent decade for which the data are available. The first interesting point is the very large proportion of income derived from employment and self-employment, approaching 80% of the whole.

This is an important economic fact, but the figures probably over-state the proportion of earned income and understate the proportion of investment income for two reasons. First, following Inland Revenue practice, self-employment income

Table 1. *Components of Personal Income before Tax in the UK, 1967, 1972 and 1977.*

	1967	*1972*	*1977*
	%	%	%
Earned income			
Employment	70.1	69.6	68.6
Self-employment	8.4	9.8	9.3
Investment income			
Rent, dividends and net interest (including imputed rent of owner-occupiers)	11.7	9.6	9.8
Transfer income			
National insurance and other cash benefits from public authorities.	9.4	10.7	12.1
Total personal income	100	100	100

Source: Report No 7, *Royal Commission on the Distribution of Income and Wealth,* HMSO 1979, Table 2.2.
Note: Percentage columns do not exactly add up because of rounding.

is all treated as earned income, whereas part of it should properly be attributed to a return on capital. Secondly, although investment does include an estimate for the imputed rent of owner-occupied houses based on rateable values, the value has almost certainly been under-stated. The second feature of most interest is the growth in transfer incomes.

Distribution of Income by Personal Share

Table 2 summarises the changes in shares of personal income since 1949. While the year-to-year changes have generally been small, the overall trend has been a marked fall in the shares of the top one per cent of the income group and a somewhat less marked fall in the top 10% both before and after income tax.

The biggest relative gains have gone to the other income groups in the top half of the distribution. Over the period the share of the bottom 50% of the distribution has risen very

Table 2. *Changes in shares of total personal income in the UK, 1949, 1959 and 1976–7*

Quantile group	*Income shares*			*Lower limit of income range 1976–7*
	1949	*1959*	*1976–7*	
	%	%	%	£
Before Tax				
Top 1%	11.2	8.4	5.4	11,258
Top 2–10%	22.0	21.0	20.4	5,686
Top 11–50%	43.1	47.5	49.7	2,615
Bottom 50%	23.7	23.1	24.5	- -
After Tax				
Top 1%	6.4	5.3	3.5	7,330
Top 2–10%	20.7	19.9	18.9	4,418
Top 11–50%	46.4	49.7	50.0	2,160
Bottom 50%	26.5	25.0	27.6	- -

Source: Report No 7, *Royal Commision,* Table 7.1.
Notes: Percentage columns do not always exactly total to 100 because of rounding.
The income unit is the tax unit.

little either before or after tax; but in any one year the post-tax share of the bottom half of the distribution is perceptibly higher than the pre-tax share.

We have said, above, that variations in quantile shares may not give an unambiguous answer to whether income distribution has become more or less uneven. In fact between 1959 and 1976–7 there was an undoubted move towards equality in income distribution. This is shown most clearly by the Lorenz curve in figure 1. This plots the cumulative percentage shares of income, after tax. If income were distributed equally, then the curve would be a straight line at 45° to the horizontal axis; the closer the curve represented by any actual distribution is to the 45° line, the less unequal is the distribution. Figure 1 shows the 1976–7 distribution nearer to the 45° line at all points than the 1959 distribution.

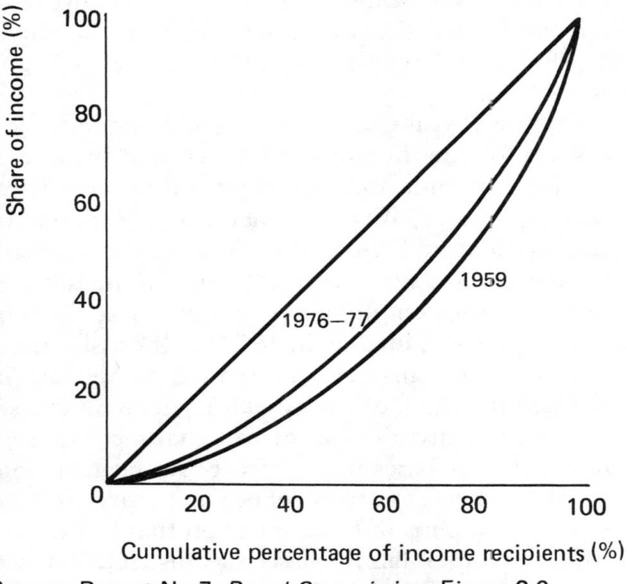

Source: Report No 7, *Royal Commission,* Figure 2.6.

Figure 1. Cumulative percentage share of income after tax in the UK for the years 1959 and 1976–7

International Comparisons of Income Distribution

Some perspective on the distribution of personal income in the United Kingdom can be gained by international comparisons. If the statistics on income distribution in a single country are deficient, comparisons between nations, which compile their data on different bases, are particularly hazardous . Such comparisons cannot therefore usefully go beyond broad generalisations.

Lydall (1975) has conveniently summarised the existing data on the distribution of income in fifty-six countries. The estimates suggested that the typical share of pre-tax income received by the top 5% of households in the poor countries was 30%; this included almost all Africa and Asia and parts of Latin America. Among the countries of Western Europe other than Scandinavia, the typical share of pre-tax income received by the top 5% was about 20%, whilst in Scandinavia, USA and Australia it was nearer to 15%. The latest figure of the top 5% in the United Kingdom, derived from the Royal Commission (1979), and relating to 1976–7, was 16% pre-tax and 13% post tax.

More recently the Royal Commission (1977) undertook a comparative study of the distribution of personal income in the United Kingdom and that in eight other countries: Australia, Canada, France, West Germany, The Republic of Ireland, Japan, Sweden and USA. Comparisons of the *structure* of personal incomes revealed a broadly similar picture: in most cases income from employment amounted to 70% or more of the total personal income in 1974; self-employment income and investment income had tended to decline in most countries and the share of social security income to rise.

Comparisons on the distribution of personal income were made on three different bases between the United Kingdom and those of the other countries whose data permitted a reasonably reliable comparison to be made on that basis.

On a tax unit or inner family basis the distribution was found to be more unequal in the USA and Canada than in the United Kingdom and Ireland. On a consumer unit basis the distribution was much less unequal for the United Kingdom than for the USA or Canada; thus the top fifth in the United

Kingdom had 40.3% on income, in the USA 46.0% and in Canada 43.6%; the bottom two-fifths in the United Kingdom had 16.8%, in the USA 13.5% and in Canada 14.1%. The household basis permitted the most wide-ranging comparisons, though with more reliability and variability than the other methods, so that results have to be treated with more reservation. From this comparison it was concluded that Australia has a less unequal distribution than the United Kingdom, while the USA, France, Japan, Germany and the Republic of Ireland have more unequal distributions than the United Kingdom.

Structure of the UK Income Tax

As already mentioned, income tax is the most important fiscal instrument currently available to British governments for the purpose of redistributing income. Let us now examine this income tax in more detail and look at its economic consequences.

We can distinguish three main characteristics of the United Kingdom income tax:

1 The existence of various allowances and reliefs, so that everyone has at least some income which is not taxable. Besides personal allowances applying to every adult either as a single or married person, there are additional personal allowances such as those for the old and the deaf, and a variety of other tax reliefs of which the most common are mortgage interest relief for house owner-occupiers, relief for contributions to approved pension funds and relief for life insurance premiums.

2 A tax schedule, which is characterised by a 'basic rate' of tax which applies to a very wide band of taxable income; there is a short reduced rate band at the lower end of taxable income and a fairly rapid increase in rates at the upper end.

3 An additional tax on investment income, known as the investment income surcharge (IIS), above a threshold level of investment income.

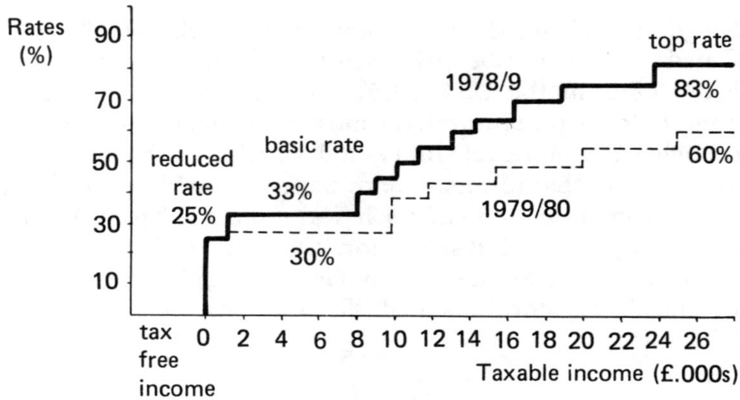

Notes:	1978/9	1979/80
Single person allowance	£985	£1,165
Married allowance	£1,535	£1,815
IIS	10% on £1,700 to £2,250, 15% above £2,250	15% above £5,000
Maximum rate on investment income	98%	75%

Figure 2. Tax structure and rates 1978/9 and 1979/80

In his first Budget the Conservative Chancellor, Sir Geoffrey Howe, made sweeping reductions in income tax with promises of more to come. To provide an adequate perspective we need to look both at the rates of tax in force in the last year of Labour's office 1978–79, and at those introduced by Sir Geoffrey for 1979–80. The position is summarised in figure 2.

Besides the income tax so-called, there is the national insurance contribution (NIC) which is compulsory in relation to most categories of workers. Views differ on the real incidence of the employers' contribution and hence how this should be treated; but there is no doubt that the employee's contribution is equivalent to an income tax. In 1979–80 for the employed worker who was not partially contracted out into an occupational pension scheme, the NIC was 6½% of all income up to £7,020 per year.

The United Kingdom income tax is progressive throughout the whole range of income, i.e. the higher the income level the larger the *proportion* of income taken in tax. Even for taxpayers with different incomes but on the same marginal rate band this is true, because for two taxpayers with the same allowances, the larger the income the smaller the *proportion* of income which is tax free, i.e. the larger the proportion of income taken in tax. Nonetheless the existence of the very wide basic rate band of income reduces the degree of progression for those at the upper end of the band, and also reduces the smoothness of the progression. The existence of tax relief for mortgage interest and the like also tends to favour the better off, partly because the benefit is felt at the marginal rate of tax. Thus, if I am too poor to pay income tax (my marginal rate is zero), an extra £100 of tax relief brings me no benefit; if I am paying tax at a basic rate of 30%, then an extra £100 of tax allowance is worth £30 to me; whilst if my marginal rate of tax is 75%, it is worth £75. So that the income tax reliefs probably reduce the overall progressiveness of the tax. Finally if the proportional NIC is taken in conjunction with income tax, the progression is further reduced and a regressive kink appears part-way along the basic rate band at the income level at which NIC ceases.

Before Sir Geoffrey Howe's 1979 Budget, whilst the overall weight of income tax and NIC was not out of line with other Western nations, the top marginal rates were abnormally high. Indeed, the 98% rate on investment income was sheer nonsense. The effect of the Conservative Budget was to reduce top income tax rates to around the European average.

The Economics of Income Tax

A major subject for examination is whether a heavy income tax, especially one with marginal rates intended to reduce inequality in income distribution, adversely affects the supply of the factors of production. Does income tax reduce willingness to work, save and take risks?

This is a big subject and we can only summarise the main lines of approach. Let us start with the effect on the supply of labour and look first at theory and then at the empirical evidence.

The usual model which economists use for examining the

effect of income tax on work effort assumes that all time is divided between work and leisure. Thus a tendency to take more leisure implies a reduced willingness to work and *vice versa*. We can then investigate the effect of a change in tax on the demand for leisure. If an income tax is imposed, or an existing tax increased, two effects are generated which work in opposite directions. There is an income effect: the taxpayer has been made worse off in terms of the goods and services he normally consumes. He can thus afford less of most goods including leisure. Hence the taxpayer will tend to do *more* work – an incentive effect. At the same time there is a substitution effect: income tax has reduced the price or cost of leisure. To take an extra hour of leisure involves less sacrifice of other things than before. If, pre-tax I received £2 per hour, and a 50% tax reduces that to £1 per hour, an extra hour of leisure costs only half what it previously did. On that score the taxpayer will tend to substitute leisure for work – a disincentive effect.

The net result for the individual taxpayer will depend on the relative strengths of the two effects; but theory can take us some way further. The income effect works through the change in aggregate income, whilst the substitution effect is concerned with the terms on which leisure can be acquired at the margin; therefore we can say that the more the marginal change relative to the average, the more the disincentive or the less the incentive effect is likely to be. As redistributive taxation implies high marginal tax rates, the danger is obvious.

What, then, of the empirical evidence? Various surveys have been undertaken and some econometrical work. All can be regarded as deficient in some respects; but taking them together, the story that emerges is a consistent one. The net effect of tax on the supply of labour appears to be small. If anything, at lower tax levels, there is a slight incentive effect. There is some evidence that, at the highest income levels, as one would expect, there is rather more disincentive effect; and there may also be some tendency for tax to discourage married women from entering the labour force on a full-time basis.

In reality there are numerous complications. Some workers cannot readily adjust the amount of work which they do, at least in the short run. Individual reactions vary according to financial and other circumstances: thus Mr A, a married man with a young family, a mortgage and heavy hire-purchase commitments, may react to an increased tax rate by working more, whilst the same person, twenty years on, with some liquid savings and far fewer financial obligations would opt for leisure. Some taxpayers may maintain their work effort not so much for current consumption as to keep up income to establish pension rights. Again, the outcome may depend on how people wish to spend their leisure. For some, leisure and income are complementary goods; more leisure is not much use without more income, for they enjoy expensive leisure pursuits like horse-racing or foreign travel; for the walkers and television-viewers this is not so.

Even if there is little evidence to suggest that income tax in the United Kingdom has been a disincentive to work effort, there are other bad economic consequences. A heavy income tax undoubtedly encourages Do-it-Yourself activities. Thus, Mr B is a writer and his marginal tax rate is 50%. Suppose it would cost him £300 to pay a professional painter to paint his house. To be able to find that money from extra writing he would need to earn £600. He may decide that, whereas he could earn £300, £400 or perhaps even £500 in the time it would take him to paint the house, he could not earn £600. Therefore he may decide to paint the house himself. The effect of tax has then been to break up the advantages of division of labour.

A further influence of high marginal tax rates is the encouragement they give to evasion (illegal tax dodging) and avoidance (perfectly legal methods by which the taxpayer can reduce his tax bill). The higher marginal tax rates, the greater the gains from successful evasion and avoidance. Although evidence is fragmentary, there would appear to have been substantial increases in the amount of income evading tax in recent years and there is little doubt of a growing trend to avoidance over the past few decades. The existence of relatively easy and safe evasion possibilities, together with avoidance loopholes, may indeed help to account for the limited disincentive effects on work effort which income tax appears to have had.

Tax avoidance, with accompanying distortions, is very evident when we turn to the effect of income tax on saving and enterprise. Just as with work effort, we can distinguish two opposing effects of income tax on aggregate saving. On the one hand, where people are saving for a given future income, the existence of income tax requires and encourages them to save more. Conversely, the more income from saving is taxed, the less worthwhile saving may appear to be. But if the effect on *aggregate* saving is unclear, where there are high marginal *income* tax rates combined with tax concessions for particular forms of saving, as in the UK, the outcome on the direction of saving is not in doubt. Housing, insurance policies and pension funds have boomed as forms of saving, whilst personal holdings of ordinary shares have markedly declined in the past decade or so. Similarly, where investment income carries a maximum rate of tax of 98%, no rich person is going to invest in assets which are predominantly income-yielding. Rather he will buy low-interest gilts, which are approaching maturity, to benefit from a tax-free capital gain; or he will invest in assets which yield only psychic income, like pictures or antiques, but from which a capital gain may be expected. The net effect in the United Kingdom has been a major distortion in the pattern of investment, with rentier assets being favoured at the expense of entrepreneurial and risk assets.

An Expenditure Tax?

This investment distortion arising from the UK income tax was one of the main findings of the Meade Committee's Report (1978). The Committee concluded that the present so-called income tax was neither a true income tax, as income was narrowly defined and on top of that the tax base had been eroded by concessions to some forms of saving, nor was it a genuine expenditure tax, under which all saving would be tax exempt and the tax base would be consumption. The Committee went on to advocate the replacement of the present income tax by an expenditure tax. A full expenditure tax would not be an indirect tax, like VAT or excise duties, but a direct tax, which could be given any desired structure of rates and which would require the completion of tax returns by taxpayers.

An expenditure tax was considered by the Committee to have a number of advantages. In particular the tax would offer greater encouragement to the accumulation of capital, since savings out of income would be exempt from tax while the marginal rate of expenditure tax would be levied on consumption out of capital gains. Also the equal treatment by the tax system of all forms of saving would enable the capital market to operate more efficiently in allocating finance to those investments yielding the highest real return.

At the same time an expenditure tax would involve a number of special problems, including a difficult transitional period. For example, special provisions would be necessary for those who were retired or were approaching retirement; they would have been taxed under an income tax regime on such of their saving as did not benefit from tax concessions and then would be caught for expenditure tax if they ran down their assets in retirement. The indications are that there is no real prospect of the implementation of an expenditure tax in the United Kingdom.

The Distributional Impact of Indirect Taxes and Benefits

So far in examining income distribution we have looked only at the distribution on the basis of tax units, before and after income tax. The Central Statistical Office (CSO) makes an annual estimate of the effects of taxes, including indirect taxes, and benefits on household income using data from the FES. The analysis is conducted in a series of stages. The starting point is the 'original income' of the sample, i.e. income before any cash receipts or other benefits from the State and before deduction of any taxes. Then cash transfers like family allowances and State retirement pensions are added (to give a figure sometimes referred to as 'gross income') and direct taxes are deducted to arrive at 'disposable income'. An estimate of the value to the household of subsidies (most notably housing subsidies) is added, an estimate of the amount paid in indirect taxes deducted and an assessment of direct benefits in kind added to arrive at a figure of 'final income'.

Some of the limitations of the procedure need to be appreciated. Taking the 1977 figures, the taxes which it is felt can be directly allocated to households represented only 63% of total government receipts, whilst only 47% of government expenditure (comprising cash transfers to individuals, subsidies on housing, food and rail travel, and health, education expenditure) was allocated as direct benefits to households. Benefits in kind in education and health are assessed on a formalised basis taking account of the household composition and age. The assumption is made that the average cost of a service measures the benefit to the recipient. In allocating indirect taxes the assumption is made that the incidence of the indirect tax falls wholly on the consumer of the product (whereas in practice part is likely to fall on the producers and perhaps part on the producers and consumers of other goods and services). As the latest CSO article (1979) puts it: 'It must be emphasised that the analysis in this article provides only a very rough guide to the kinds of household which benefit from government expenditure and by how much, and to those which finance it.'

With these caveats, let us look at some of the results. Table 3 is an extract from the summary table for the latest year available at the time of writing, 1977. The analysis is by decile groups – the total sample, of some 7,200 households, is divided into ten groups of equal numbers and ranked by size of original income. To avoid undue detail we have extracted the first, fifth, sixth and tenth deciles, together with the results for all households. It may be noted that for all households taken together the taxes paid exceed the benefits; but this simply reflects the fact that a larger proportion of government revenue than of benefits is allocated to households.

Table 3 indicates the extent of distribution from rich to poor – the poorest decile, from an original income of only £20, enjoys a disposable income of nearly £1,400 and a final income of over £1,700, whilst the original income of over £11,000 for the richest decile is reduced to under £8,000 final income. The table also offers clues to the complex nature of distribution and redistribution amongst households.

Table 3. *Effect of taxes and benefits on income of households, 1977, selected decile groups*

Average	*1st*	*5th*	*6th*	*10th*	*All Households*
No. of workers per household	0.1	1.4	1.6	2.4	1.4
No. of persons per household	1.6	2.9	3.1	3.7	2.8
No. of adults per household	1.3	1.9	2.0	2.7	2.0
No. of children per household	0.3	1.0	1.1	1.0	0.8
No. of persons per worker	16.0	2.1	1.9	1.5	2.0
£ per household per year (to nearest £10) *Average*					
Original income	20	3,610	4,410	11,080	4,230
plus cash benefits	1,360	370	280	220	570
less direct taxes	--	660	890	2,750	890
Disposable income	1,380	3,320	3,800	8,550	3,910
plus subsidies	230	100	100	90	120
less indirect taxes	280	760	860	1,560	820
plus direct benefits in kind	390	610	670	810	600
Final income	1,710	3,270	3,710	7,890	3,810

Source: CSO, *Economic Trends*, January 1979.

Thus the first decile consists almost exclusively of the old, retired person of whom just a few have small part-time earnings. Conversely what stands out about the tenth decile is the very high average number of persons per household. The process of redistribution to an important extent reflects life-time patterns and vicissitudes. Thus there is a transfer of income from the working population to the retired; from those without children to those with; and, though it fails to come through in the figures, from the well to the sick, the employed to the unemployed.

One feature of particular interest in the CSO figures is the incidence of indirect taxes. The conventional assumption has always been that indirect taxes are regressive, i.e. that the lower the income the larger the *proportion* of income taken in tax. Taking all indirect taxes together as a proportion of disposable income, this appears to be true; though the regressiveness is not perhaps as pronounced as might have been

Table 4. *The progressivity/regressivity of direct taxes, 1977 as per cent of disposable income*

Quintile	*Domestic Rates*	*VAT*	*All indirect taxes*
Lowest	5.9	2.45	22.05
Second	4.1	3.0	23.9
Third	3.25	3.25	22.8
Fourth	2.85	3.4	21.25
Highest	2.3	3.2	19.25
Average	3.1	3.2	21.1

Source: CSO, *Economic Trends*, January 1979

expected. Rates are the most regressive, though the impact on the poorest households is over-stated because no account is taken of the component within supplementary benefit which is expressly for household costs. But, primarily because of widespread zero rating, covering food, transport, children's clothes, rent, VAT emerges as slightly progressive (table 4). This is a very significant finding in view of the Conservative strategy of switching from income tax to VAT.

The Relationship of Tax and Social Security Provisions

Clearly, apart from benefits in kind, the social security plays a vital part in redistributive policies; but the whole area is bewildering in its variety and complexity. Some cash benefits are paid universally, without reference to means tests or contributions, but simply according to circumstances; the former family allowances were in this category as is the new child benefit. Other benefits are paid without a means test according to circumstances, like sickness or unemployment, but are dependent on a sufficient record of national insurance contributions. Supplementary benefits are a general means-tested benefit to those in need. In addition there have grown up a whole series of means-tested benefits, each designed to meet a particular circumstance; over forty such benefits exist. One of the most important is Family Income Supplement (FIS) introduced in the early 1970s, which is available to those in full-time work, with at least one child, whose income falls below a prescribed level; the payment under FIS is half the difference between actual pay and the prescribed level, subject to a maximum. Other important means-tested benefits are rent rebates (on council houses), rent allowances (on private accommodation), rate rebates and free school meals.

In addition, as we have seen, the income tax itself has an implicit welfare structure built into it, with its allowance for single and married persons (and, until recently, child allowances), its special personal allowances such as those for the old and the blind and its 'subsidisation' of housing.

But if the income tax is an implicit welfare system, means-tested benefits are an implicit income tax. If the original income of those on means-tested benefits increases, then the benefit is reduced, e.g. in the case of FIS by 50p for every £1 of addition to income – the equivalent of a tax rate of 50%.

To add further to the confusion, some of the social security payments are themselves subject to income tax whilst others are not, without any clear rationale for the difference of treatment. Thus child benefit is untaxed whilst state retirement pensions are taxed. Short-term benefits like sickness and unemployment benefits are not taxed because of the administrative difficulties.

The overlap between tax and social security provisions and lack of coordination in means-tested benefits have generated a number of unfortunate consequences of which possibly the worst is the 'poverty trap'. A married man with several children may be paying income tax and national insurance contributions and at the same time receiving FIS and other means-tested benefits like rate and rent rebates and free school meals. If he earns an extra £1 per week he may find himself paying extra tax and contributions, losing 50p of FIS benefit and smaller sums from the other benefits, with the result that he may actually lose more than the extra £1 he has earned: his marginal rate of explicit and implicit tax is more than 100%. Such an extreme situation is exceptional and would not happen all at once, partly because eligibility to benefits relates to different time periods; but very high rates of 'poverty surtax' are a reality. Such a situation means that poverty is not being properly relieved; that there is a big disincentive to extra work and it is almost impossible for the poor to pull themselves out of poverty; and it may make nonsense of an incomes policy designed to help the low paid.

It is universally accepted that the present situation is intolerable and that the social security provisions and the tax system need to be examined together. Various approaches to reform have been suggested and we shall briefly consider three main ones, each capable of considerable variation.

One approach is that of the Social Dividend or minimum income guarantee. Each citizen, by right of being a citizen, should receive, say through the Post Office giro, a social dividend related to his status (single, married, parent), which in principle would be sufficient to keep him/her above the poverty line. At the same time all tax allowances and national insurance benefits and contributions would disappear and the whole of income except the dividend would be taxed. The attractions of the scheme are its basic simplicity; its assurance that poverty would be relieved and that take-up would be 100%; and the removal of the tax/social security overlap. Its most fundamental defect, however, is the high rate of income tax required to sustain the benefits at the necessary level – estimated to require a basic rate of around 55% – which might prove a severe disincentive. Attempts to reduce the marginal rate by a high surcharge at the lower end of the scale or to reduce the cost by a two-tier dividend system are ingenious but bring their own problems (Meade 1978).

Another approach is that of negative income tax or tax credit schemes which would utilise the income tax machinery. Again, there are a number of variants (e.g. Lees 1967, IEA 1970) but the most practicable is the tax-credit scheme produced by the Conservative Government in 1972, which was to have been implemented in 1977 if the Conservatives had won the 1974 election. Under the tax-credit proposals the basic personal and most of the other income tax allowances would have disappeared for the majority of the population and been replaced by tax-credits (for a married couple, for a single person, for a child). If the credit exceeded the tax due then the balance would be paid as an addition to income; if not, then the credit became an offset to tax. Apart from the credits, all income would be taxed. The objections to the tax-credit scheme were that, as proposed, it was very limited in its scope: it did not abolish national insurance contributions or benefits; it did not apply to the self-employed; it did not even apply to the very poorest; and it left nearly all the means-tested benefits intact. It would have replaced FIS and, at the illustrative rates proposed, it would have taken many pensioners and others out of supplementary benefit; but how many would have been floated off supplementary benefit, and how effective it would have been as an agent of redistribution, was a matter of controversy, because the Green Paper proposing the scheme did not explain how the extra £1,300m necessary to finance it was to be found.

Finally, a third approach is that usually referred to as 'New Beveridge' (Meade 1978). It entails a return to some of the principles of the Beveridge Report on which the present social security system was based. Whereas the two previous approaches sought to integrate tax and social security provisions, the New Beveridge proposals seek rather to coordinate them and make them complementary. Beveridge envisaged that most needs would be covered by national insurance benefits, which would be supplemented by family allowances and by national assistance (or supplementary benefits), which would be a means-tested benefit scheme to act as a safety net and the need for which, it was envisaged, would gradually diminish. In fact the calls on supplementary benefits have grown massively, because the national insurance benefits and family allowances were set at a much lower level than the supplementary benefit (SB) scale. New Beveridge envisages that the income tax thresholds shall be equated with supplementary benefit levels, so that no one on SB would pay tax. Further, the various national insurance benefits would be up-rated to the SB level and the new child benefit would likewise be up-rated to the SB child allowance level. The disadvantages of the proposal are that it would be extremely costly, involving making considerable payments, for example to wealthy pensioners and the better off with children, who do not need them; it would also retain the structure of national insurance payments and contribution conditions which some consider is cumbersome and outmoded. Perhaps its biggest attraction is that is is closely related to the present system and could therefore be implemented on a piece-meal basis.

Conclusions on Policy

Two brief comments may be made by way of conclusion. The first follows immediately from the various proposals for reform of the social security system. On the face of things the proposals may seem very diverse, but the reality could be different. The much-needed reform has to start from where we are, and necessarily has to proceed step by step. This is likely to mean beginning with an approach on New Beveridge lines, up-rating some existing benefits to take a particular class of citizen altogether out of the need for supplementary benefit. But the up-rating could take the form of a special credit – for example, a pensioner credit. If such a credit were made universal at retirement age, irrespective of contributions, it would then be a step on the way to a tax credit and indeed a social dividend scheme. Something similar happened with child benefit. Although the full Conservative tax-credit scheme has not been implemented, the new child benefit can properly be thought of as the implementation by the Labour Government of part of its predecessor's plans.

Secondly, with the 1979 Conservative Government we appear to be moving into a period in which a rather different view is being taken of inequality and redistribution. Whilst it seems likely that, at least in terms of the direct effects, the poorest especially pensioners, gained from the 1979 June Budget and the up-rating of the social security payments which went with it, the second quantile in the income scale may have lost – gaining less in income tax reductions than they will have to pay in higher indirect taxes. Indisputably, those on the highest incomes gained substantially from the reduction of higher-rate tax. Whether reduced inequality at the very bottom combined with increased inequality elsewhere in the income distribution is desirable in itself is a matter of personal judgement.

Further, Conservative strategy is based on the belief that the income tax changes will generate incentives to work and enterprise. If this strategy is successful, the egalitarians will have to ask themselves what increase in real incomes throughout the whole income scale justifies an increase in inequality.

References

Christopher, A., *et al*, *Policy for Poverty*, IEA Research Monograph, No 20, 1970.

Lees, D., 'Poor families and fiscal reform', *Lloyds Bank Review*, October 1967.

Lydall, H., 'The economics of inequality', *Lloyds Bank Review*, No. 117, July 1975.

CSO, 'The effect of taxes and benefits in household income, 1977', *Economic Trends*, No 303, January 1979.

The Meade Committee Report, *The Structure and Reform of Direct Taxation*, IFS/George Allen & Unwin 1978.

The Royal Commission on the Distribution of Income and Wealth, Report No 5, Third Report on the Standing Conference, Cmnd 6999, HMSO 1977.

The Royal Commission on the Distribution of Income and Wealth, Report No 7, Fourth Report on the Standing Conference, Cmnd 7595, HMSO 1979.

Suggestions for Further Reading

Break, G.F., 'Effects of taxation on incentives', *British Tax Review*, June 1957.

Brown, C.V. and Levin, E., 'The effects of income tax on overtime: the results of a national survey', *Economic Journal*, December 1974.

Fields, D.B. and Stanbury, W.T., 'Incentives, disincentives and the income tax, further empirical evidence', *Public Finance*, No 3, 1970.

Rhys Williams, Sir Brandon, *The New Social Contract*, Conservative Political Centre 1967.

Sandford, C.T., *Social Economics*, Heinemann 1977.

Proposals for a Tax Credit System, Cmnd 5116, HMSO 1972.

Select Committee on Tax Credit, HC 341–1, HMSO 1973.

PART III

Macroeconomic Policy

9. The objectives and instruments of macroeconomic policy in the UK

RODNEY B. CROSS
Lecturer in Economics,
University of St Andrews

Introduction

Economic policy is conventionally thought of as having a trinity of aims: one relates to the allocation and efficiency of use of economic resources; another concerns the distribution of income and wealth; while the third is concerned with the 'stabilisation' of economic activity. Macroeconomic policy is conventionally identified with the third objective, stabilisation. In the context of macroeconomic policy, stability is usually used to refer to the constancy of output, employment and prices (or their rates of change) over time, and also the ability of the economic system to return to some equilibrium values for output, employment and prices (or their rates of change) after experiencing supply or demand disturbances.

Macroeconomic policy differs from stabilisation policy in that it specifies the particular levels of output, employment and prices (and/or their rates of change) around which the economy ought to be stabilised. Macroeconomic policy can thus be considered as stabilisation policy together with a specification of the goals towards which that policy is directed. The purpose of this chapter is to provide an overview of the broad issues involved in UK macroeconomic policy. The chapter discusses first the ends or objectives of policy, then proceeds to examine the instruments of macroeconomic policy employed in the UK. As we shall see, in contrast to elementary textbook expositions of macroeconomic stabilisation policies, macroeconomic policy making in the UK is far from being a precise science. Not only are governments frequently unclear and inconsistent over the objectives they wish to pursue, but economic policy must be formulated under conditions of uncertainty as to the current state of the economy and the likely impact of policy variables. In this chapter attention is given to the different views which economists hold concerning the operation of the economy and the appropriate policies for correcting macroeconomic problems.

In the UK five main schools of macroeconomic thought can be discerned. The *Orthodox Keynesian* school has dominated official opinion since 1945. A basic tenet here is that the private sector is likely to respond in an unstable manner to supply or demand shocks and that as a result the government should play an active role in stabilising the economy by controlling the level of aggregate demand. Until recent years, monetary factors have not been seen to have an important influence on economic activity and inflation.

The *Monetarist* school on the other hand holds that the private sector left to its own devices is not likely to respond in an unstable manner to disturbances (e.g. the oil price increases of 1973 and 1979). Largely as a result of this tenet, the government is advised not to allow its own policies to provide a source of disturbance to the economy, the idea being that governments should only gradually change their policies or organise their policies inside a set of non-discretionary rules. Monetary factors, of course, are seen to be dominant in explaining fluctuations in economic activity and inflation.

The *New Cambridge* school of thought has developed as a critique of orthodox Keynesianism. The principal effects of fiscal policy are taken to be felt primarily on the balance of payments rather than on the domestic level of economic activity. The authorities are advised not to indulge in discretionary policies of the 'fine-tuning' variety and import controls are seen as a necessary component of any successful plan for the UK to sustain a higher rate of economic growth.

The *International Monetarist* school has principally developed as an extension (rather than revision) of orthodox Monetarism, though in the UK such ideas have also been grafted on to a basically Keynesian system of thought in the

London Business School analysis of economic policy (see Ball and Burns 1978). This extension of Monetarism particularly stresses the influence monetary factors exert on the balance of payments or the exchange rate (according to whether exchange rates are fixed or flexible), the direct domestic influence of monetary factors being de-emphasised.

Finally the *Marxist* school stresses the endogenous tendency of capitalism to develop via a series of booms and slumps, analyses government policy as a reaction to such tendencies and emphasises the class conflicts which are involved in the economic processes producing fluctuations in inflation and unemployment.[1] For expositional purposes, the following discussion will attempt, primarily, to highlight the contrasts between Keynesian and Monetarist approaches.

The Objectives of Macroeconomic Policy

Conventionally, macroeconomic policy is regarded as being directed towards four targets: (1) achieving the lowest rate of unemployment consistent with the achievement of other objectives; (2) achieving the lowest or most stable rate of inflation possible given other objectives; (3) achieving a long-run balance between international payments and receipts (though in the short run a surplus or deficit may be aimed at for various reasons); and (4) securing the macroeconomic conditions most conducive to economic growth in the economy.

Of the above policy targets, the economic growth objective may appear as the ultimate aim of macroeconomic policy. This follows if, as advocated by a long line of eminent economists including Keynes, consumption is regarded as the end of all economic activity and if maximising output per head is regarded as synonymous with maximising consumption per head over time. The pre-eminence of growth as the primary objective of macroeconomic policy in the UK is underlined by the failure of the UK to attain a rate of economic growth approaching that of other industrialised nations. Indeed, it could be argued that the other deficiencies of UK macroeconomic performance – unemployment, inflation and balance of payments difficulties – stem from an inadequate growth of productive capacity. But it is the very seriousness of these other economic problems that has prevented the orientation of macroeconomic policies towards the objective of economic growth. While the problems of low growth are long term and pervasive, those of unemployment and the balance of payments are concentrated and immediate. Increases in unemployment above 'acceptable' levels result in electoral unpopularity for the government and the loss of the cooperation of the trade unions in economic policy. Deficits on the balance of payments and associated pressure on the exchange rate of sterling have involved the British government in heavy overseas borrowing and in the contravention of its international commitments, the result being that overseas governments and international agencies (e.g. the IMF) have been able to exert substantial influence over UK economic policy. The post-war history of macroeconomic policy in the UK has been one of expansionary measures to reduce unemployment, alternating with panic measures to support sterling and correct deficits in the current account of the balance of payments. This orientation of macroeconomic policy to short-term objectives has largely precluded the pursuit of policies which would create a macroeconomic environment conducive to economic growth. Moreover, it has been suggested that the lack of success of macroeconomic policies even to achieve these short-term objectives has had a destabilising influence on the economy which has been positively detrimental to economic growth.

The Unemployment Objective

An implicit assumption behind the full-employment policies of post-war British governments is that unemployment is an undesirable social evil. This assumption fails to distinguish between voluntary and involuntary unemployment. Clearly employment policies which involve economic measures will influence only involuntary unemployment.[2] The distinction which concerns us here is between unemployment that can be cured by macroeconomic policy measures and that which cannot. Two approaches to the analysis of the unemployment problem may be identified, one Keynesian, one Monetarist.

The *Keynesian* approach is to divide unemployment into different categories. Surprisingly enough, a taxonomy produced by Keynes himself in a 1942 Treasury Paper (cited by Kahn 1976) typifies this approach. Five categories are distinguished: (1) the hard core of unemployables; (2) the seasonally out of work; (3) transitional unemployment between jobs; (4) structural and regional unemployment; and (5), after eliminating the above categories, a residual due to deficiency in aggregate demand. Adopting this conceptual framework, conventional Keynesians would today probably consider that approximately a third of the 1,300,000 unemployed (excluding school leavers) at the end of 1978 were unemployed owing to demand deficiency and could be re-employed by appropriate demand management policies providing other constraints could be overcome.

The *Monetarist* approach to unemployment as a policy objective proceeds by distinguishing between an equilibrium or *natural* rate of unemployment and the *actual* rate of unemployment. The determinants of the 'natural' rate are mainly microeconomic in nature and so the natural rate will be largely invariate with regard to macroeconomic policy measures. The latter measures can affect the actual rate of unemployment, though only at the cost of a *rising inflation rate* if the actual is pushed *below* the natural unemployment rate, the *rate of inflation falling* if the actual is pushed *above* the natural unemployment rate. In the long run the economy will experience the natural unemployment rate. Thus, macroeconomic policy measures can reduce (or increase) unemployment in the short run, but long-run reductions in unemployment can only be achieved by influencing the largely microeconomic factors which determine the natural rate of unemployment.

The natural rate of unemployment (the term is due to Friedman 1968) depends upon a large number of factors including the occupational and geographical mobility of labour, the balance between those entering and leaving the labour force, the balance between unemployment benefits and after tax wages and the amplitude of cyclical fluctuations in the economy. Thus changes in actual unemployment can be separated into changes in the natural rate of unemployment and any change in the deviation of the natural from the actual rate. A recent study (Sumner 1978) estimates that the natural rate of unemployment for the UK averaged 3.4% between 1952 and 1974. The natural rate rose sharply in the late 1960s and early 1970s, reflecting an increase in the numbers of young persons entering the labour force, employment protection measures which made employers more reluctant to offer jobs and a rise in the ratio of unemployment benefits to post tax earnings (for a married man with two children and average wages, unemployment benefit was 36% of post-tax wages in 1952–54 and 71% in 1972–74). This rise in the natural rate meant a decline in the amenability of unemployment to macroeconomic measures.

The Inflation Objective

As pointed out in greater detail in Chapter 11, the main costs of inflation stem from inflation which is unanticipated, although certain costs arise with fully anticipated inflation due to the decline in the value of non-interest bearing money balances and the effect of the UK tax system which is not indexed to the rate of inflation. Since the more the rate of inflation changes the more difficult it becomes to anticipate correctly the inflation rate, it may be argued that the main task for macroeconomic policy is to ensure that the inflation rate does not change greatly over time, rather than to achieve the lowest rate of inflation possible.

The latter argument, however, ignores the open nature of the UK economy, where about a quarter of goods are imported and substantial amounts of capital flow across the foreign exchange market. If macroeconomic policy were to be concerned only with ensuring that the current rate of inflation of, say, 10% does not change much over time, this would be fine if on average other countries had the same 10% inflation rate. If, however, other countries had rates of inflation which on average were substantially less than 10%, then over time the UK economy would, in a fixed exchange rate system, experience a balance of payments deficit, or, in a floating exchange rate system, experience a depreciation of the pound sterling against other currencies. Thus, for international reasons major costs are going to be associated with the *level* of the rate of inflation (if different from other countries) as well as with *variations* in the rate of inflation.

It is this relationship between the UK's relative rate of inflation and its external transactions that has been the principal concern of British governments in seeking to lower the rate of inflation. Under the fixed exchange rate regime of the 1960s, the UK's relatively high rate of inflation was identified as the major cause of balance of payments difficulties and policies to control inflation were seen as the appropriate cure. Under flexible exchange rates, exchange rate adjustments should, in principle, allow the attainment of balance of payments equilibrium under any domestic rate of inflation. The experience of 1974–76 cast doubt upon the equilibrating role of the exchange rate and raised the spectre of a vicious circle of high inflation, current account deficit, depreciating currency leading to higher inflation, etc. The unprecedently high rate of inflation of the period 1975–77 also made evident the costs of inflation itself, notably in the form of adjustment costs and increased uncertainty. It seems likely therefore that the objective of a low rate of inflation will continue to be a primary objective of UK macroeconomic policy, despite the relief to the balance of payments provided by North Sea oil.

The way in which the rate of inflation appears as a macroeconomic policy target differs between the major schools of thought. Again we illustrate such differences by drawing a crude distinction between Keynesian and Monetarist views.

The tendency of British Keynesian economists is to view the rate of inflation as primarily determined by microeconomic or sociological factors and thus not to be a major target for macroeconomic policy. The approach usually focuses attention to the individual prices that make up the price index from which the figure for the overall rate of inflation is derived. Individual prices are usually taken to be determined by sellers adding a profit mark-up onto their costs, the centre of attention thus shifting backwards to the determinants of costs.

The principal *domestic* influence on UK costs is the level of wages and salaries. Wages and salaries are taken to be determined by trade union militancy (Hines 1971); trade unions seeking to achieve a target net-of-tax real wage (Sargan 1971); sociological factors such as 'relative deprivation and the perception of social justice' (Turvey 1971); or similar factors equally distant from macroeconomic policy influence (see Hicks 1974, Chapter 3). Other domestic influences include the level of indirect taxes and changes in the degree of monopoly power which may affect mark-ups. International influences on the UK rate of inflation include movements in the exchange rate and changes in world raw material prices. As a result, British Keynesians envisage macroeconomic policies as playing a relatively minor role in influencing inflation. While policies to influence the level of aggregate demand will influence price and wage changes, such policies do not tackle the root causes of inflation.

In contrast, the Monetarist school takes the determinants of the rate of inflation to be predominantly macroeconomic in nature and thus very much a concern of macroeconomic policy.

The first plank in the UK Monetarist explanation of inflation is the natural rate of unemployment theory mentioned earlier. If unemployment is held below the natural rate, the rate of inflation will rise, and *vice versa.* Deviations of the actual from the natural rate of unemployment will be symptomatic of the state of excess demand (the differences between demand and supply), excess demand driving unemployment below the natural rate, excess supply driving unemployment above the natural rate. The second plank in the Monetarist position explains excess demand as being principally a function of the difference between the rate at which the money supply is expanded and the rate at which members of the public wish to increase their money holdings, the latter being determined by a stable demand for money function.

The Monetarist analysis of the role *international* factors play in determining the rate of inflation differs according to the exchange rate regime. If the UK authorities have *fixed* the sterling exchange rate against other currencies, this will set a limit to the amount by which the UK inflation rate can differ from that in countries reciprocally holding exchange rates fixed against sterling, the proposition being that in the long run the UK will tend to experience the same inflation rate as that prevailing in other countries. Thus the UK inflation rate would be primarily determined by factors outside the control of domestic macroeconomic policy once the exchange rate is fixed – see Chapter 13 for an explanation of the above proposition.

If the UK authorities allow the sterling exchange rate to *float*, however, the proposition is that the exchange rate will tend to depreciate (appreciate) to reflect the excess (shortfall) of the UK inflation rate over that on the average prevailing in other countries. Thus the UK inflation rate reverts to being primarily determined by UK macroeconomic policy. The UK exchange rate system since 1971 has been a 'dirty floating' one, with the authorities intervening to help determine the rate of exchange during certain periods and allowing private supply and demand to determine the rate during other periods. Thus there have been periods in which the fixed exchange rate propositions of the Monetarists apply and periods in which the floating propositions apply, thus complicating matters.

The Balance of Payments Objective

Here we define the balance of payments policy target as a state of equality between the international payments and receipts of the UK. To examine the nature of the balance of payments as a policy objective, it is necessary to discuss the costs of imbalance between payments and receipts

In the fixed exchange rate case a private sector deficit (surplus) is financed by the central bank using (accumulating) foreign exchange reserves. If the UK were continually to run a deficit, the central bank would eventually run out of reserves and the country would face insolvency. In the event of this extreme position not being reached, the costs of the deficit would correspond to the costs of reducing expenditure, lowering the exchange rate or taking other measures to correct the deficit. These costs may be considerable. The recurrent balance of payments difficulties of 1961 to 1968 necessitated deflationary measures which increased unemployment and reduced the rate of economic growth. On the other hand, if the UK were to run a surplus, this would not only involve the costs of the higher inflation rate engendered by the inflow of money, but would also involve the costs associated with the accumulation of foreign exchange reserves which tend to bear lower interest rates than could be earned elsewhere in the economy. In the case of a floating exchange rate, a deficit will cause depreciation of the exchange rate. The costs of this are adverse movement in the country's terms of trade and the increase in inflation which higher import prices are likely to cause.

It was one consequence of the 'Keynesian Revolution' that the balance of payments came to be viewed as a policy target rather than as a self-regulating mechanism (see Johnson 1958). The approach of British Keynesians to the balance of payments is to break it down into its structural components and to identify the relationship between macroeconomic variables and the various components. Thus the current account is seen as determined, *inter alia*, by the domestic and foreign levels of demand and by relative costs and prices in the UK compared to the rest of the world. Of the above factors, domestic aggregate demand and the exchange rate are the variables which domestic macroeconomic policy can influence according to this position. The *capital* account is viewed as being influenced primarily by UK rates of interest relative to those of other countries.

In contrast, Monetarists look at the balance of payments in terms of the outflow (inflow) of money which corresponds to the excess (shortfall) of private sector international payments over receipts, and combine all items on both private current and capital accounts together for this purpose. A deficit means that UK residents are running down their sterling money balances, the authorities in a *fixed exchange rate* regime exchanging such sterling balances for the foreign currencies required by the foreigners who are running a surplus, thus leading to a reduction in the UK's foreign exchange reserves. In a *floating exchange rate* regime such pressure leads to exchange rate depreciation, foreign exchange reserves not being used to support the exchange rate.

The next step in the Monetarist analysis is to identify the outflow (inflow) of money corresponding to the deficit (surplus) with the difference between the rate at which the authorities expand the money supply and the rate at which the private sector wishes to increase its money holdings. In a closed economy the money supply increasing at a faster (slower) rate than money demand will tend to push down (up) unemployment and up (down) the rate of inflation. In an open economy, however, UK residents can offload (acquire) the excess (required) money balances through the balance of payments in a manner lucidly described by David Hume many years ago (Hume 1752), the excess (required) money supply affecting unemployment and inflation overseas rather than domestically. A distinction is drawn between the *ex ante* increase in the money stock, which is called Domestic Credit Expansion (DCE) and the part of the increase in this money stock which remains in the UK, this being called the *ex post* change in the money supply. Thus controlling DCE is the key to achieving the balance of payments target.

If a freely floating exchange rate is adopted, no distinction between *ex ante* DCE and the *ex post* change in the money supply is drawn, the exchange rate depreciating (appreciating) to reflect any excess (shortfall) of the rate of monetary expansion over the increase in demand for money. Again controlling DCE appears as the key to achieving any balance of payments target.[3]

The Growth Objective

Inadequate economic growth has been identified by successive British governments as the fundamental problem of the UK economy. Although the benefits of economic growth have been questioned by those who stress the costs associated with growth (Mishan 1967), those who stress the scarcity of natural resources (Meadows *et al.* 1972) and those who note the social tensions arising from continued economic expansion (Hirsch 1977), there is virtually unanimous agreement that it is in the national interest that the discrepancy between the growth rates of the UK and its European neighbours should be narrowed. However, in no other area of economic policy has failure been more conspicuous and the range of policy suggestions more varied.

British Keynesians have tended to ascribe to macroeconomic policy an active role in promoting economic growth, in that a sufficient level of demand has to be forthcoming if the potential growth rate is to be realised. Policies to promote the growth objective, however, have not been notably successful and expansions in aggregate demand have not been sustained in the light of subsequent balance of payments deficits. The response of British Keynesians to the experienced inability of governments to sustain aggregate demand increases has been, *inter alia,* to advocate exchange rate depreciation (Kaldor 1966) or import controls (Godley and May 1977).

In contrast, British Monetarists have tended to see active macroeconomic policy measures as more likely to hamper the achievement of any economic growth objective, and thus accord to macroeconomic policy the negative role of ensuring that policy measures do not provide sources of disturbance to the economy. The underlying assumption here is that private sector behaviour is stable. This means that disturbances such as the oil price rise of 1973 can lead to a reduction in demand, employment and growth, but that such changes will only be temporary, there being adjustment mechanisms at work in the private sector which will eventually move the economy back to its equilibrium level of demand, employment and growth. The key word in the above statement is 'eventually' – the Monetarist who thinks that 'eventually' might mean a long time, tending to have a more open mind as to whether active macroeconomic policy measures with regard to aggregate demand might be advisable in certain circumstances.

As has been noted, the concentration of macroeconomic policy upon the short-term objectives of unemployment and the balance of payments has effectively precluded the consistent application of fiscal and monetary policies towards the stimulation of economic growth. Consequently British governments have introduced various additional policy measures to encourage growth. Many of these have been microeconomic in nature, such as policies to stimulate innovation and increase investment in particular industries and raise the educational standard of the labour force. At the macroeconomic level policies towards economic growth have been built around notions (often vague ones) of medium-term economic planning. Economic planning at national and individual industry level has been closely associated with the National Economic Development Council (NEDC).

Fiscal Policy

A simplistic approach to policy formulation would be to attempt to discover the policy instruments which could most effectively be used to achieve each of the policy objectives discussed above. Such an approach is quite impractical. Not only are policy objectives interdependent (e.g. a policy measure to reduce unemployment may tend to increase inflation), but the policy variables themselves cannot be adjusted independently. For example, an expansionary fiscal policy will lead to an expansion in the money supply or upward pressure on interest rates. Thus, while we discuss the main instruments of macroeconomic policy separately, it must be recognised that in practice policy implementation is complicated by the inter-relationships between the various instruments.

Fiscal policy can be defined as 'any change in the level, composition or timing of government expenditure, or any change in the rate of taxation or the timing and composition of fiscal receipts' (Shaw 1977). Fiscal policy works by influencing directly, via government expenditure, or indirectly, via taxation, the level of aggregate demand in the economy.[4] This instrument has conventionally been seen to be *the* anti-depression or counter-cyclical tool of demand management to have emerged from the Keynesian revolution in economic thought.[5] In the 1970s increasing doubt has been cast on the effectiveness of expansionary fiscal policy in achieving a *lasting* reduction in unemployment and increase in output, this change in attitude being evident not only in the academic literature but also in the public pronouncements of senior Labour and Conservative Cabinet ministers in the late 1970s. Even more doubt has been cast on the effectiveness of 'fine tuning' fiscal policies in smoothing the trade cycle.

Before turning to look at the effectiveness of fiscal policy as a whole, it is worthwhile to discuss some of the issues which arise with regard to government spending and taxation receipts considered separately.

Government Spending

The public spending of central government, local government and nationalised industries accounts for just over 45% of GDP in the UK if we define public spending as that which has to be financed by taxation, national insurance contributions or government borrowing; though this figure can vary from about 30 to almost 60% according to whether we include transfer payments, private or overseas finance of investment spending by nationalised industries, net or gross debt interest and so on. Public spending has grown more rapidly than GDP over the last thirty years and this growth of the public sector has been held by some to have been responsible for the UK's poor growth performance (Bacon and Eltis 1978) or poor inflation record (Friedman, *Financial Times*, Jan. 6, 1977).

Government spending plans are reviewed annually, each spending department submitting expenditure plans for the coming four years which are reviewed by the interdepartmental Public Expenditure Survey Committee (PESC). Ministers then rejoin the debate about priorities and, after Cabinet level discussions, the government publishes its plans in an expenditure White Paper at the beginning of the calendar year. The process culminates in the presentation of detailed 'Supply Estimates' to Parliament by the government on the March/April Budget day. Besides detailed expenditure estimates, the government also announces a 'Contingency Reserve' fund which is designed to allow for any unanticipated increases in the cost of expenditure programmes while at the same time keeping the total level of public spending within the amount planned.

Spending is initially planned in real terms (numbers of teachers, for example), such plans being then converted to money equivalent at 'survey prices' pertaining usually to the autumn of the preceding year. The higher rates of inflation of recent years have created problems in terms of keeping actual money spending under control, *vide* the substantial overspending in the mid 1970s. To cope with this problem 'cash limits' for certain building programmes were introduced in 1974/75, the system being extended to cover most of public spending in 1975/76 (transfer payments excepted). The 'cash limit' involves embedding an allowance for inflation into each spending programme, which implies a ceiling on money spending. The April 1976 White Paper on cash limits (Cmnd 6440) was not clear as to what would happen should the actual inflation rate turn out to be substantially higher than budgeted. The pronouncements of the current Conservative administration, however, imply that the ceilings would be rigidly adhered to, involving a cut in the volume of spending. Here the aversion of treasurers in charge of public projects to the risk of breaching the expenditure ceiling has to be taken into account. The substantial underspending in 1977/78 was in large part due to this risk aversion.

The usefulness of variations in public expenditure as an instrument of macroeconomic policy is limited and complicated by several factors. First, public expenditure is not primarily an instrument of macroeconomic policy. Public spending is geared to the provision of public services and the achievement of social objectives. It is not obvious that any gains from varying public spending as an instrument of demand management outweigh the costs involved in varying public provision. Second, changes in different items of government spending can be expected to have different effects on the economy. The marginal consumption, tax and import ratios for different items of expenditure will usually be different. Third, not all changes in public spending will occur as a result of active policy choices. Transfer payments to the unemployed, for example, will vary with the level of economic activity; therefore government spending will be higher in the trough and lower at the peak of the trade cycle.

Finally, the success of changes in public expenditure in stabilising the economy depends crucially upon the ability of the authorities correctly to estimate the time lags involved in policy changes taking place. These lags include the *recognition lag* before the authorities receive reliable information that, say, a downturn in economic activity has begun; the *implementation lag* while the authorities organise and put into effect the required policy measures; and finally the *behavioural lag* while the private sector adjusts its responses to the policy change. If time lags are estimated incorrectly, then policies designed to smooth cyclical fluctuations in the economy may be positively destabilising. Thus if the government pursues a 'proportional' stabilisation policy whereby public spending is actively increased at the trough of the trade cycle, such measures will only take effect once economic activity has already picked up. To avoid such problems a 'derivative' element needs to be incorporated into such counter-cyclical policies, whereby public spending is actively increased (reduced) most, the faster economic activity is falling (rising). Such a policy, however, would be politically difficult to introduce given that it would imply an active reduction in public spending immediately the economy comes to recover from a depression, economic activity and employment being still low in this phase of the cycle.

The shift of opinion away from using public spending as a discretionary instrument of demand management, with increases in spending following rises in unemployment and cuts following balance of payments crises, is reflected in the 1974 report of the Expenditure Committee of the House of Commons: 'We recommend that therefore in managing the economy . . . changes in public spending should only be used in the last resort . . . short term demand management by fiscal means should primarily be carried out by changes in taxation' (HC 328, page xi).

Taxation

Taxation policy influences aggregate demand indirectly by either changing private sector disposable income through taxes on income, or by changing the costs of producing and consuming commodities, the division of the tax burden between consumers and producers depending on the relevant elasticities of demand and supply. The influence is indirect, in contrast to that of public spending, reliance being made on the private sector changing its behaviour in a reasonably stable way in response to tax changes. Recently emphasis has been placed on the effects of taxation on aggregate supply. In particular, a shift of taxation from income to expenditure has been recommended (see Chapter 8, pp. 200–201). The desire of the Conservative Party to create incentives for productive effort by reducing marginal rates at high income levels, and shift taxation from income to expenditure, is reflected in the Budget of June 1979. The extent to which the level and structure of UK taxes has been responsible for the poor performance of the economy has attracted considerable debate.

International comparisons suggest that the UK is out of line with most other Western industrial countries only in terms of relatively high marginal tax rates on high incomes and this discrepancy was largely removed with the June 1979 Budget. In terms of the percentage of GNP at factor cost associated with taxes and social security contributions, the tax take was 41% in 1975, which placed the UK on a par with France (41%) and West Germany (42%); below Denmark (50%), the Netherlands (53%) and Sweden (52%); and above the US (33%) and Japan (22%) (see *Economic Trends,* December 1977, p. 111). Thus the link between UK taxation policy and its poor growth performance is not as obvious as commonly alleged (see Chapter 8).

A further important role for taxation policy is often involved in the Keynesian school's analysis of inflation. The idea here is that trade unions respond to any change in direct taxes by demanding higher money wages in order to maintain the real wages of their members after tax, the idea sometimes being referred to as the *real wage resistance hypothesis* (see Sargan 1971). Providing the effect is symmetric, taxation policy could thus be used as an instrument to reduce inflation – lower income tax rates leading to lower money wage demands and lower average costs above which prices need be marked up. This instrument formed part of the 1974–79 Labour Government's anti-inflation policy. Monetarists, on the other hand, tend to argue that the influence of taxation on the rate of inflation is relatively small.

The Inland Revenue and Customs and Excise are responsible for the collection of direct and indirect taxes respectively.

Whereas indirect taxes and taxes on capital are permanent, income taxes need to be renewed annually. The latter is achieved by the Chancellor tabling Ways and Means Resolutions immediately after the Budget speech; now taxes or changes in permanent taxes are also being introduced by such a method. Such Resolutions provide the government with the temporary authority to collect taxes until the Finance Bill on them becomes a Finance Act. The particular tax rates and allowances are decided by the Chancellor in consultation with his colleagues, part of the background advice being provided by the February forecast from the Treasury macro-econometric model as to what the likely course of the economy is going to be on the basis of unchanged policy and the contemplated changes in policy. Up until 1973 anyway, changes in taxes have been used more than changes in public spending in attempts to 'fine tune' the economy via changes in aggregate demand (see Wass 1978).

The qualifying remarks made with regard to public spending also apply to taxation policy: it is not purely a macro policy instrument; different tax changes can be expected to have different effects; total tax receipts will depend on the level of economic activity, so not all tax changes will occur as a result of active policy choices; and there are profound timing problems to be faced in any attempt to frame a successful counter-cyclical policy. Worthy of particular note is the way different tax revenues vary with inflation. Given unchanged tax rates, income tax revenue will rise faster than the rate of inflation given the progressive rate structure; VAT revenue at the same rate; and fixed sum excise taxes on tobacco, alcohol and petroleum remain constant with inflation. Thus in the absence of changes in the tax rates and allowances the proportion of total tax revenue contributed by direct taxes would rise in the face of continuing inflation. This problem of 'fiscal drag' has been to a certain extent ameliorated by the commitment placed on governments to adjust income tax allowances for inflation. This was introduced by a back-bench (Rooker–Wise) amendment to the 1977 Finance Act.

Besides the movement to shift the burden of total taxation from direct to indirect taxes, the main change in policy practice over the last four years has concerned an increased reluctance to make large changes in the total tax take in any one year. This can be partly traced back to the effects of the 1972 Budget, where tax cuts to the almost unprecedented value of £1,200 million were introduced at a time when economic activity was already showing strong signs of recovering from the trough which had seen unemployment hover around its highest post-1945 level of one million. This policy succeeded in stimulating a 5% rate of output growth in the succeeding 18 months, and in reducing unemployment to around half a million by the end of 1973, but only at the cost of exerting strong upward pressure on the rate of inflation and turning the balance of payments round from a current account surplus to a deficit. Certain doubts were recently expressed by the Permanent Secretary to the Treasury: '... if the brunt of short-term fiscal policy falls on the tax side, the burden of adjustment falls on the private sector. The consequent costs of disruption may well be as great as the costs of disruption in the public sector (had public spending changes been used)' (Wass 1978, p. 100).

Fiscal Policy as a Whole

The net effect of fiscal policy is measured by the fiscal deficit, the difference between public spending (G) and taxation (T), thus $G-T > 0$ indicates an expansionary fiscal policy, $G-T < 0$ a contractionary policy. Given the tendency of G and T to vary automatically with the level of economic activity and the rate of inflation, however, a more sophisticated measure is required to measure the stance fiscal policy is taking as a result of active policy choices. Such a 'full-employment fiscal deficit' figure is arrived at by estimating what the G and T figures would have been on the basis of current policies, had the economy been at full employment.

It is on these adjusted fiscal deficit figures that much of the appraisal of UK fiscal policy in the post-1945 era has been based. The stabilisation performance of fiscal policy has largely been appraised by comparing the course the economy would have followed in the absence of active fiscal policy measures, with the course actually taken. Here the comparison will obviously partly reflect the view of the way the UK economy would function in the absence of active fiscal policy measures which is used as a basis for comparison. The fact that several detailed studies by economists have concluded that fiscal policy measures have been at best not stabilising, and at worst destabilising, must be regarded as casting severe doubts on the efficacy of the fiscal policy instrument as used in the UK in achieving its counter-cyclical objectives. Here it is sufficient to quote two influential Keynesian economists: 'As far as internal conditions are concerned then, budgetary and monetary policy failed to be stabilising, and must on the contrary be regarded as being positively destabilising' (Dow 1964, p. 384); and 'The record of demand management over the last twenty years has been extremely poor. Throughout this whole period fiscal policy has been operated in alternating directions to produce periods of strong demand expansion, followed by periods of reversal in crisis conditions. Thus in 1953–54, 1958–59, 1962–63, and most notoriously in 1971–72, demand-expansionary policies were introduced . . . Then always, just two years later, the direction was reversed, demand-deflationary policies being initiated in 1955–56, 1960–61, 1964–65 and now again in 1973–74 . . . Demand, output and the balance of payments might have been more stable than they were had some simple rule been followed through thick and thin, such as that (the) tax yield . . . cover . . . some fixed proportion of public expenditure' (Godley, House of Commons HC328, p. 1). Further doubt has been cast on the thesis that Keynesian fiscal measures have been responsible for the relatively low unemployment rates (compared with the inter-war period) experienced by the UK in the post-1945 era (Matthews 1970, though see Stafford 1970 for a critique).

The New Cambridge school offers a different, though fundamentally Keynesian, view of the influence of fiscal policy. The starting point is a rearrangement of the equilibrium condition for national income:

$$(G-T) + (I-S) = (M-X)$$

where I, S, M and X refer to investment, savings, imports and exports respectively. There follows an empirical proposition that $(I{-}S)$ is stable. This means that the private sector wishes to accumulate assets in some well-defined way, or, alternatively, that fluctuations in the balance between personal savings and investment tend to be offset by countervailing fluctuations in the balance between company retained profits and investment. This implies that $\Delta(I{-}S) \approx 0$ and thus:

$$\Delta(G{-}T) \approx \Delta(M{-}X)$$

Thus the main effect of an expansionary fiscal policy will be to produce an increase in the balance of payments deficit. The school's prescription is that the fiscal policy instrument be used to achieve the balance of payments target; and that, given the planned level of G, the government should fix a 'par' rate of tax which should not be changed for stabilisation reasons. Orthodox Keynesians have criticised the New Cambridge school regarding the empirical validity of the $\Delta(I{-}S) \approx 0$ relationship, and Monetarists have pointed out flaws in the analysis of asset holding behaviour underlying the New Cambridge position.

The Monetarist school emphasises the importance of the financial consequences of fiscal policy rather than the direct influence of fiscal measures upon aggregate demand. This involves an interdependence between fiscal policy and monetary policy to which we now turn.

The Public Sector Financing Identity

This can be written as:

$$(G{-}T) \equiv \Delta M + P_D \, \Delta B + \Delta F$$

where $(G{-}T)$ is the fiscal deficit in nominal terms, or public sector borrowing requirement (PSBR); ΔM is the increase in government borrowing from the banking system which represents an increase in the money supply; P_D is the price of government debt and ΔB the increase in the amount of such debt held outside the banking system; and ΔF is the increase in foreign borrowing.

The above financing identity means that the effect of a

change in fiscal policy will depend on how it is financed and that it is misleading to consider a change in one of the fiscal or monetary instruments in isolation. An increase in G, for example, has to be financed by an increase in T, in which case effects of the balanced budget multiplier type will follow; or by an increase in ΔM, in which case there will be downward pressure on interest rates and an expansion in the money supply; or by an increase in ΔB, which will be accompanied by upward pressure on interest rates; or by an increase in ΔF; or, most usually, by some combination of the above financing instruments.

The Monetarist approach sees the effects of fiscal policies depending primarily on the financing of the PSBR. If a fiscal deficit is financed by borrowing outside the banking system, then the expansionary fiscal impact will be offset by the rise in interest rates caused by the increased supply of government debt. Only if the fiscal deficit is financed by an increase in the money supply would the effects be strongly expansionary, and even then the lags involved make such policy unsuitable for stabilisation and the expansionary effects would be only temporary before the real impact of monetary growth was replaced by the longer-term inflationary impact. Evidence of this process is provided by the effects of the 1972 Budget, where the strong fiscal expansion financed primarily by an increasing money supply resulted first in rapid real growth of GNP followed by a sharp increase in inflation in 1974–76.

Monetary Policy

The main instruments of monetary policy are the supply of money and interest rates; in addition controls over particular forms of credit (such as hire purchase and trade credit) have been employed. As we have already noted, monetary policy is interdependent with fiscal policy. In a closed economy the change in the money supply is equal to the PSBR *PLUS* the change in bank lending to the private sector *MINUS* the change in private sector lending to the government. In an open economy the above will provide a formula for the determination of domestic credit expansion, (DCE), the figure for the change in the money supply being arrived at by subtracting the balance of payments deficit from the DCE figure. DCE can be thought as the *ex ante* increase in the money supply, the *ex post* change being balances held in the country after UK residents have settled any payments deficit with the external world.

The money supply and interest rates are highly interdependent; hence by controlling one variable the authorities effectively lose control over the other. Interest rates will influence the amount that the private sector is willing to lend to the government and the amount that the private sector wishes to borrow from the banking system. In fixing interest rates, the authorities must accept whatever financial flows are generated at that particular level of interest rates. Assuming that the PSBR is determined independently of monetary policy, the level of interest rates chosen will largely determine the increase in the money supply. Similarly, control of the money supply means that the authorities must accept whatever rates of interest are determined by the financial markets.

The Money Supply

Variations in the rate of monetary expansion influence the economy by affecting private sector demand for goods and non-money assets. If the money supply expands at a faster rate than the private sector wishes to increase its holdings of money balances, this will lead the private sector to divest itself of the excess money balances by increasing current spending and accumulating non-money assets. This, according to the Monetarist school, will, in the short run, lead to an increase in economic activity, it taking one or two years for the maximum effect to be felt. Such real increases in activity will then fade, being replaced by upward pressure on the rate of inflation which will reach maximum effect after two or three years. In the case of the money supply expanding at a lower rate than that desired by the private sector, the opposite effects will be felt – a decrease in economic activity followed by downward pressure on the rate of inflation. For the open economy, the relevant concept of monetary expansion is DCE, too high a DCE leading to balance of payments deficit under a fixed exchange rate and a depreciating exchange rate with a floating currency.

These effects of monetary expansion on external transactions, together with the domestic effects on economic activity and inflation, amount to the money supply being regarded by the Monetarist school as a very powerful instrument of economic policy, in contrast to the subsidiary role which the Keynesian and New Cambridge schools attribute to it. But despite the importance attached to the role of money, the Monetarist approach does not advocate the use of the money supply as a discretionary instrument of economic management. Because of the long and variable lags in monetary measures taking effect, the money supply is an unreliable instrument of macroeconomic control. The central Monetarist prescription is for the maintenance of some long-term target rate of growth of the money supply, with little or no variation for the purpose of counter-cyclical stabilisation.

Such a policy requires that the authorities can control the supply of money. The first issue is the definition of the money supply. Notes and coins held by the private sector and private sector current accounts within the banking system would be included without controversy in any definition of the money supply, this definition being known as M1. In addition there is a wide array of relatively liquid, interest-bearing assets which can be converted into M1 balances without much fear of capital loss at reasonably short notice. These include bank deposit accounts, building society deposits and various marketable fixed-term deposits. M3 is the most widely used broader definition. It has been used by the IMF and Bank of England to set monetary expansion targets. M3 consists of M1 plus deposit accounts within the UK banking system. Keynesian economists tend to deny the distinct role of money, viewing money as distinguished by its extreme liquidity, but also as being readily substituted for other financial assets. Hence Keynesians tend to regard wider definitions than M3 as being relevant for monetary policy.

Accepting M3 as the key monetary variable, how are the monetary authorities to control it? Creation of money by the government depends upon the size of the PSBR, and the proportion of the PSBR which is financed by sales of debt.

Sales of government debt will tend to depress its price, raising interest yields. Partly because the authorities thought the variation in interest rates involved would make public sector debt less attractive and more difficult to sell, and partly because of the political sensitivity of variations in mortgage rates which would tend to follow any changes in the yields on public sector debt, monetary policy up until 1976 was concerned chiefly with stabilising the yields on public sector debt rather than with controlling the money supply. The April 1976 Budget saw the introduction of the first official target for monetary expansion in UK history (excepting the monetary target implicit in the DCE ceiling involved in the 1967 IMF loan), and since then the Bank of England has on several occasions changed substantially the yields offered on public sector debt in order to achieve the monetary expansion targets which have continued in operation since then.

The second source of variation in M3 is changes in bank lending to the private sector. Here control implies the ability of the Bank of England to exert a strong influence over the behaviour of the banking system. The basic system of control is through the requirement that banks hold a certain proportion of their assets in a *reserve asset* – some asset, such as cash or bankers' balances at the Bank of England, whose supply can be controlled by the Bank of England. Given stable bank and non-bank demand functions for such an asset, the authorities would then be able to exert a strong measure of control over the total assets and hence liabilities of the banking system, and thus over the current and deposit accounts that constitute most of M3. In practice, however, the authorities when wishing to control the money supply have tended to rely on direct controls of the banking system.

Interest Rates

Interest rate variations can be used as a policy instrument to control aggregate demand by influencing private consumption and investment expenditure. An important issue here concerns the responsiveness of these variables to changes in the rate of interest – empirical studies show only a small response. For

UK policy purposes, balance of payments effects have been the most important consideration in interest rate policy. Interest rates have been raised sharply on several occasions to try and stem the outflow of capital associated with balance of payments crises.

The governments control over interest rates is exerted through setting the *Minimum Lending Rate* (MLR), the rate at which the Bank of England lends to the banking system via the discount houses. Prior to October 1972[6] this rate was known as Bank Rate. Because of the close inter-relationship of financial markets, changes in MLR normally lead to general movements in interest rates. However the ability of the Bank of England to change interest rates for domestic reasons is strongly influenced by the international mobility of capital. Hence changes in UK interest rates tend to have strong balance of payments and exchange rate effects.

Since the introduction of monetary targets in 1976, the interest rate instrument has occupied a subsidiary role in monetary policy formulation. Given the large PSBR of the 1970s, and the authorities method of selling public sector debt by tender rather than by auction, sharp increases in public sector debt yields have often been necessary in order to tempt tenders sufficient to achieve the debt sales required.

Credit Controls

In the past British governments influenced by orthodox Keynesian views have attached little importance either to control of the money supply or variations in interest rates to influence spending behaviour. Direct controls on credit availability, however, have been thought to be capable of exerting fast-working direct effects on spending. Restrictions on hire purchase (HP) lending, and directives to the banks to restrict lending to the private sector, have been the main instruments used. During the 1950s and early 1960s, HP controls in the form of minimum deposit rates and maximum repayment periods were particularly prominent. Two major problems arise with the use of credit controls. The first involves the free market argument that such controls lead to a misallocation of resources and encourage inefficiency by inhibiting competition between banks and other financial institutions. The second is that direct controls encourage the development of alternative financial institutions and instruments to which the controls do not apply, and which reduce the effectiveness of the controls. The application of direct controls greatly encouraged the growth of near and secondary banks, money brokers and the inter-corporate loan market.

The use of credit controls as a policy instrument was largely abandoned in 1971, when the Bank of England announced that '. . . impediments to competition arising from existing liquidity and quantitative lending controls should be replaced by other means of influencing lending' (*Bank of England Quarterly Bulletin,* June 1971), as part of its new 'competition and credit control' (CCC) approach to monetary policy. Further, the Crowther Report of 1971 recommended abandoning HP controls, although formal dismantling has yet to take place.

Monetary Policy During the 1970s

During the 1970s there has been a remarkable transformation both in the application of monetary instruments and in the role accorded to monetary policy within the framework of macroeconomic management. During the 1950s and 60s heavy reliance was placed on credit controls, almost none on the money supply – with Bank Rate being varied sharply to deal with balance of payments crises. The view of monetary policy in this period is stated in the Radcliffe Report of the Committee on the Workings of the Monetary System (Cmnd 827, HMSO 1959). The report is notable for the lack of importance which it attributes to monetary control. The only specific innovation in monetary policy arising from the report was the introduction of Special Deposits, whereby banks were required to lodge additional balances with the Bank of England. From 1961 Special Deposits were increasingly relied on as a means of controlling bank liquidity and credit.

During the later 1960s, however, the official, Radcliffe-dominated view of the role of monetary policy was seriously undermined and a significant change in policy practice occurred in 1967 when the government accepted a ceiling on

DCE for the period 1968–70 as a condition for IMF credit. The change in official attitudes was marked by a complete revision of the framework of monetary control in the UK. This was announced in May 1971 with the publication of the Bank of England's consultative document *Competition and Credit Control.* Quantitative controls over bank lending and credit were to be abandoned and future monetary policies were to be consistent with the maintenance of free competition in financial matters. In addition to measures to increase competition between banks and between banks and other financial institutions, the Bank announced its intention not to intervene to stabilise the prices of gilt-edged securities. A new reserve ratio system was established which required banks to hold at least 12½% of their liabilities in the form of balances at the Bank of England, 'call' money with the discount houses (and similar institutions), Treasury bills, local authority and commercial bills, tax reserve certificates and government stock with less than one year to maturity. It should be noted that the new system of control was directed more towards the objective of increasing competition than towards exercising control over the money supply. Indeed, the inclusion in the definition of reserve assets of certain assets which the authorities could not directly control (e.g. call money and commercial bills) indicated that the reserve assets ratio was not intended as a means of controlling the money supply.

Two factors were mainly responsible for the abandonment of the new system late in 1973. First was the massive expansion in the money supply during the period: M3 grew by 28% in 1972 and 26% in 1973. Second was the financial crisis of 1973 involving the collapse of several secondary banks. The extent to which these developments were due to the new system of financial and credit supervision is open to question; the relevant point is that the government came round to the view that greater control over monetary aggregates, particularly bank lending, was necessary.

Since 1973 British governments have reverted to direct controls over the banking system, involving ceilings on bank liabilities with the imposition of supplementary Special Deposits should the ceilings be exceeded. This system, known as the 'corset', imposes a scale of Special Deposits depending upon the size of the breach of the ceiling. The main difference between controls before 1971 and after 1973 is that since 1973 liabilities rather than assets are controlled, this allowing more control over money supply growth.

The shift towards a monetary policy which emphasises control over the supply of money rather than control over interest rates has also involved a more aggressive approach to the sale of public sector debt. The authorities have been prepared to raise interest rates dramatically in order to reduce debt prices sufficiently to attract buyers. Then interest rates are reduced slowly to encourage continued buying as debt prices rise and so offer the prospect of capital gains.

Most significantly, targets for the expansion in the money supply have been continually in operation since the 12% target for 1976/77. The targets now take the form of a target range, as in the 9–13% range for 1977/78, which has been reduced to 8–12% and 7–11% in succeeding years. Up until the arrival of the Conservative administration in 1979, it has been by no means obvious that the adoption of monetary rules reflected a conversion to Monetarist philosophy. The targets have not tended to be seen as imposing rigid constraints on monetary policy, as indicated by the 16% overshoot of the 9–13% target for 1977/78. Even with the present Conservative administration, the pursuit of money supply targets appears to be a subsidiary objective to the principal aims of cutting public expenditure and taxation and reducing the PSBR.

Wage and Price Controls

Despite the continual efforts by government to use fiscal and monetary instruments to manage macroeconomic aggregates, the persistent tendency of the UK economy to generate a rate of inflation in excess of other industrialised countries has resulted in successive governments resorting to direct controls over wages and prices. Between 1961 and 1978 controls over wages have been in operation almost continuously, while prices have been subject to control for a substantial part of the period. The focus of control has been upon wages. Control on prices and on other forms of income (such as dividends) have been introduced primarily to make wage controls more acceptable to trade unions. Wage controls have existed in a variety of forms: voluntary wages policies were in operation in 1948–50, 1956, 1961–64, 1964–66 and 1974–75; statutory controls existed in 1966–70 and 1972–74; while the compulsory controls of 1974–78 were enforced without statutory backing. For certain periods wage increases were prohibited, but in general controls have involved a percentage limit on annual increases, or some more complex formula.[7] The administration of wage and price controls has often been delegated to an independent agency: the National Incomes Commission (1962–64), the National Board for Prices and Incomes (1964–70), the Pay Board (1973–74) and the Price Commission (1973–79). Here we shall not be concerned with the details of particular prices and incomes policies, but only with the general arguments for and against and an overall assessment of the effectiveness of controls. For a more detailed account by an advocate of wage and price controls see Blackaby (1978) and for an opposing view see Brittan and Lilley (1977).

The extent to which wage and price controls have been based upon a coherent theory of inflation is difficult to determine. In many instances the introduction of controls has involved an element of desperation by government following the failure of demand management or a reluctance by government to introduce the deflationary measures necessary to lower inflation. Thus both the 1970–74 Conservative administration and the 1974–79 Labour administration, after resolutely rejecting wage controls, were led to introduce comprehensive wage and price controls. However, the eagerness with which governments have embraced wage–price controls is indicative of the influence of the Keynesian analysis of inflation. The Keynesian approach sees the wage bargaining power of the trade unions as crucial in determining the rate of wage increases which, together with the other components of business costs, determines the rate of price inflation. Given that fiscal and monetary factors are not taken to be major influences on inflation, some additional policy instrument is required to control inflation. Since measures to weaken the monopoly power of trade unions are likely to be socially divisive and politically unacceptable, wage controls are proposed as the appropriate policy.

The main criticism of the use of wage–price controls as a means of limiting inflation has been voiced by the Monetarists. Given the dominant influence of the money supply on inflation, incomes and prices policies have at most only a very short-run impact. Not only are such policies usually viewed by Monetarists as irrelevant to the control of inflation, but they are positively harmful because of their costly side effects on resource allocation and efficiency.

Between the extreme Keynesian and Monetarist positions regarding incomes policies comes the view that, while controls are not capable of effectively controlling the long-run rate of inflation (this being determined by monetary factors), controls can serve as a useful short-term policy instrument. The idea here is that controls can help the process of adjustment to a lower rate of inflation by providing a shock to inflation expectations. If union wage demands are based upon some target real-income level, their demands will be influenced by expectations of inflation in the subsequent period. If wage controls can be used to moderate wage increases in the short run, this can create the downward revision in inflationary expectations which will enable a transition from a higher to a lower rate of inflation, without the temporary increase in unemployment which would result from a monetary contraction.

The empirical evidence on the effectiveness of wage and price controls is difficult to assess, particularly since it involves distinguishing between the impact of controls and the effects following the dismantling of controls. There is little doubt that the wage freezes or severe controls – which have usually been imposed at the start of policy periods – have been effective in the short term. The freeze and severe restraint controls from mid-1966 to mid-1967 were accompanied by earnings rising at 2% p.a. compared to 8% p.a. before the freeze; earnings rose at 3% per annum during the November 1972 to March 1973 freeze compared with 17% previously; while the Labour Government's controls introduced in mid-1975 were accompanied by a remarkably rapid deceleration in the rate of increase of earnings during the following two years.

Less obvious is the success of the controls during the whole of the policy period. The objectives of the authorities during the 1964–69 Labour and late 1972 to early 1974 Conservative policy periods have been estimated by one experienced commentator to have involved 4–5% and 8% increases in money earnings respectively (Blackaby 1978, pp. 390–391). The actual outcomes were 8% and 12% increases respectively. Judged in terms of the objectives sought the policies failed, although it could still be maintained that the policies exerted a moderating influence on inflation which would have been higher in the absence of the policies. But even if incomes policies achieve some measure of success in their periods of operations, critics argue that any beneficial effects are subsequently offset by a re-adjustment of wage rates following the dismantling of controls. Thus, the 1964–69 period was followed by an acceleration in the rate of earnings increase from 8% to 15%, and the 1972–74 period, when earnings increased by an average of 12% per annum, was followed by a 25% increase in 1974/75.

Apart from their effectiveness in reducing inflation, any assessment of wage and price controls must consider the cost of such controls in distorting resource allocation. Wage controls tend to prevent adjustment of relative wages in accordance with shifts in the demand and supply of labour, thereby causing shortages of labour in particular industries and occupations. Price controls similarly hamper the allocative role of the price mechanism in the goods market. Price controls may also have the effect of depressing profit margins to the extent that new investment is discouraged. A further problem of those wages policies which have increased the incomes of low-paid relative to higher-paid workers, has been the emergence of shortages of skilled workers in much of manufacturing industry. Such problems arise only to the extent that the controls are effective. In practice a great variety of methods is adopted by the private sector to circumvent wage and price controls. Thus, wage controls have been avoided by upgrading particular jobs or workers and by increasing the non-wage remuneration attached to jobs. A particular problem is that controls have been more effectively imposed in the public than the private sector. A familiar pattern has emerged of public sector wages falling behind private sector wages during the control periods, followed by public sector unions (largely successfully) pushing strongly to restore their relative wages at the end of control periods.

Balance of Payments Policies: Exchange Rate Management and Import Controls

Exchange Rates

As we have noted, balance of payments problems have been a dominant factor influencing the conduct of macroeconomic policy in the UK. Policies towards correcting balance of payments deficits have involved restrictive fiscal and monetary measures, with very little use of exchange rate variations or import controls directly to influence the balance of payments. Prior to 1971, government commitment to fixed exchange rates meant that only in the severe crises of 1949 and 1967 did governments reluctantly devalue sterling. Otherwise the authorities reacted 'like Pavlovian dogs' (Brittan 1969) to balance of payments crises, with deflationary fiscal policies and increases in Bank Rate rather than adjustments in the exchange rate. Under the IMF rules member countries were allowed to change their exchange rates to correct any 'fundamental disequilibrium' in their balance of payments. Even in the face of such disequilibrium, UK governments before 1971 were reluctant to devalue, due partly to the reserve currency role of sterling and partly to the identification of the value of sterling with the international prestige of Britain. In the years prior to 1967, devaluation was 'the great unmentionable' (Brittan 1969). The abandonment of a fixed parity for the pound in 1978 has allowed much greater scope for government to use the exchange rate as a policy instrument and the extent to which government should intervene to influence the value of the pound has been a major policy issue since then.

Differences of opinion concerning policy towards exchange

rates partly reflect different views as to the size and nature of the relationship between the exchange rate on the one hand and output, inflation and the balance of payments on the other. The orthodox Keynesian view is that movements in the exchange rate will enable a lasting correction to any balance of trade disequilibrium, the quantitative effects depending upon the various demand elasticities involved. In practice adjustment takes some time, the initial period after devaluation seeing a balance of payments deterioration before the supply responses take place (the 'J-curve'). Such devaluation will at the same time have potentially lasting effects in boosting domestic output and employment. Higher import prices caused by devaluation will increase domestic inflation, the size of this inflationary effect depending upon the ratio of imports to total domestic expenditure. The official view on the effectiveness of exchange rate variations has been modified in recent years, with the Treasury now placing a higher estimate on the inflationary effects and a lower estimate on the balance of payments and domestic output effects of exchange rate depreciation (Treasury Economic Progress Report, March 1978). The small size of the balance of payments and output effects of exchange rate movements is the main reason for the scepticism of the New Cambridge economists concerning the usefulness of the exchange rate as a policy tool. To achieve significant results the exchange rate would have to be used 'more violently than would be acceptable at home or abroad' (Wynne Godley, *The Times*, Nov. 1976).

The Monetarist view, on the other hand, places little emphasis on the exchange rate as a policy instrument. Variations in the exchange rate by the authorities are likely to have only temporary effects, since any depreciation will lead to domestic prices rising by approximately the same proportion as the depreciation, nullifying the effects on the balance of payments. The Monetarist analysis suggests that the exchange rate is primarily, therefore, an instrument to affect the rate of inflation. The prescription here, however, tends to be that exchange rate effects should be taken into account when formulating the target for the rate of monetary expansion, rather than that the exchange rate should be used as a policy instrument *per se.* The money supply and the exchange rate are taken to be too interdependent to be used as separate policy instruments.

In practice it is very difficult to identify the effects of exchange rate policy upon the balance of payments, let alone the effect on other macroeconomic variables. While the 1967 devaluation of sterling appears to have been an outstanding success in moving the balance of payments into strong surplus during the late 1960s, it is impossible to separate the effects of devaluation from those of fiscal deflation and IMF-imposed monetary restraint. In the period of floating since the abandonment of the fixed exchange rate regime in 1971, the degree of official intervention in foreign exchange rate markets has varied. The long-term weakness of sterling between 1945 and 1977 has made governments cautious about committing sterling to any new system of pegged exchange rates, particularly since Britain's forced withdrawal from the first EEC Monetary Union in June 1972. The principal aim of government appears to have been the avoidance of short-term fluctuations in the value of the sterling. To this end the authorities appear to have been remarkably unsuccessful, uncertainty as to the intentions of the Bank of England being a major source of additional uncertainty to the foreign exchange markets.

During 1979 the extent to which government should seek to manage the exchange rate has been a major issue in the policy debate, the focus of disagreement being whether the appreciation of sterling was damaging to the long-term economic prospects of the UK and, if so, whether government intervention to exert downward pressure would create more problems than it would cure. The main argument in favour of intervention to secure a currency depreciation is that some restoration in the price competitiveness of UK exports is essential to produce a demand-induced increase in domestic output and employment. While there is little doubt that during the first eight months of 1979 sterling appreciation was such as significantly to influence the relative cost of UK exports, it is suggested by some that price effects are of limited importance in influencing long-term export performance, non-price factors having been paramount in explaining the

UK's poor export performance. On the other side are those who argue that the authorities should encourage a high exchange rate. Here stress is placed on the effects of the exchange rate on the rate of inflation, a high or even increasing value for the exchange rate being postulated to feed through quickly into lower domestic price and wage increases.

Import Controls

A further balance of payments policy measure which has been advocated in recent years is the imposition of import controls in the form of an external tariff or quantitative controls over imports (quotas). Because of Britain's international obligations which were formally established in the General Agreement on Tariffs and Trade (GATT) and the Treaty of Rome, import controls have been generally imposed only during the period of severe balance of payments disequilibrium between 1964 and 1970. Between 1964 and 1966 an import surcharge was imposed on all manufactured imports, while between 1968 and 1970 the import deposit scheme had similar effects to a general tariff. The effect of the import surcharge in reducing imports was less than was intended at the time, while no significant balance of payments effect of the import deposit scheme is discernible (Artis, pp. 344–347 and 349 in Blackaby 1978).

More recently the New Cambridge school has advocated the use of import controls, the idea being that they are a less costly way of correcting the UK's balance of payments problems than either fiscal or monetary policies which depress output and employment, or devaluation which must be too drastic if it is to be effective. Further, import controls are necessary to enable a high level of demand and higher rate of growth to be sustained, without running into the balance of payments problems which have been the culmination of most previous phases of high growth in the UK economy. The prescription is an expansionary fiscal policy together with the introduction of import controls, to prevent the high levels of output and income from drawing in the additional imports which are implied by the UK's high marginal propensity to import.

The precise mechanics of the import control system have not been clearly spelled out by the New Cambridge school. Stress is laid on the need for general controls, that is controls which do not discriminate between the country of origin or type of good. A tariff on all imports would be a possible instrument to use, a system whereby licences would be required by importers (such licences covering a money value of imports and being auctioned off to the highest bidders) would be another. Such a system would contravene the rules of GATT and the EEC.

Opponents of the use of import controls as a policy instrument emphasise the undesirable side effects of controls and cast doubt upon their effectiveness. The central issue is the notion that import controls would, if they worked, restrict free trade, and if adopted on a global scale would ultimately reduce world prosperity and world economic growth. The crucial issue is whether other countries would retaliate or not. If retaliation took place, then the benefits to the UK from import controls would be either removed entirely or severely reduced. But even without retaliation, critics of import controls argue that the tendency of controls to 'feather-bed' inefficient producers in the UK and reduce incentives to efficient producers might result in a long-term trend towards growing inefficiency and an ultimate ossifying of UK industry. This tendency towards inefficiency will mean that the protection provided by import controls is only temporary because of the escalation of UK costs. Hence the severity of import controls would have to be progressively increased. At the same time import controls tend to reduce consumer welfare by restricting consumer choice. While the advocates of the New Cambridge position do not deny that import controls do involve some real costs, their position is that such costs are a small price to pay for extraditing the UK economy from the long-term industrial decline which is the consequence of two decades of free trade.

Notes

1. For examples of the Marxist approach see F. Green and P. Nore (1977) chapters 7–12.
2. A few words about unemployment figures are in order. An unemployed person is defined as someone who has registered at an employment office looking for work. The 1971 population census revealed 300,000 adults as saying they were looking for work but had not registered as unemployed – primarily because they were not entitled to employment benefits, and thus had no financial incentive to register. Also, high unemployment need not imply that no job vacancies exist. At the end of 1978, some 1,300,000 registered unemployed coexisted with some 230,000 notified job vacancies; moreover, many vacancies are not notified to employment offices, people being hired via other channels. Finally, the unemployed form a constantly changing group; in 1972, for example, 50% of those registering as unemployed left the register within 14 days (Smee and Stern 1978) and of those unemployed in 1978, only 24% had been unemployed for longer than 52 weeks (Department of Employment Gazette).
3. In a very real sense the balance of payments always balances. The surpluses and deficits referred to above relate to the *total currency flow* in UK statistics. This figure is the sum of the current account (exports minus imports), the invisible account (services and transfer payments) and capital account transactions – the last consisting of private plus public autonomous flows of capital. For accounting reasons, any surplus or deficit in the total currency flow must be balanced by an equal and opposite amount of *total official financing.* It is in this sense, the sense in which the total currency flow is balanced by an equal and opposite amount of total official financing that the balance of payments balances. The former indexes the private sector and autonomous public sector balance of payments, whilst the latter denotes the induced amount of official financing required by the former. The argument is analogous to the value of goods sold being equal to the value of goods bought.
4. The June 1979 Budget introduced by the incoming Conservative administration involved the use of fiscal policy to influence aggregate supply. The idea here is that the reduction in income tax rates will be accompanied by a substitution effect in favour of higher work effort which will not be outweighed by the opposing income effect. However, empirical evidence fails to show much relationship between income tax and the supply of labour (see Chapter 8).
5. The use of public works to alleviate unemployment was advocated during the 1920s and 1930s by economists other than Keynes (see Winch 1969, chapters 8–14). Keynes's contribution to the policy debate was directed against the 'Treasury view' that increases in government spending would be offset by reductions in private

spending. The revolution associated with Keynes is found more in his *theory* of effective demand than in his specific policy advice.

6. From this date to 1978 MLR was determined by the level of market interest rates, being ½% above the Treasury Bill rate of interest; this formula was only occasionally over-ridden by the authorities. Since then the Bank of England has returned to determining MLR by dictat.
7. An element of income redistribution in favour of low wage earners has sometimes been introduced by combining a fixed sum wage increase with a percentage limit.

References

Bacon, R.W. and Eltis, W.A., *Britain's Economic Problem: too few producers*, Macmillan 1976.

Ball, R.J. and Burns, T., 'Stabilisation policy in Britain 1964–1981', in M. Posner (ed.), *Demand Management*, Heinemann 1978.

Blackaby, F.T. (ed.), *British Economic Policy 1960–74*, Cambridge University Press 1978.

Brittan, S., *Steering the Economy*, Secker and Warburg 1969.

Brittan, S. and Lilley, P., *The Delusion of Incomes Policy*, Temple Smith 1977.

Committee on the Workings of the Monetary System, *Report*, Cmnd 827, HMSO 1959.

Dow, J.C.R., *The Management of the British Economy 1945–1960*, Cambridge University Press 1964.

Friedman, M., 'The role of monetary policy', *American Economic Review*, 1968.

Green, F. and Nore, P. (eds), *Economics: an Anti-Text*, Macmillan 1977.

Godley, W., 'What Britain needs is growth – but it must be the right kind', *The Times*, 1 November 1976.

Godley, W. and May, R.M., 'The macroeconomic implications of devaluation and import restriction', Chapter 2 of *Economic Policy Review* No. 3, University of Cambridge Department of Applied Economics, March 1977.

Hicks, J.R., *The Crisis in Keynesian Economics*, Blackwell 1974.

Hines, A.G., 'The determinants of the rate of change of money wage rates and the effectiveness of incomes policy' in H.G. Johnson and A.R. Nobay (eds), *The Current Inflation*, Macmillan 1971.

Hirsch, F., *Social Limits to Growth*, Routledge and Kegan Paul 1977.

House of Commons, Ninth Report from the Expenditure Committee, 'Public expenditure, inflation and the balance of payments', HC 328, *HMSO* 1974.

Hume, D., 'Of the balance of trade' in D. Hume, *Essays, Moral, Political and Literary* Vol. 1., Longmans Green 1752, republished in 1898.

Reprinted in R.N. Cooper (ed.), *International Finance*, Penguin 1969.

Kahn, R.F., 'Unemployment as seen by Keynesians' in G.D.N. Worswick (ed.), *The Concept and Measurement of Involuntary Unemployment*, Allen and Unwin 1976.

Kaldor, N., *Causes of the Slow Rate of Economic Growth of the United Kingdom*, Cambridge University Press 1966.

Matthews, R.C.O., 'Why has Britain had full employment since the war?, *Economic Journal*, 1968.

Matthews, R.C.O., 'Why has Britain had full employment since the war? – reply', *Economic Journal*, 1970.

Meadows, D.H., Meadows, D.L., Randers, J. and Behrens III W.W., *The Limits to Growth*, A Report for the Club of Rome's Project on the Predicament of Mankind, Earth Island Limited 1972.

Mishan, E.J., *The Costs of Economic Growth*, Staples Press 1967.

Sargan, J.D., 'A study of wages and prices in the UK, 1949–68', in H.G. Johnson and A.R. Nobay (eds), *The Current Inflation*, Macmillan 1971.

Shaw, G.K., *An Introduction to the Theory of Macroeconomic Policy*, 3rd edn, Martin Robertson 1977.

Smee, C.H. and Stern, J., 'The unemployed in a period of high unemployment', *Government Economic Service Working Paper*, No. 11, 1978.

Stafford, G.B., 'Why has Britain had full employment since the war? – comment', *Economic Journal*, 1970.

Sumner, M.T., 'Wage determination', in J.M. Parkin and M.T. Sumner (eds), *Inflation in the United Kingdom*, Manchester University Press 1978.

Turvey, R., 'Some features of incomes policy and comments on the current inflation', in H.G. Johnson and A.R. Nobay (eds), *The Current Inflation*, Macmillan 1971.

Wass, Sir D., 'The changing problems of economic management', *Economic Trends*, March 1978.

Winch, D., *Economics and Policy*, Fontana 1972.

Worswick, G.D.N., 'The end of demand management?', *Lloyds Bank Review*, January 1977.

Suggestions for Further Reading

Blackaby (1978).

Brittan, S. *Second Thoughts on Full Employment Policy*, Barry Rose for Centre for Policy Studies 1975.

Brittan and Lilley (1977).

Shaw (1977).

Wass (1978).

10. The formulation of macroeconomic policy

JOHN D. HEY

Lecturer in Social and Economic Statistics,
University of York

Introduction

The previous chapter described in some detail the main theoretical principles involved in the formulation of macroeconomic policy in the United Kingdom. This chapter is concerned with describing and discussing how such general principles are put into practice, and with explaining the kinds of problems with which governments are faced when they try to implement the theoretical advice proffered by their economic experts. In other words, we are here concerned with the practical day-to-day problems of running, and monitoring the performance of, the complex economic state that the UK is today.

It will be recalled from the previous chapter that a discussion of macroeconomic policy can usefully start with a statement of the *targets,* or objectives, of the policy. Four targets are usually signalled out as being of particular importance (though other minor targets exist from time to time):

1. achieving the lowest rate of *unemployment* consistent with the achievement of other objectives;
2. achieving the lowest or most stable rate of *inflation* possible given other objectives;
3. achieving a long run *balance* between the *international payments* and receipts of the private sector;
4. securing the macroeconomic conditions most conducive to *economic growth* in the economy. (See p. 215 above.)

Two important points should be noted at this stage. First, as the above quotation emphasises, the targets of macroeconomic policy are usually framed in terms of key aggregate economic variables; the four explicit in the target descriptions above being:

1. unemployment (the percentage of people willing to work who are unable to find work);
2. inflation (the rate of change of some appropriate price index);
3. the balance of payments (usually on the current account);
4. growth (the rate of change of Gross Domestic Product).

Second, as the qualifying phrases in the above quotation emphasise, there may be some inherent *conflict* between the various targets: for example, it may be the case that unemployment can only be reduced below a particular level at the expense of an excessively high inflation rate. If such a case exists, then the government must balance the various targets using weights determined by their political inclinations.

Needless to say, in a mixed economy such as that of the UK, the government is unable to control *directly* the key target variables of macroeconomic policy (except in a few rather uninteresting special cases). Instead, as was discussed in the previous chapter, the government is forced to operate *indirectly* through the medium of the *instruments* (or means) of macroeconomic policy. The most important of such instruments include fiscal instruments (such as government spending, tax rates, and the government surplus or deficit), monetary instruments (such as the money supply and interest rates) and various direct interventionist controls (such as incomes and prices policies and import quotas).

Macroeconomic policy in practice, therefore, consists of the government selecting the 'best' values of the various instruments under its control, so that the various targets are achieved as optimally as possible given any constraints that may exist between the target variables.

It is clear, therefore, that the successful operation of macroeconomic policy requires that the government is aware of the likely consequences of its actions; that is, that it is aware of the effect that any changes in the instruments are likely to have on the target variables. In other words, the government should know the relationships between targets and instruments. Unfortunately, because of the presence of uncertainties and the vagaries of human behaviour, it is highly unlikely that the government can ever know the precise form of these relationships. However, it can find estimates of these relationships and economists can strive to improve and refine the accuracy of these estimates. The next section considers ways in which this is done.

Estimating the Relationships Between Targets and Instruments

In an advanced economy the relationships between the targets and instruments of macroeconomic policy are usually very complex. However, the principles involved can be more readily expounded if attention is confined to a highly simplified abstract model of the economy. Consider the simplest possible macro-model: one in which there is just one policy instrument – the level of government expenditure; and just one policy target – the attainment of full employment income. Such an economy is usually represented by two equations:

$$C = a + bY \tag{1}$$
$$Y = C + G \tag{2}$$

where (1) is the consumption function and (2) is the equilibrium condition. (*C* is aggregate consumption, *G* is government spending and *Y* is aggregate income; all investment is assumed to be undertaken by the government.) In this simple economy, as is well known, increases in government expenditure *G* lead to multiplied increases in income *Y*, the multiplier depending upon the marginal propensity to consume *b*. Algebraically this can be demonstrated by solving equations (1) and (2) in terms of *G* by eliminating *C*. This yields:

$$Y = \frac{a}{1-b} + \frac{1}{1-b}G \tag{3}$$

Equation (3) shows the relationship between instrument *G* and target variable Y. In order to achieve the desired value of Y, the appropriate value for G can be selected by using equation (3) if $a/(1-b)$ and $1/(1-b)$ are known. Clearly this is possible if a and b are known. In practice, of course, a and b are not known – they are not God-given constants. However, economists can try and *estimate* the values of a and b. The method by which this is done is to study the way the economy has behaved in the past, and to use this information to show how economic variables are related and thus to infer what the values of the relevant economic parameters might be. (One then hopes that the economy continues to behave in the future in the same way as it did in the past; otherwise, the past is of little use as a guide to the future!) There are clearly two possibilities as far as a and b are concerned. First, economists can look at the past relationship of C with Y – and thus estimate the values of a and b using equation (1). Alternatively, economists can look at the past relationship of Y with G – and thus estimate the values of $a/(1-b)$ and $1/(1-b)$ (and hence, rather indirectly, the values of a and b) using equation (3). In practice, economists tend to prefer the first of these alternatives: this is because the relationship (1) is immediately interpretable in terms of the economic behaviour of a particular group of economic agents (consumers). If, for example, a is estimated to be negative, or b is estimated to be negative or greater than one, immediately warning lights begin to flash – indicating that something looks wrong. In other words, economic theory provides a check on the estimated relationship.

If the model above was a correct description of the economy, then knowledge of a and b would be necessary and sufficient for the successful operation of macroeconomic policy. Unfortunately, this model is too simple to describe real-world economies, though one element is a remarkably good approximation. Consider figure 1, which plots UK aggregate consumption against GDP (both in real terms) for the years 1948 to 1977.

The relationship between the two can be fairly well approximated by the straight line drawn on the figure. This line has an intercept of £4,526m (i.e. C = £4,526m = a when $Y = 0$) and a slope of 0.629; this latter, of course, is an

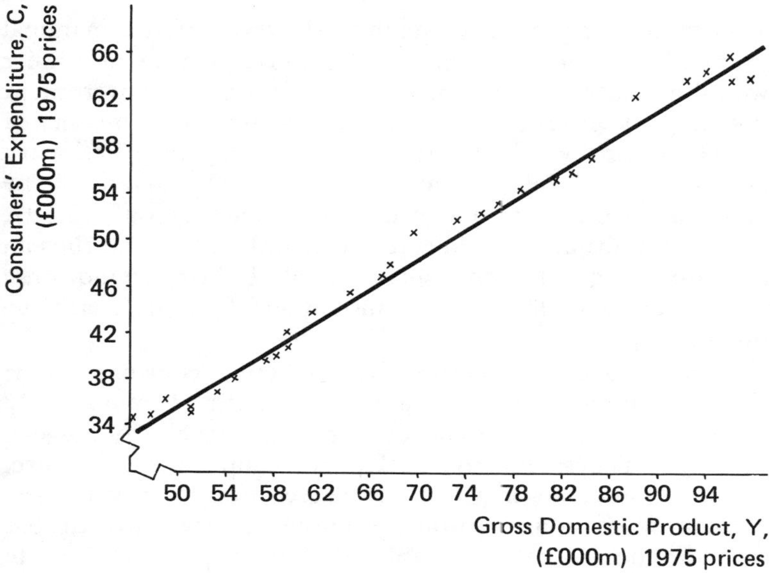

Figure 1

estimate of b, the marginal propensity to consume (MPC). Visually it appears that the relationship between consumption and income can be fairly well represented by equation (1) (with a = £4,526m and b = 0.629), and indeed it can be shown that 98% of the variation in consumption is 'explained' by income. However, for the purpose of operating macroeconomic policy this degree of accuracy is not sufficient. It is not certain that the marginal propensity to consume is exactly 0.629 – in fact, given the information portrayed in figure 1, the most that can be said[1] is that one can be 'reasonably confident' that the marginal propensity to consume lies between 0.597 and 0.661. To place this margin of uncertainty in perspective, suppose that the government knows that, without intervention, income next year will be £1,000m below full employment income; suppose, further, the government takes 0.629 to be the marginal propensity to consume, and thus calculates the multiplier to be $1/(1-b) = 1/(1-0.629) = 1/0.371 = 2.695$. On this basis an increase in government spending of £371m would be required to achieve full employment income. However, if the marginal propensity to consume was actually 0.661, then the multiplier would actually be 2.950 and thus an increase of government spending of £371m would lead to an increase in income of £1,094m; this would be £94m too much, and inflationary pressure would be generated. On the other hand, if the marginal propensity to consume was actually only 0.597, then the multiplier would actually be only 2.481 and thus an increase of government spending of £371m would raise income by only £921m, an amount insufficient to achieve full employment.

A more accurate method of predicting consumption is clearly desirable. Indeed, as a glance at figure 1 immediately shows, and as intuition and economic theory clearly suggest, other factors besides income affect consumption expenditure. Thus, in order to improve the degree of accuracy (of the prediction of consumption), economists have investigated the influence of other variables on consumption – the rate of interest is an example that springs to mind. It is noteworthy that, whereas four or five years ago economists were fairly confident about their ability to explain and predict consumption with the aid of a few key economic variables, their confidence has been shaken badly in the past few years. In particular, it seems that consumers have reacted in an unexpected fashion to the experience of the very high inflation rates of the mid-1970s (this point is graphically illustrated by the half-dozen points on the top right of figure 1). This emphasises an important point: as time passes, not only may economists discover new variables which help to explain some other variables, but also the actual economic relationship may change as economic agents adapt their behaviour to different economic situations; estimates of key economic parameters also change (for example, using data available at the time of the first edition of this book, the MPC was estimated to be 0.61 – in contrast with the 0.629 reported above). Such changes constitute continuing headaches for macroeconomic policy-makers.

In addition to finding new explanatory variables, experience has also shown that accuracy may be improved by considering the various sub-components of aggregate consumption separately. For example, separate equations can be estimated for spending on durable goods, and for spending on non-durable goods. Certain factors (such as the existence and stringency of hire purchase controls) are more likely to affect the first category than the second and *vice versa*. The process of disaggregation can continue virtually indefinitely. However, this process is not without its disadvantageous side effects: every extra variable that is introduced to explain or predict (some of) consumption must itself be explained or predicted. There is little value, if one wants to predict consumption, in knowing that the rate of interest influences consumption, unless one is also able to predict the rate of interest. Thus, for every explanatory variable introduced, an extra equation must be added, showing how it, in turn, is determined. (This, of course, does not apply to variables directly under government control – such as tax rates, the strength of hire purchase restrictions and so on.)

The economic model given by equations (1) and (2) is over-simplified as a representation of the UK economy, not only because of its over-simplified consumption function, but also because of the other assumptions underlying it. First, not all investment is undertaken by the government, indeed private investment is an important, and volatile component of total expenditure. Second, the UK economy is not closed, so that total expenditure includes exports less imports. Third, the existence of stocks (of raw materials and fuels, of work in progress, and of finished goods) means that any increase in such stocks constitutes an increase in total expenditure and thus in GDP. Now, in order for the government to be able to assess how its policy measures will affect total income, it will need to know how such policy measures affect each component of aggregate expenditure. It will therefore need to know how each component is determined; that is, not only does it need to know the factors determining consumers' expenditure, but also it needs to know the factors determining private investment, exports, imports, stockbuilding and so on. However, the requirements do not end here: this list simply includes *some* of the key variables describing the real economy. In addition, the government needs to know about monetary phenomena: the rate of change of prices and wages, the growth of monetary aggregates, and the rate of interest, for example.

For each of these key economic variables, a procedure similar to that discussed for consumers' expenditure is followed. Taking private investment as an example, the first step may be to investigate whether the accelerator theory (Lipsey 1975, pp. 537–9) is valid, by seeing if there is a relationship between investment and the change in income. If there proves to be some relationship, but not a perfect one, then the rate of interest may be tried as an additional explanatory variable. Other variables that economic theory would suggest as being potentially important as explanatory factors might include, for example, the rate of investment allowances, investment grants, and the rate of corporation tax. With investment, as with consumption, it may be found that accuracy of explanation is improved by considering the various subcomponents separately. Here again, of course, each variable that is used as an explanatory variable must itself, in turn, be explained.

Proceeding in this way, using past data on the UK economy to investigate the relationships between variables, and being guided by economic theory as to the choice of the (hopefully) relevant variables, economists can build up what is termed an *econometric model* of the UK economy. As is apparent from the above discussion, an econometric model consists of a set of equations, or estimated relationships, each of which is an attempt to discover how a particular economic variable is determined. The *number* of equations in the model will depend upon the degree of disaggregation and the number of variables introduced as explanatory variables. In any econometric model of a country's economy, a distinction is usually made between two different kinds of variable – *exogenous* and *endogenous*. The former term refers to variables determined *outside* the model, that is, those not influenced by the model. In the category of exogenous variables would fall variables directly under government control (the instruments of macro policy), variables determined outside the economy (for the UK such variables would include the GDP of the USA and the volume of world trade[2]) and variables whose value is determined outside the period to which the model refers (for example, last year's GDP or last year's consumers' expenditure). Endogenous variables are those determined *within* the model, that is, those influenced by both exogenous and other endogenous variables. Indeed, it can be seen (as is apparent from any textbook discussion) that the values of the endogenous variables are *simultaneously* determined. For example, the values of the two endogenous variables, income and consumption, depend on each other: consumption depends upon income (through the consumption function) and income depends upon consumption (since consumption is a large element of income, one person's consumption being some other person's income).

The number of equations in an econometric model must be the same as the number of endogenous variables (loosely speaking, this means that to each endogenous variable there must correspond an equation explaining it) so that, given any set of values for the endogenous variables, the model can then be simultaneously solved to yield values for the endogenous variables. Clearly the *size* of an econometric model (the number of endogenous variables it contains) can be indefinitely large, and will depend on the degree of disaggregation and on the explanatory variables introduced. Probably the smallest meaningful model of the UK economy that one could build would contain nine equations: a consumption function, an investment function, a stockbuilding equation, an export function, an import function, a demand-for-money function, a wage inflation equation, a price inflation equation and a production function. Such a model might be able to explain consumption, investment, stockbuilding, exports and imports (and hence GDP), the rate of interest (or the money supply if the rate of interest were exogenous), wage and price inflation and employment (and hence unemployment). Exogenous variables that would need to be considered would probably include government spending, world trade, world prices, the money supply (or the rate of interest if the money supply were endogenous) and various tax instruments. For an example of a model somewhat along these lines, the reader is referred to Surrey (1971).

While a nine-equation model may be the smallest one could feasibly construct, it is almost inevitable, when one is involved with model construction, that one finds the size of the model growing at an alarming rate. It may at first be thought that the larger the model the better; but this is not necessarily so. By introducing extra explanatory variables into an equation explaining a particular endogenous variable, the explanation of that variable may be improved *if we know the value of the explanatory variables*; but, since they in turn need to be explained, their introduction may actually make matters worse. To clarify this point, consider the following illustration. Suppose an econometrician is trying to decide which of the following two (aggregate) consumption functions is 'best' as far as his econometric model is concerned:

$$C = a + bY \qquad (4)$$
$$C = a + bY - cr \qquad (5)$$

(C is aggregate consumption, Y is aggregate income and r is the rate of interest). Suppose he has collected the relevant data, and has 'fitted' the two functions to the data, thus finding estimates of the coefficients a, b and c. Suppose that he finds that equation (4) explains (as in our example above) 98.9% of the variation in consumption while (5) explains 99.9%; that is, the inclusion of r (the rate of interest) improves[3] the explanation of C. In other words, knowledge of the value of r, and use of equation (5) instead of equation (4), leads to a more precise prediction of the value of C. Now, suppose that r is *not* exogenous; then, if the econometrician uses (5) instead of (4) as the consumption function in his econometric model, he must add an extra equation to his model to explain r. If (as is quite likely) he is unable to explain r with a very high degree of accuracy, then the prediction of C using the expanded model may well be worse than the prediction of C using the smaller model, since the error in predicting r may offset the improved (when r is known) explanatory power of equation (5).

The question of the optimal size of an econometric model remains an unresolved issue, though clearly this depends on the use to which the model is to be put. If the government is interested solely in the effects of its policy measures on the four target variables mentioned earlier (unemployment, inflation, balance of payments and growth), then it may be able to operate with a smaller model than that needed to assess the impact of its measures in wider terms.

The section has spent some time discussing the question of econometric model-building in general terms; the next section describes the main econometric models that currently exist (and are accessible to the public) in the UK.

The Major Econometric Models of the UK Economy

At any one time, there are usually a large number of econometric models of the UK economy in existence. Most of these are fairly small-scale models and are developed by private firms and institutions for their own use. However, there are a small number of large-scale models which have been in existence for some years and which are available for public inspection. Indeed, even the very model that is used to advise the Chancellor of the Exchequer – namely, the Treasury model – is now open to public scrutiny. The model constructed and used by the National Institute of Economic and Social Research (a body often considered as providing an independent check on the Treasury's economic forecasting and policy making) is also public knowledge, as is the model constructed by the London Graduate Business School.

Because such models are, as discussed above, continually undergoing a process of revision, experimentation and updating (in response to changing economic structure and changing information), it is almost impossible to describe what the 'present state' of any model is.

It may help to relate the discussion here to the state of the models as described in Laury, Lewis and Ormerod (1978), so that the interested reader may refer to that source for further details. This article describes the three major models referred to above: the Treasury model, the London Business School (LBS) model and the National Institute of Economic and Social Research (NIESR) model. At the time of that article, the Treasury model was considerably larger than the other two and contained about 875 variables: of this total, 230 were exogenous and 645 were endogenous. This means that the Treasury model consisted of 645 equations – considerably larger than four years previously. Of course, not all these equations were behavioural – many were simply identities.[4] The LBS model contained 430 variables of which 150 were exogenous and 280 were endogenous. The NIESR model was the smallest, containing 233 variables of which 84 were exogenous and 149 were endogenous. (A simplified version of the NIESR model, as it existed in 1971, is described by Surrey 1971).

Laury *et al.* (1978) point out that the Treasury model is larger partly because it is put to uses different from the other two, in particular, '. . . the Treasury forecasters are required to produce a detailed set of accounts for the public sector, and much of this takes the form of quasi-exogenous data input' (p. 54). It is interesting, and important, to note that all three models were developed from the same initial structure – the income–expenditure framework of Keynesian economics. However, the models have taken somewhat different paths as they have evolved through time, depending upon the model-builders' predilections towards new (or revised) economic theories popular in recent years.

The Treasury and NIESR models are most similar in basic structure; both use an income–expenditure framework for determining real income. In both models the consumption function is of crucial importance, though the models use different sets of explanatory variables and accordingly derive different estimates of the economic parameters (for example, the long-run MPC is unity in the Treasury model, but 0.7 in the NIESR model). The investment equations (and indeed the stockbuilding equations) are modified forms of the accelerator equation (discussed above). Exports are related to world trade, relative prices and capacity utilisation. Imports are related to output or expenditure, capacity utilisation and relative prices. Employment is determined by output, modified by productivity changes. As far as inflation is concerned, wage inflation is explained by a Phillips curve (named after Phillips 1958), 'augmented' by a price inflation expectations variable. Prices in turn are determined as a mark-up on costs (including wages, import prices, and taxes).

As far as monetary variables are concerned, econometricians

have had considerable difficulty in incorporating such variables into their models. Not only is it difficult to explain them satisfactorily, but also their influence on the real variables of the economy is erratic and difficult to estimate. However, both the Treasury and the NIESR have made vigorous attempts to incorporate such variables. A version of the Treasury model with a fully integrated monetary sector does exist, but relatively little confidence is placed on the monetary equations relative to the real equations. This is a particularly worrying problem, especially when the prevailing opinion amongst economists, financial experts and politicians has clearly undergone a marked shift towards monetarism.

The LBS model is different from the other two models in two main respects: the consumption function and the system of wage and price determination. In particular, inflationary movements are more closely related to international inflationary trends. The reader is referred to Laury, Lewis and Ormerod (1978) for further details.

One common feature of all these models is that none of them is perfect; none of them is able to explain (let alone predict) the endogenous variables with complete accuracy. This is due partly to a shortage of data (though this is becoming less acute as time passes), partly to poor quality data (about which more will be said shortly), partly to the relative youthfulness of economics as a science, and partly to the fact that the models are trying to account for human behaviour, which inevitably contains some random element. In general, it seems fair to say that accuracy is improving as time passes, though setbacks do occur from time to time (when behaviour undergoes fundamental shifts). However, the shortcomings of such models continue to cause problems for the efficient operation of macroeconomic policy.

Forecasting the Future

The government and the Treasury maintain a constant watch on the performance of the economy, to see how well the targets are being achieved, and to see whether any changes are required to the policy instruments. At one time, major changes to the instruments were a once-a-year affair (confined to the annual Budget statement). However, nowadays changes to the instruments occur with much greater frequency. (Whether this is a good thing is often hotly disputed; see Budd 1975 for a discussion of some of the issues.) Before any changes in policy instruments are considered, the past and likely future course of the economy is carefully assessed. The latest statistics on key economic variables are studied closely, not only for the evidence they provide on the performance of the economy in the recent past, but also for the indications they give for its likely future course. In determining whether any changes in instruments are needed, a key role is played by forecasts of the future economic situation. These forecasts are provided by a variety of methods, both formal and informal, though the use of formal econometric models is becoming increasingly predominant. (For an interesting discussion of the role of informal methods in forecasting, see Surrey and Ormerod 1977.)

The first type of forecast that is used in deciding whether any policy changes are needed is a forecast of the movement of the economy over the next eighteen months or so, in the absence of any such changes. The forecast is then studied to see how closely it satisfies the various targets of the government. If it diverges considerably from such targets, consideration is given to possible changes in policy instruments which might reduce the divergences. If some changes are considered necessary, then further forecasts are produced indicating the likely effect of the changes. In order to generate a set of forecasts using an econometric model, forecasts of the exogenous variables must first be provided. Given such forecasts, the model can then be solved to provide forecasts of the endogenous variables. Clearly then, any set of forecasts of endogenous variables is conditional on the forecasts of the exogenous variables, and thus the accuracy of the former depend heavily on the accuracy of the latter. Earlier, three basic types of exogenous variables were described. The first type, namely the policy instruments directly under government control (should) pose no problem – since the whole point of the forecasting exercise is to determine the effect of changes in these variables. The second type, those determined outside the country (examples given were the USA GDP and the volume of world trade), are much more difficult to forecast accurately. Errors in predicting this type of exogenous variable will lead to errors of forecasting and thus to errors of policy. A recent example is provided by the policy decision of the 1974–79 Labour Government to allow sterling to find its own level on foreign exchanges; this decision led to considerable problems for the non-oil account of the balance of payments because of sterling's unexpected popularity. The third type of exogenous variable, those determined outside the time period to which the model relates, are in fact determined by prior forecasts produced by the model. For example, suppose that, in a quarterly model, it is found that last quarter's consumers' expenditure is an important determinant of this quarter's consumers' expenditure (due to some kind of habit or persistence effect). Suppose further that quarterly data on consumption (and all the other variables in the model) are available up to and including the final quarter of 1978, and that forecasts are required for the six quarters up to the middle of 1980. By using the figure of consumption for the fourth quarter of 1978 (and forecasts of the other exogenous variables), forecasts can be produced for consumption (and other endogenous variables) for the first quarter of 1979. This, in turn, is used to provide a forecast for the second quarter of 1979, and so on. It is important to note, however, that errors can well accumulate, since an error in the forecast of consumption for the first quarter of 1979 will lead to an error in the second quarter's forecast, and so on. This is one of the reasons why forecasts of the more distant future are likely to be less accurate than forecasts of the more immediate future.

The article by Laury, Lewis and Ormerod (1978) presents a set of forecasts, showing the net effect of certain policy changes on the future behaviour of the economy. The policy changes examined include increases in government spending, decreases in tax revenues, and changes in exchange rates; the Treasury, NIESR and LBS models were compared in terms of the forecasts produced. The results are of considerable interest – sometimes startling divergencies are revealed (the consequences of differing model structures), but other times quite remarkable similarities are obtained.

All three of these models are regularly used to provide

published forecasts for the UK economy. The formal Treasury forecasts are usually published in the annual *Financial Statement and Budget Report* (published coincidentally with the main Budget of the year). The forecasts produced with the aid of the NIESR model are published quarterly in the *National Institute Economic Review*, while the London Business School also issue regular quarterly forecasts (published in the *Sunday Times*). Also of considerable interest are the forecasts now published regularly in *The Guardian* by members of the ITEM Club: The Independent Treasury Economic Model Club. As its name suggests, this club consists of a set of economists, independent of the Treasury, but who use the Treasury model to generate their forecasts. The reasons why their forecasts generally differ from the official Treasury forecasts lie in different assumptions about the future behaviour of the exogenous variables of the model. Accordingly, a comparison of the unofficial and official forecasts provides an indication of the sensitivity of the model to changing exogenous predictions.

The Accuracy of Forecasts of the Future

Clearly, if macroeconomic policy is to be based largely on the forecasts of the short-term economic situation, it is of paramount importance that such forecasts be accurate. Macroeconomic policy can fail in its purpose for other reasons besides incorrect forecasts, such as totally unexpected shocks to the system (for example, the world-wide recession following the oil price rises of the winter of 1973/74, and the industrial unrest of the winter of 1978/79); but without a solid base of good forecasts, macroeconomic policy may aggravate the situation rather than improve it. (That this is, in fact, what has happened is the view of Polanyi 1973 amongst others.)

Certainly no economist would pretend that present day forecasts are accurate or that there was no room for improvement; the crucial question, however, is whether the availability of such forecasts (despite their inaccuracies) provides the policy makers with more and better information than would otherwise be the case. An affirmative answer to this question is the conclusion of the comprehensive study by Ash and Smyth (1973) into the accuracy of various UK forecasters' predictions. Indeed they remark (p. 262)

> Our evaluation of UK short-term macroeconomic forecasts gives no support to the view that economic forecasting is a waste of time. With few exceptions, the forecasters' predictions are significantly more accurate than simply extrapolating or averaging past outcomes . . .

As this study shows, the assessment of the accuracy of forecasts is considerably more difficult than might appear. First, many forecasts are based on a particular set of assumptions about government policy over the forecast period; if these assumptions are subsequently falsified, adjustments need to be made to the forecasts before their accuracy can be assessed. Second, it is not always clear what forecasts should be assessed against – since published figures often undergo several revisions before being presented in a 'final form'. Third, the accuracy of a set of forecasts may well vary depending on the degree of aggregation, and it may thus be difficult to give an overall measure for the accuracy of the set as a whole. For example, as intuition might lead one to expect, and the Ash and Smyth study confirms, forecasts of a whole year tend to be more accurate than forecasts of individual quarters; similarly, though perhaps more surprisingly, Ash and Smyth find that errors in the forecasts of individual components of GDP tend to offset each other, so that GDP is forecast more accurately than its components.

The accuracy of forecasts can be assessed in various ways: the simplest and most naive is to assess whether the forecasts are correct on average, or whether there is a persistent tendency to over- or under-estimate the variable being predicted. In the crucial case of GDP forecasts, Ash and Smyth observe that 'the forecasters tend to under-estimate the average rate of growth of the economy' (1973, p. 257). This result is also apparent in a study of National Institute forecasts over a later period by Dean (1976), who also shows how inflation has tended to be under-estimated. Of course, errors of forecasting of this type may well lead to over-inflationary policy recommendations. The National Institute has developed a method for adjusting their forecasts in the light of such persistent under- or over-estimation (see Surrey and Ormerod 1977).

Even if a set of forecasts is correct on *average* (over a period of time), there is still clearly scope for forecasting errors in particular time periods. A comparison of the forecasting *magnitude* of fluctuations with the actual magnitude thus provides a further check on the accuracy of forecasts. Interestingly, Ash and Smyth found that (as with the level) UK forecasters tended to under-estimate the magnitude of the fluctuations, particularly in the more volatile series, notably investment. The implication of this type of forecasting error is that, if the authorities under-estimate the cyclical fluctuations in the economy, their anti-cyclical policy would not remove all the fluctuations but only part of them. However, it may be considered safer to err on the side of under-estimation of fluctuations, since an error in the other direction would actually reverse the cyclical fluctuations (i.e. turn a boom into a slump and *vice versa*).

An even more important test of the accuracy of forecasts is their ability to predict turning points. For example, when monitoring the rate of growth of the economy (as measured, say, by GDP), it is crucial to know when the rate of growth is going to fall (or rise), as this indicates the onset of a 'slump' (or 'boom'). Suppose, for instance, the government is told by its forecasters that the rate of growth of GDP will rise from 3% this year to 4% next year, and that this rate of growth would cause inflationary pressure because of supply constraints. If the government acts on this advice, it would take measures to deflate the economy – that is, reduce aggregate demand – so as to lower the growth rate. Suppose, however, that the forecasters have mis-forecast a turning point, and that (in the absence of government intervention) the rate of growth of GDP next year would in fact be only 2%. In this case, the effect of the deflationary measures makes matters worse by making the down-turn in the rate of growth much sharper than would otherwise be the case. Clearly, similar problems arise if the forecasters predict turning points which do not materialise. Thus, if errors in forecasting turning points are at all frequent, then the effect of government policy may well be de-stabilising – making fluctuations in activity worse than they would otherwise have been. The Ash and Smyth study shows that turning-point errors of prediction were unfortunately common among UK forecasters.

Errors of forecasts arise for a variety of reasons, not least of which concern the inadequacies of published data on economic statistics. These inadequacies also create problems for another aspect of macroeconomic policy, namely that of determining the precise state of the economy at any particular time.

Forecasting the Past and the Present

Clearly an essential prerequisite for successfully forecasting the future path of the economy is knowledge of where it has been in the past and where it is at the time of the forecast. Unfortunately, since the collection and processing of large quantities of data take time, there are often lags (sometimes of considerable length, though they have become shorter in recent years) in the publication of economic data. In order to reduce the delay in publication, provisional estimates of key variables are often prepared. By their very nature, these provisional estimates are derived from partial information, and as more information is accumulated they are likely to be revised. Often these revisions are considerable and may continue for several months, if not years. Thus it may be some time before a clear picture emerges of the movement of the economy in the past, and thus 'forecasting the past' constitutes an essential part of formulating macroeconomic policy. It should be noted that revisions to data are not a short-term phenomenon but continue for many years. A useful source for any reader interested in getting some idea of the magnitudes involved is Ormerod (1978).

Even if a published series 'settles down' (that is, no further revisions are forthcoming), this does not guarantee that the final figure is accurate. Because of the way the data are collected, some margin of error inevitably remains – though its magnitude varies from series to series. For example, the Central Statistical Office estimates that its figures for GDP are accurate only to within ± 3%, while the figures for stock changes may show a margin of error up to 10% either way.

The inevitable delays in the publication of key economic variables mean that it is often difficult to assess how the economy is behaving at any particular time. However, some insight may be gained by the study of proxy variables, or of other economic indicators whose publication is faster or more frequent than that of the variables of direct concern. Indeed, heavy reliance is placed on such indicators by the National Institute in forecasting the past. Thus, before the figure for consumers' expenditure for a particular quarter has been published, the Institute makes use of the published monthly figures on the volume of retail sales and the figures on new car registrations to provide an estimate. Similarly, an estimate of GDP is obtained with the use of the monthly figures on industrial production (and with the help of an equation showing the relationship between GDP and industrial production that held in the past). Such indicators may also be used to provide forecasts of the future; for example, the number of new houses whose construction has been initiated in one month gives some measure of investment in housing in subsequent months, while data on new orders placed with contractors and with engineering firms also give indications as to the future movement of capital formation. Information from investment intentions surveys (as carried out by the Department of Industry and the Confederation of British Industry) also provides evidence in this direction; most major forecasters make use of such surveys.

Although the use of indicators reduces the margin of uncertainty as to the behaviour of the economy in the recent past, some error inevitably remains. As with mistakes in forecasting the future, macroeconomic policy can be blown off course by mistakes in forecasting the past. Here again, errors in spotting turning points are likely to cause the most serious problems. Several examples of such instances are given in the article by Ormerod (1978), while Osborne and Teal (1977) examine the effect of such revisions on forecasting accuracy.

Conclusions

The inaccuracies of forecasting and the inadequacies of economic data pose problems for successful implementation of macroeconomic policy; this suggests that the full potential welfare gain may not be realised. If the problems are sufficiently small, so that at least some of the potential gain is realised, then macroeconomic policy is worthwhile. If, however, the problems are so large that economic management actually reduces welfare rather than increases it, then it may be preferable to play down the role of macroeconomic policy.

While it may be difficult to assess the degree of success of macroecomic policy, and to disentangle the reasons for its failures, certain broad conclusions do emerge. First, assuming that society does not wish to repeat the experience of the Great Depression, some government intervention at a macroeconomic level is necessary. Second, such intervention can be beneficial, as a comparison of the post-war with the pre-war situation indicates. Third, because of the continuing deficiencies of forecasting and of economic data, there is inevitably some margin of uncertainty over the precise effects of macroeconomic policy and thus care should be taken not to expect too much from, or to place too much reliance on, such policies. For instance, the manifest absurdity of policy changes which attempt to alter the rate of growth of GDP by one or two percentage points should be recognised, since it is impossible to measure, let alone forecast, the rate of growth of GDP this accurately. Clearly we need to walk before we can run; while our ability to explain economic phenomena remains imperfect, we must keep our ambitions in this field appropriately modest.

Perhaps the final word can most fruitfully be left to Sir Douglas Wass, Permanent Secretary at the Treasury (1978):

> I believe that faced with the challenge of uncertainty and of ignorance, we must not give up the patient search for truth no matter how disappointing our endeavours may at times appear. We must have more, not less research into the behaviour of the economy. For there is no adequate alternative. As Alfred Marshall once said of an earlier generation, let us hope that posterity will say of us: 'Though economists have not yet succeeded in bringing that study to a successful issue the cause of their failure lies in the profound obscurity and ever-changing form of the problem: it does not lie in any indifference on their part to its supreme importance.'

Notes

1. This statement is the result of standard statistical techniques; see Hey (1974, pp. 281–285). The details of the techniques need not

detain the reader at this stage. The main point to be grasped is that there is a margin of error in the estimate of the marginal propensity to consume.

2. Strictly speaking, what happens in the UK may influence the US GDP or the volume of world trade slightly; however this dependence is usually considered so slight as to be insignificant. This example shows that the distinction between exogenous and endogenous variables may not always be clear cut, and may sometimes be more a question of degree than of kind.
3. The discussion here is very heuristic statistically; the purist is referred to any statistics text (e.g. Hey 1974) for a more precise discussion of the relevant technical points.
4. In the very simple model represented by equations (1) and (2), (1) is a behavioural equation and (2) is an identity.

References

Ash, J.C.K. and Smyth, D.J., *Forecasting the United Kingdom Economy*, Saxon House 1973.

Budd, A.P., 'The debate on fine-tuning: the basic issues', *National Institute Economic Review*, No. 74, November 1976, pp. 56–59.

Dean, A.J.H., 'Errors in National Institute forecasts of personal incomes, inflation and employment', *National Institute Economic Review*, No. 78, November 1976, pp. 48–57.

Hey, J.D., *Statistics in Economics*, Martin Robertson 1974.

Laury, J.S.E., Lewis, G.R. and Ormerod, P.A., 'Properties of macroeconomic models of the UK economy: a comparative study', *National Institute Economic Review*, No. 83, February 1978, pp. 52–72.

Lipsey, R.G., *An Introduction to Positive Economics*, 4th edn, Weidenfeld and Nicolson 1975.

Maurice, R. (ed), *National Accounts Statistics: Sources and Methods*, Central Statistical Office, HMSO 1968.

Ormerod, P.A., 'The effects of revision to Central Statistical Office data for the UK economy', *Oxford Bulletin of Economics and Statistics*, Vol. 40, No. 2, May 1978, pp. 165–171.

Osborne, D.R. and Teal, F., *An Analysis of National Institute Forecasting Error in 1975*, National Institute Discussion Paper No. 2, 1977.

Phillips, A.W., 'The relation between unemployment and the rate of change of money wage rates in the United Kingdom, 1861–1975', *Economica* NS, Vol. 25, November 1958, pp. 283–299.

Polanyi, G., *Short-term Forecasting: A Case Study*, Background Memorandum 5, Institute of Economic Affairs 1973.

Shaw, G.K., *An Introduction to the Theory of Macroeconomic Policy*, 3rd edn, Martin Robertson 1977.

Surrey, M.J.C., *The Analysis and Forecasting of the British Economy*, NIESR Occasional Paper 25, Cambridge University Press 1971.

Surrey, M.J.C. and Ormerod, P.A., 'Formal and informal aspects of

forecasting with an econometric model', *National Institute Economic Review*, No. 81, August 1977, pp. 67–71.
Treasury, *Financial Statement and Budget Report*, HMSO.
Wass, D., 'The changing problems of economic management', *Economic Trends*, No. 293, March 1978, pp. 97–104.

Suggestions for Further Reading

For an elementary introduction to the theory of macroeconomic policy, see Lipsey (1975). For a fuller discussion see Shaw (1977).

Discussion of forecasting methods, and comparisons of different econometric models, can be found in Surrey (1971); Laury, Lewis and Ormerod (1978).

For an analysis of the accuracy of forecasts, see Ash and Smyth (1973); Dean (1976); Osborne and Teal (1977).

A description of the methods used in collecting and processing economic statistics at the CSO is given in Maurice (1968).

Discussion of the revisions to CSO data is provided by Ormerod (1978).

For an analysis of the practical problems of operating macroeconomic policy see Wass (1978).

11. Inflation and its control: a monetarist analysis

DAVID LAIDLER
Professor of Economics,
University of Western Ontario

Inflation[1] is a process of generally rising prices. This is not to say that, as inflation proceeds, all prices rise at the same rate. In any economy the relative prices of different goods and services will change as conditions of supply and demand for individual items change over time. However, during an inflation the cost in terms of money of a representative bundle of goods and services, such as might be consumed by an average household, continually goes up; or to put the same point another way, the purchasing power of money, its value, steadily declines. Inflation is usually regarded as undesirable; but what harm does it do if prices in general rise over time? The answer here depends critically upon whether inflation is *anticipated* or not. By anticipated inflation we mean not just that inflation is expected, but that that expectation has also been acted upon. Many of the adverse effects that are usually associated with inflation arise not as a result of a rising price level *per se*, but rather because the people affected by that rising price level did not anticipate that it would rise in their earlier decisions.

Unanticipated inflation has effects on the distribution of income and wealth. For example, suppose that a person borrows £100 from another with the promise to repay the sum at 5% interest at the end of the year. Suppose, furthermore, that both expect the price level to remain stable over the year in question. If instead the price level rises at, say, 10% per annum, the wealth positions of both the borrower and the lender are affected by their transaction in a way they did not foresee. The lender receives £105 at the end of the year, but it will buy goods that would have been worth about £95 at the prices prevailing at the time the loan was made. He has earned a real rate of interest of minus 5% when he hoped to earn plus 5%; he has been made unexpectedly worse off. The borrower, by exactly parallel reasoning, has gained unexpectedly. These effects are the result of disappointed expectations about the behaviour of the price level rather than of inflation *per se*. Suppose the 10% rise in prices had been expected: in order to get a real return on his loan of 5%, the lender would have asked for £115 to be repaid at the end of the year, the extra £10 to take care of rising prices. Furthermore the borrower, provided that he too expected prices to rise at 10% a year, would have acquiesced in this. Inflation would have been anticipated.

The matter is of course far more general than an affair between an isolated borrower and lender. Anyone who holds any asset denominated in money terms, or any claim to an income – a pension say – whose value is fixed in money terms, loses if the price level rises unexpectedly. Similarly, any debtor, the value of whose debts is fixed in money terms, gains. On the other hand, if debtors and creditors form correct expectations of inflation, and allow for these expectations in the interest rate at which they strike their bargains, or, in the case of pension rights and such, in the terms of the pension contracts into which they enter, then in thus anticipating inflation they ensure that it does not redistribute wealth between them.

While unanticipated inflation redistributes wealth from creditors to debtors it should be clear that unanticipated deflation just as surely redistributes wealth from debtors to creditors. There is a general rule here: if the price level rises faster than anticipated (and this phrase includes situations in which the rate of fall of prices is smaller in absolute terms than the anticipated one) then debtors benefit, while if it is smaller they lose. A zero rate of change of prices when a 10% rate of fall is anticipated discriminates against creditors in just the same way, and to just the same extent, as does a 10% inflation when a constant price level is anticipated. A zero rate of change of prices when 10% inflation is anticipated, on the other hand, works in favour of creditors just as much as 10% inflation when constant prices are anticipated.

Now the redistribution we have discussed so far takes place between private individuals, or at least between institutions and individuals in the private sector of the economy. But one of the most important characteristics of inflation is its capacity for redistributing income and wealth between the private sector and the government. To begin with, the real value of government debt held by the public falls with inflation, just as does the real value of private debt, and unless inflation is anticipated by both lenders and borrowers (in this case the government) this fall in real value will not be compensated for by the interest paid. The redistribution implicit here works just like that between private borrowers and lenders and there is no need to analyse it in any further detail.

Inflation redistributes income from the private sector to the government through the effect of price-level changes on the real level of taxes. Tax laws, as they relate both to individuals and companies, are usually written on the assumption of a constant price level. Thus individuals are allowed to claim certain allowances fixed in money terms against their income before they become eligible for tax; thereafter the higher their money income the higher their marginal rate of income tax. Inflation erodes the real value of tax allowances, and by increasing money income pushes individuals into higher and higher tax brackets, even though, in real terms, their incomes are not increasing. Thus inflation increases the revenue accruing to the government from income taxes without the need for unpopular legislation to increase tax rates. Dealings between taxpayer and government are not automatically subject to renegotiation, even when both sides recognise and come to expect inflation; it is only if the government decides to adjust tax allowances and rates automatically and regularly in order to keep the real burden of taxes the same – if it decides to 'index' the income tax structure – that inflation comes to be anticipated by that tax structure and this redistributive effect is avoided.

Inflation has similar effects on the revenue that accrues from capital gains taxation. This is levied on the difference between the price at which individuals purchase and later sell a wide variety of assets. To the extent that, with inflation, the prices of certain assets rise in money terms but not in real terms, nominal gains reflect no real addition to the wealth of the person who holds the assets. Nevertheless, because capital gains taxation is levied on gains measured in money terms, a tax liability is generated by the sale of an asset at a higher money price than that at which it was purchased, even if the gain in question is purely the result of inflation. Also, conventional tax procedures interfere with the attempts of individuals to anticipate inflation by seeking higher interest rates on the loans they make. They must, after all, pay tax not just on that part of their interest income which represents a real return, but also on that part which represents compensation for inflation. Thus, even if the before-tax interest rate adjusts fully for inflation, the after-tax rate of return will be driven down by this effect, with the government being the beneficiary.

Inflation affects company taxation too. Here a key factor is its effect on the market value of inventories of goods held by companies. To see what is involved, consider the simple example of a grocery shop that must keep its shelves stocked with goods in order to carry on business. When prices are rising such goods will appreciate in money terms while they remain on the shelves; this rise in nominal value shows up as part of the shop's profit and is subject to taxation. But when goods are sold they must be replaced at a new higher price. Appreciation in the money value of inventories brings no real gain to the shop. Although the original stock of goods was sold at an increased price, that stock must be replaced at the same high price if business is to be carried on. But the shop is taxed as if the gain was a real one and wealth is redistributed from its owners to the government. Again, it is possible for tax laws to be re-written in order to avoid the type of redistribution implicit in this example; but there is no automatic mechanism that can ensure that it will happen even if both taxpayer and tax collector are fully aware of what is going on. It is up to the government, if it so desires, to change its regulations.

The redistributive effects of inflation stem, not from rising prices *per se*, but from unanticipated fluctuations in the time path of prices. To the extent that one is worried about them and desires 'price stability' to avoid them, the policy objective implied by this phrase is not a zero rate of change of prices, but a stable and predictable rate of change of prices with taxation practices being adapted to take price-level changes into account. However, there are costs even to anticipated inflation; when these are considered, a zero rate of change of prices comes to look more desirable than a positive one. Such costs arise from the fact that many assets used as money in the United Kingdom, and in every other advanced economy for that matter, bear a zero rate of interest. The rate of return on holding them is given by the rate of change of their purchasing power, that is by the rate of inflation. A positive rate of inflation produces a negative real rate of return on money. It constitutes a tax on holding money.

Cash balances will still be held when inflation is anticipated. The imposition of a tax on any good does not usually lead people to cease consuming it altogether. However, if they expect inflation, people will hold less cash than they otherwise would, and inasmuch as cash provides services to those who hold it, they will be that much worse off as a result. The more money one holds either as currency in the pocket or in the form of a deposit at a commercial bank, the easier it is to design one's expenditure pattern in the way found most convenient and the more independent it can be made of the time pattern of receipts; moreover, the more cash one has on hand, the easier it is to make unexpected but advantageous purchases when the occasion arises; and so on. When inflation is seen to be eroding the value of money kept on hand, people begin to cut back on their money holdings, to sacrifice these advantages rather than face the losses which holding money imposes. They will devote more time and trouble to arranging their affairs in order to economise on cash than they would in the absence of anticipated inflation.

These costs of anticipated inflation would not occur if it was possible to pay interest on money holdings to compensate for the erosion of their value by inflation. It would be difficult to do this for currency, but not so difficult for bank deposits.

The main obstacle here is rigidity in the institutional structure of the banking system rather than any real practical difficulty. Even so, anticipated inflation has other costs too. When prices are rising, even if everyone expects them to rise, producers still have to notify their customers about the timing and extent of particular price changes; shops still have to change the price tags on the specific goods they have for sale; consumers find that it pays to spend more time shopping around for bargains, and so on. All this activity takes time and trouble, and consumes resources which might otherwise have been devoted to more productive uses.

Now these arguments suggest that, on balance, a stable price level is to be preferred to a rising one, even if its rate of rise is fully anticipated; but this would be the case if there were no benefits to be had from rising prices and it is often argued that such benefits do exist. In particular it is argued that rising prices enable the economy to be run at a higher level of employment and with more efficiency in the use of productive resources. This argument is of dubious validity, although it stems from the plausible proposition that money wages are relatively sticky downwards – that it is easier, in any particular industry, for these to rise than for them to fall.

In any well functioning economy the pattern of output is going to change over time in response to changing patterns of consumer expenditure, changes in technology, and so on. Such a changing pattern of output requires that resources, including labour, be re-allocated between sectors of the economy. Such re-allocation is accomplished by having relative prices and wages vary; by having them rise in the expanding sectors and fall in those areas where a contraction of output is needed. Now if some particular prices are going to rise against a background of an overall stable price level, then others must fall. If it is difficult to get wages and prices to fall, then it is difficult for the allocative mechanism to work efficiently. However, if the overall price level is permitted to rise, the required changes in the pattern of relative prices can be brought about by permitting the prices of some goods, and wages in some industries, to rise faster than those elsewhere, but without actually trying to force any absolute falls in wages and prices on any sector of the economy. Thus, it is argued, a steady rate of inflation might actually be conducive to the more efficient working of the economy and might produce a lower overall level of unemployment.

Now the key to this argument is the proposition that there are downward rigidities in wages and prices. But why should wages and prices be downwardly rigid? The answer usually given has to do with the reluctance of wage earners in particular industries to take cuts in real income. When dealing with an economy in which a zero rate of change of prices has been the norm, and hence has come to be expected to continue, it might make more sense to argue that individual wages and prices will tend to downward rigidity and that this tendency will to some extent interfere with the effectiveness of the price mechanism in re-allocating resources in response to a pattern of demand that changes over time. It would equally make sense to argue that a rising general price level will then help to make the allocative process work smoothly, *but only so long as a zero rate of increase of prices was expected.*

If prices and wages tend to be downwardly sticky because of the desire of wage earners to protect the level of their real wages, then if they expect that rising prices rather than stable prices are the norm they will attempt to ensure that their money wages, and hence the price of their output, rise at least as fast as the general price level. Wages and prices will be sticky relative to the expected rate of change of prices and any tendency for a particular wage or price to rise less rapidly than the overall expected rate of inflation will be resisted. In short, the benefits in terms of the smoother functioning of the allocative mechanism and of associated lower unemployment rate that one might get from inflation exist only if inflation is unanticipated. Anticipated inflation may do relatively little harm, but it will not do any good either as long as downward stickiness in wages and prices is itself the product of wage earners' expectations about inflation.

Wage earners seem to be at least as adept as their employers at anticipating inflation, though for a long time many economists did not believe this. A widely held theory of the interrelationship of inflation and economic growth was based on the proposition that wages lag behind prices in inflationary situations. Were this the case, then the resulting fall in real wages would lead to an increase in profits and the incentive to accumulate capital would be greater. Hence inflation would lead to more rapid capital accumulation. Plausible though it may be, the result of testing this 'wage lag' hypothesis has been to show that there is no systematic tendency for real wages to fall in response to inflation, suggesting that the labour force is just as adept at predicting inflation as any other section of the population. Thus the proposition that inflation leads to more rapid capital accumulation than would occur in its absence is probably false.

To summarise then, if inflation is unanticipated it redistributes income and wealth from creditors to debtors, with the government being prominent among the debtors who gain; it also distorts the effects of taxation and increases government revenue. Anticipated inflation has no such effects, provided that tax regulations are adapted to nullify the effects of cost of living changes. However, fully anticipated inflation also has its costs. Where money bears no interest it leads to people taking more time and trouble over arranging their trading activities in order to economise on their holdings of depreciating cash balances. Moreover, the very process of changing prices and disseminating information about them uses up resources that could be devoted to more productive uses.

Inflation has its drawbacks and seems to yield no lasting benefits. It is therefore worth controlling and curing. The key to understanding its causes lies in the very meaning of the word inflation: a sustained fall in the value of money. Supply and demand analysis tell us that, given a stable demand function for anything, its price will fall continuously only if the supply of it increases continuously. There have been inflations for as long as there is recorded history, and there has never been a sustained inflation in any country without a sustained increase in the supply of money in that country; nor has there ever been a sustained increase in the supply of money in any country without inflation. Both elementary economic theory and an immense body of evidence point to an increasing quantity of money as a key factor in the inflationary process.

A simplified example will help the reader to understand

the complex process whereby monetary expansion generates rising prices. Consider an economy in which there is no economic growth and no foreign trade, in which, initially, there is full employment with a stable price level, and in which there is initially a constant quantity of money, that is volume of currency in circulation and of bank deposits. Now let the quantity of money increase *unexpectedly* (and that is a vital qualification) by 10%. Before the increase, all the firms and households in the economy were holding enough money to satisfy their desire for convenience in carrying on their trading activities. After the increase, people find that they have more cash on hand than they really want to hold, given that it can be used by them to purchase other assets or even goods and services. Different economic agents will spend their excess cash in different ways. One man may buy a bond, another may pay off a debt, another may purchase a new car, another may take an extra holiday, but one way or another they spend their excess cash. But when it is spent by one person, cash does not disappear. It passes on to another who accepts it in exchange for whatever it is he is selling, not because he wants cash to hold, but because he in his turn can use it to buy something. Thus an unexpected increase in the supply of money leads to an increase in the overall level of demand for goods and services.

Producers, faced with this increase in demand for their output, try to meet it by increasing output, but in an already fully employed economy there is little scope for this. They bid against one another for a supply of labour and other productive services that can only be increased marginally and succeed not so much in increasing their output as in driving up wages and other costs of production. Hence the price of output also rises. Now with a once-and-for-all increase in the quantity of money, this process comes to an end soon enough. As prices rise, people find they require more money to finance their day-to-day market activity; indeed the amount of money so required rises in proportion to the level of prices at which such activity is being carried on. Once a 10% increase in the quantity of money has led to a 10% increase in prices, there will be no excess cash holdings left to bid up prices further and prices will stabilise at a new higher level.

If, instead of a once-and-for-all increase in the money supply, we think in terms of an initially unexpected continuous expansion of the quantity of money, continuous inflation will be set in motion by the mechanisms we have just discussed. However as the process continues over time another vital element comes into play. If people learn from experience, then once they see wages and prices rising they will come to expect that they will continue to do so. Such expectations in turn get built into the pricing policies of firms and into the wage bargaining process. Wages increase because prices are expected to increase and, because wages increase, prices do indeed increase. However this phenomenon of wages pushing up prices, so visible in any actual inflation, is not a sign that the labour force, represented or not by trade unions, 'causes' inflation. Rather it is a sign that the labour force has come to expect inflation to continue and is seeking to protect itself from it. It is a sign that inflation has become anticipated in the wage bargaining process and is generating its own momentum. When this stage of an inflation is reached, monetary expansion allows people to have sufficient cash on hand to carry on their economic life without being inconvenienced by rising prices. It becomes something that permits inflation to continue rather than something which drives it along.

The assumptions we made about expectations are crucial to the foregoing description of an inflationary process. It was assumed that monetary expansion was not expected at the outset, so its first effect was to cause excess demand. Only as resulting inflation began to generate expectations that it would continue, did expectations exert direct influence on wages and prices. Some economists, advocates of the 'rational expectations hypothesis', would say that such assumptions credit private agents with too little intelligence. They would argue that, if it is widely recognised that monetary expansion causes inflation, people will be led to monitor the behaviour of the money supply in order to form expectations upon which to base their behaviour *vis-à-vis* wage and price setting. If they do act in such a way, and provided adequate data are available, then a monetary expansion such as we have been discussing would from the outset lead directly to an increase in the rate of wage and price inflation by way of its effects on expectations. Excess demand would not have been needed to set inflation in motion. Moreover, if expectations are formed in such a 'rational' manner then money has a much more fundamental causative role to play in the process of ongoing anticipated inflation. Wages and prices keep on rising because of expectations, but the expectations themselves, instead of being the effect of the past behaviour of the inflation rate, are the direct result of the current behaviour of the money supply.

As we shall see, the way in which expectations are formed is a crucial matter in determining the way in which an economy reacts when the rate of monetary expansion is slowed down in the face of ongoing inflation. First, however, we must deal with an important extension of the foregoing arguments, modifying the analysis to make it more relevant to the case of any economy that has significant trade links with the rest of the world. Here, much depends upon whether the economy operates a fixed or a flexible exchange rate for its currency.[2]

A fixed exchange rate involves the central bank of the country concerned standing ready to buy and sell its currency in exchange for foreign currencies in unlimited amounts at a fixed price; the ultimate effect of this is to ensure that any one country cannot for long sustain an inflation rate that differs substantially from that prevailing elsewhere. Suppose prices in one economy did indeed begin to rise more rapidly than those in the rest of the world as a result of domestic monetary expansion. Potential and actual exporters in that country would find it less and less profitable to sell their goods abroad instead of selling them at home. The price available to them in terms of their home currency from selling abroad would not rise as quickly as that available from selling at home and so they would begin to divert some of their output to the home market. Foreigners selling to the more rapidly inflating country would find the practice increasingly attractive and the volume of imports would tend to increase.

Implicit here is a tendency for the balance of payments of the more rapidly inflating economy to go into deficit. To keep the exchange rate stable, its central bank would have to act as a net purchaser of its own currency on the foreign exchange market and would have to carry out its purchases with its reserves of foreign currency. Since its stocks of reserves are finite it can only do so for a limited period, and if the value of the exchange rate is to be maintained, domestic policy actions must be taken to bring prices into a relationship with those ruling in the rest of the world that will permit balance of payments equilibrium. This must involve having a domestic rate of change of prices that is very much the same as that ruling elsewhere.

The process described above would work in reverse if inflation in the rest of the world were to accelerate relative to that ruling at home. Producers of export goods would divert output from home markets and increase prices there to keep pace with those available abroad. The price of imports would also begin to rise and so the domestic inflation rate would accelerate. A balance of payments surplus would be generated and the central bank of our relatively small open economy would find itself buying up foreign exchange with domestic currency, hence generating the monetary expansion needed to support the new inflation rate. This surplus would be permanent if the central bank was willing to acquire foreign exchange reserves indefinitely. If it was not, then it would have to set in motion the policies necessary to make domestic prices and their rate of change behave in such a way as to keep the balance of payments in equilibrium.

In short when an economy is open to the rest of the world and small in relationship to it, *and operates a fixed exchange rate*, the inflation rate is, in the long run, very much an imported item. Advocates of 'rational expectations' argue that in such an economy, agents recognise this, and form their expectations about inflation on the basis of what is happening abroad, rather than on the basis of domestic considerations, thus making domestic prices relatively insensitive to disturbances of purely domestic origin. If the economy operates a flexible exchange rate, however, things are very different, because in such circumstances the exchange rate is determined by the supply and demand for the country's currency on foreign exchange markets – in the limiting case, with no central bank intervention at all.

If domestic monetary expansion leads to a relatively fast inflation rate, we have already seen that a tendency to an outflow of domestic currency is the result. Under a flexible exchange rate, this tendency drives down the price of domestic currency on foreign exchange markets. Domestic currency prices received by exporters increase, as do the domestic currency prices of imports. Thus the stabilising forces that are at work when there is a fixed exchange rate are nullified by a flexible rate. Such a rate will fall for just so long as domestic policies imply a more rapid inflation rate than that ruling in the rest of the world and will ensure that the domestic price level behaves very much as it would in a closed economy. These relationships between a falling exchange rate, rising import prices, and domestic inflation are easily (and often) misinterpreted as showing that a falling exchange rate causes inflation. In fact causation runs in just the opposite direction. Just as rising money wages are in the first instance a consequence of inflation, and at the very most a factor tending to keep it going once it is under way, rather than being an independent causative factor, so exactly the same is true of a falling exchange rate.

As the reader should easily be able to satisfy himself, the existence of a flexible exchange rate insulates the domestic economy from inflation originating abroad. However it cannot insulate it from all shocks. In particular, no matter what the exchange rate regime, if there occurs a change in the real terms of trade, as for example when the world price of oil was raised so steeply in late 1973, that will have domestic consequences – consequences for the level of real income and the structure of relative prices, rather than the long-run time path of the inflation rate however. Under a flexible exchange rate, it is domestic monetary policy that is the dominant influence on domestic inflation, just as in a closed economy.

There are good reasons for regarding inflation as undesirable but it is difficult to bring and keep it under control. The problems are at heart political. Debtors gain from inflation and the government is a prominent debtor. Government, uniquely among debtors, has the power to generate the monetary expansion that brings about and sustains inflation. It is always politically easier for an elected government to provide state-financed benefits for the community than it is for it to increase the taxes that might pay for such benefits, so there is always an incentive for governments to borrow to finance some of their expenditure. To borrow from the public at large involves the government in bidding against would-be private borrowers. In doing so, it drives up rates of interest and causes some private borrowers to go out of the market and to give up the expenditure which they planned to finance by borrowing. Government expenditure, financed in this way, 'crowds out' private expenditure and the private sector of the economy is no fonder of cancelling expenditure plans in the face of higher interest rates than it is of cancelling them in the face of higher taxes.

Thus an elected government is under political pressure to find somewhere else to borrow and it alone has the power to borrow at will from the central bank. When it does so the central bank creates deposits for the government which are then spent and put into circulation. The effect on the money supply is exactly the same as if the government had literally printed the notes with which to finance its expenditure. As long as the government continues to finance expenditure by borrowing from the central bank in this way, the money supply continues to increase. If it increases more rapidly than the real output of the economy, then we get inflation. To get rid of inflation requires a lower rate of monetary expansion, but that in turn requires either a cut in government spending, an increase in taxes, an increase in the private sector's borrowing costs, or indeed a combination of all three. The political problems involved here are obvious, and this is not to mention those raised by the consequences of a lower rate of monetary expansion for real income and employment.

As we have seen, there is a strong element of the self-fulfilling prophecy about anticipated inflation. Prices are expected to rise and so wages rise; therefore prices do in fact rise. The process continues so long as monetary policy permits it. However, suppose that attempts are made to stop this spiral by reducing the rate of monetary expansion. If this policy change is unexpected, firms and households will begin to find that they have insufficient cash on hand to support comfortably their usual transaction patterns. They will all try to restore their cash positions by temporarily cutting down expenditure. Firms will face a fall in the demand for their output, but will be unsure as to whether it is temporary or permanent. Moreover, because they are tied into particular wage contracts, they will be unwilling to cut prices below levels originally planned. They will plan temporarily to cut back on output and employment, but this cutback sets up a tendency towards further contractions as a downward multiplier process gets under way. In short, the initial effect of an unexpected monetary slow-down is not on the inflation rate at all, but on output and employment. Firms will eventually revise their planned prices downwards, and the labour force will moderate its bids for money wages in the face of unemployment. The inflation rate will begin to slow down. If people learn from experience as it does so, the expected inflation rate will also begin to fall. As long as there exists unusually high unemployment the inflation rate will fall, and eventually it will reach levels at which, given the rate of monetary expansion, there is room for income and employment to get back to full employment levels again with a lower rate of inflation.

According to the foregoing analysis, then, the cost of significantly reducing the inflation rate, in an economy where inflation has become anticipated, is a period of stagnation and unemployment that might better be measured in years rather than in weeks or months. Of course that analysis rests on the assumption that monetary contraction is initially unexpected, and that later expectations about inflation are based on past experience of the inflation rate. If expectations are instead formed 'rationally', that is if contractionary policy is announced by the government, if the announcement is believed, and if economic agents are not prevented by contracts already embarked upon from acting on the information that such an announcement yields, then the time path of wages and prices will adjust at once to conform to the new time path of the money supply, without any intervening slow-down in real activity.

The reader will need little persuasion that the list of conditions that must be fulfilled for this to happen is a formidable one, unlikely to be realsied in practice. As a practical matter, therefore, a monetary cure for inflation is likely to be a painful one. It is hardly surprising that so many governments in so many countries have resorted to direct controls upon wages and prices in order to find a way out of the harsh dilemma implicit here. There is not space here to chronicle the series of failures that have resulted, or to assess the reasons for them. Suffice it to say that, in the current state of our knowledge of how the economic system works, it is becoming increasingly apparent that the painful cure for inflation outlined above is the only sure one available. The more slowly is the inflation rate brought down, the less unemployment and stagnation must be endured in the process. This is because unemployment arises from the cuts in expenditure plans made as the community tries to maintain the level of its money holdings. The more slowly is a cash shortage generated, the smaller will be the expenditure cuts in question. However, the slower is this monetary slow-down, the longer will the community suffer from the costs of inflation in the meanwhile.

There is quite a lot that can be done to mitigate the costs imposed by inflation. Inasmuch as there is redistribution between the public and the government as a result of inflation, this can be offset by the government gearing the tax system to changes in the price level. Inasmuch as creditors of the government lose because the real value of their assets falls with inflation – and this is a particularly important factor for poorer members of the community, for whom government savings bonds are an important way of holding wealth – then the government can agree to pay interest rates at a level that will compensate for these losses. In short, the government can act in such a way that, in its dealings with the private sector, inflation becomes anticipated. As far as redistribution within the private sector is concerned, problems are not so widespread because, as we have seen, if inflation is anticipated, private contracts adjust to take account of it. Some problems do remain: certain types of contract – for example for private pensions – made long in the past, cannot now be revised, even though the expectations upon which they were based have long been shown to be false. In such cases, there is perhaps room for government intervention to iron out the redistribution that inflation brings about, even within the private sector.

Such actions as these of course would not remove all the

costs that inflation imposes. There would still be some loss in the efficiency of the financial system; the extra costs involved in administering the pricing policies of firms when the price level is rising would still have to be borne. It would still be worthwhile to cure inflation then, but, by mitigating some of its costs, the government could make it less urgent to do so. Thus, the type of 'gradualist' cure outlined above, designed to minimise the costs of curtailing inflation by spreading them out over time, would be made more viable. The solution to the problem of inflation that derives from the foregoing analysis is thus very much one of trading off one set of costs against another. In the current state of knowledge, it is not really possible to quantify these costs and there should be no presumption that they are negligible. Indeed the last few years' experience in Britain, where monetary policy has, on average, been contractionary, sometimes savagely so, suggests that they are serious. However, unless some unforeseen breakthrough in our knowledge of inflation occurs, such costs are going to have to be borne if inflation is to be banished from the economy.

Notes

1. The reader is warned that many of the views expressed here are matters of controversy among economists. This chapter is intended to provide a basis for debate on the problem of inflation, not to provide an analysis of the problem that anyone should simply read and accept as definitive.
2. The reader should compare the section that follows with Chapter 13 on the International Monetary System. He should also note that, in order to keep the exposition simple here, I have set aside the complications that arise when the capital account of the balance of payments is analysed. These complications do not alter the basic outlines of the analysis.

Suggestions for Further Reading

Brittan, S., 'Inflation and Democracy', in Fred Hirsch and John H. Goldthorpe (eds), *The Political Economy of Inflation*, Martin Robertson 1978.

Flemming, J.S., *Inflation*, Oxford University Press 1977.

Foster, J.I., 'The redistributive effects of inflation – questions and answers', *Scottish Journal of Political Economy*, February 1976, pp. 73–98.

12. Economic growth: causes, consequences and constraints

G.K. SHAW*
Reader in Economics,
University of East Anglia

The Importance of Growth

The case for economic growth is clear and compelling. Increasing income *per capita* permits increased consumption of all goods including leisure and hence generates an increase in economic welfare as commonly defined. Moreover, it is only through economic growth that poverty, whether in advanced or developing countries, will be readily overcome. In contrast, policies to redistribute income and wealth, whilst implying a once-and-for-all improvement in the lot of the extremely poor, have but a minor impact upon the existence of poverty *per se* compared to the sustained impact of rising income *per capita*.[1] This arises from the compounding nature of the growth process. To illustrate, consider a school-leaver aged fifteen finding employment at the comparatively low wage of £2,000 per year. If he could look forward to an increment of 3% per annum (in real terms), he would by the time he reached retirement age at sixty-five be earning £8,760, which would place him in the upper income group by today's standards. Economic growth is also necessary to absorb the natural increase in the labour force. Particularly where structural change reveals itself in the comparative decline of labour intensive industry, economic growth becomes a pre-requisite for the maintenance of full employment.

* I have benefited from the helpful comments of R.M. Grant and Alan Peacock.

The foregoing should not be taken to imply that there is a consensus about the desirability of economic growth. Many economists, most notably E.J. Mishan (1967, 1977), have drawn attention to the attendant costs of economic growth. These include the costs of pollution and congestion, the tensions and stresses of living in a highly complex and urbanised society and also possibly a decrease in consumer choice. This last effect derives from the adoption of highly efficient production processes which generate standardised products, with which the more varied output of handicraft manufacture cannot compete. In addition, economic growth speeds up structural change and generates displacement effects. Existing skills and techniques become outdated and unemployment results, especially amongst workers who cannot readily be retrained for alternative occupations.[2] These costs and consequences of economic growth dictate the need for government intervention and control. Moreover, the welfare implications of economic growth imply government intervention to ensure that the fruits of such growth are distributed in accordance with the prevailing standards of equity. Almost paradoxically, the concern with redistributive policies, reflected in government expenditure and transfer programmes, has increased with rising income *per capita*. For those people preferring a non-interventionist stance, the increasing regulatory power and size of government is an additional cost emanating from the growth process. Finally, economic growth inevitably hastens the depletion of natural resources, particularly energy resources, many of which are in finite supply, and also may permanently damage the environment. The consequences will be borne by those yet unborn, who have no say in determining the 'optimal' degree of resource depletion.

The Causes of Economic Growth

Considerable disagreement exists with respect to the determinants of economic growth, a disagreement reflected in widely divergent opinions concerning the optimal growth strategy. In part, these disagreements spring from the empirical difficulty of quantifying the various contributions to economic growth, but they also stem from different assumptions about the manner in which the economy behaves and responds to certain stimuli. A pioneering attempt to identify the sources of economic growth was made by Denison in his influential volume *Why Growth Rates Differ* (1967), which indicated no less than twenty-three distinct sources of growth, ranging from such factors as variations in the pressure of demand, improvements in education and learning, the changing hours of work and sex composition of the labour force, to fundamental reallocation of resources. Denison's study was important in stressing that most economies are confronted with a relatively inelastic growth potential; accordingly, growth performance is to be judged in terms of deviation from the indicated growth path and not by reference to arbitrary intra-country comparisons.

Conceptually, it is convenient to invoke the concept of a production function in analysing the sources of economic growth. Writing

$$Q = \alpha(L, K)$$

where Q is real output, L the labour input, K the capital input and α a non-factor residual, we can distinguish between changes in real output arising from the augmentation of the factor inputs, labour and capital,[3] from changes arising from all other non-factor augmenting sources. Changes in the value of α, therefore, would reflect such influences as innovation and technical progress as well as a host of cultural and sociological factors including differing attitudes to work effort, trade union behaviour, tax induced changes and so forth, which may assist or impede the growth process. It follows that we may adopt the same conceptual framework to appraise growth policies, since the latter will attempt to influence actual growth rates either by augmenting factor inputs or by influencing the residual component, α, or by some judicious combination of the two. In what follows, we will briefly review the case of the principal claimants to growth and in so doing we suggest possible insights into the comparatively disappointing growth performance of the UK economy.

The Importance of Capital Accumulation

The belief that capital accumulation may hold the key to economic growth is widely held and springs partly from the observed correlation between high growth rates and high investment/GNP ratios.[4] However, correlation need imply nothing about causation; a high level of investment to national income may be the consequence of rapid growth which creates a continuously expanding demand for increased capacity. Moreover, the issue of correlation is bedevilled by the fact that the crucial relationship is between economic growth and *net* productive investment. That is to say, for example, that if two countries were investing 15% of GNP annually, but in one case 10% of it was to meet depreciation needs whilst in the other only 5% was required, then the latter would have twice the net productive investment rate. Consequently, small variations in the aggregate investment/GNP ratio may conceal large variations in the net investment/GNP ratio.[5] Empirically, the issue is complicated by the fact that it is no simple matter to distinguish between gross and net investment, since the replacement of worn-out capital usually involves the adoption of improved and superior assets – net and gross investment being inextricably interlinked.

The theoretical basis for the advocacy of capital accumulation is closely related to the elementary Harrod–Domar growth model which equates the increase in capacity income in any period to the volume of net investment divided by the capital–output ratio. Symbolically,

$$\Delta Y = \frac{I}{C}$$

where Y refers to capacity income, I is net investment and C is the capital–output ratio. It follows that if the capital–output ratio differs between sectors of the economy, then it is possible to raise the overall growth rate by transferring resources from sectors with relatively high capital–output ratios to those with comparatively low capital–output ratios. Critics of British growth performance have pointed not only to a comparatively low investment/GNP ratio, but have also argued that much investment has been allocated into high capital–output sectors.[6]

Thus far we have discussed the concept of the capital–output ratio without specifying whether we are dealing in average or marginal terms. This is very much in keeping with the spirit of the Harrod–Domar model, since it assumed constancy – and thus equality – between average and marginal capital–output ratios. If the capital–output ratio is indeed a constant, then the logic of capital formation as a means to economic growth is unassailable. If, however, the capital–output ratio is not constant, then clearly it is the marginal concept or the incremental capital–output ratio which is crucial for policy prescription. Should increasing the amount of capital, relative to other co-operative inputs, encounter the onset of diminishing returns as neo-classical theory would predict, then clearly the incremental capital–output ratio will rise and the anticipated increase in productive capacity will not be forthcoming. This is broadly the line of argument taken by those economists who are sceptical of the claim of capital formation to be crucial to the growth process. In their view capital formation is the consequence of growth, since growth enlarges demand and broadens the scope of profitable investment opportunities, offsetting the tendency towards diminishing returns. It may be noted that this controversy cannot readily be settled by reference to the available empirical findings. Whilst the evidence, such as it is, indicates a broad constancy in the average capital–output ratio over time, this is precisely what one would expect from the existence of diminishing returns to capital investment – a rising incremental capital–output ratio – assuming profit maximising behaviour. For as diminishing returns set in, the incentive to undertake new investment ceases and investment comes to a halt, leaving the average capital–output ratio virtually unaffected. Later, when new investment opportunities have emerged, investment recommences until the next onset of diminishing returns. Such a cyclical view of the investment process would then reveal virtual constancy in the average capital–output ratio.

Despite these arguments the virtue of capital accumulation as a means to growth commands great respect. Perhaps the most extreme example of this view has been voiced by the celebrated economist Paul Samuelson (1956) who claimed: 'With proper fiscal and monetary policies, our economy can have full employment and whatever rate of capital formation and growth it wants.' The proper monetary and fiscal policies which Samuelson had in mind have been aptly referred to as the strict-fiscal easy-monetary policy for economic growth. The essential idea is that taxes can be used to force down consumption spending and the budget surplus so obtained be diverted to investment usage, either by the government spending the proceeds directly or by transferring them to the private investment-oriented sector by the purchase of government bonds. In the act of purchasing outstanding government bonds, the money supply is increased and the interest rate lowered, thus providing further stimulus to investment activity. To quote Samuelson (1963) again:

> A strong growth-inducing policy of monetary ease, if it succeeds in producing overall employment, can be combined with an austere fiscal policy, in which tax rates are kept high and/or expenditure rates low enough, so as to remove inflationary pressures of the demand-pull type and succeed in increasing the net capital formation share of our full-employment income at the expense of the current consumption share.

Unfortunately, such a policy prescription implicitly presupposes a closed economy. If the analysis is extended to the sphere of international trade, however, then even ignoring any reservations about diminishing returns to capital investment, sizeable constraints emerge with regard to the external deficit. If full employment is maintained, then *ceteris paribus* so too will the level of imports, whilst the lowering of the rate of interest will worsen the capital account and hence *in toto* the overall balance of payments. It is for this reason that recent advocacy of the appropriate monetary–fiscal mix for economic growth has been accompanied by attempts to direct investment into the export sector (export-led growth), or by permitting the exchange rate to float to overcome the balance of payments constraint. However, international trading obligations (such as GATT) specifically prohibit favourable fiscal assistance to the export sectors, whilst allowing the exchange rate to float does not always bring the adjustment predicted by elementary trade theory. In particular, the resulting rise in import prices adds to inflation, triggering off wage demands which quickly negate any competitive advantage of currency depreciation before the external deficit can be overcome.

The Importance of Technical Change

As we have already indicated, one can mentally decompose growth into two components, the one resulting from augmentation of factor inputs and a residual element encompassing all other contributing factors. In the latter category one would undoubtedly wish to emphasise the importance of technical change and innovation. Many economists have argued the latter to be the major cause of growth and far more important than the role of capital accumulation.

A pioneering work emphasising the importance of technical change was published by Robert Solow (1957). In this article Solow attempted to segregate observed variations in output per head due to technical change from those due to the increase in capital per head. Applying US GNP non-farm data for the period 1909–49, and adopting a constant returns to scale production function exhibiting neutral technical change (not inconsistent with the evidence), Solow was able to obtain an estimate of the marginal productivity of capital and consequently a measure of the increased output due to increased capital formation over a specific period of time. The excess of increased output not so explained provides a measure of economic growth arising from all other factors described in the catch-all technical change. There are all sorts of difficulties and objections involved in this approach,[7] but nonetheless Solow's conclusion was startling, indicating that of the doubling of gross output per man which occurred over the forty-year period no less than 87½% stemmed from technical change with the remainder arising from capital formation. However, the role of capital accumulation should not be dismissed lightly. As Solow was quick to emphasise, much if not all technical change is in fact embodied in new plant and investment. It is through the medium of investment that technical change is transmitted throughout the economy. A prerequisite for technical progress, therefore, would appear to be adequate incentives to invest and expand the capital stock. In this connection it is important to distinguish between pure scientific advances and technological progress as actually applied in industrial investment. Mere scientific progress and advances in knowledge are in themselves insufficient; it is the application of scientific developments to actual productive processes which is the all-important factor. Crucial in the application of new ideas will be the social climate. Opposition to change, stemming from either too conservative management or from restrictive trade union practices, may limit the degree of technological progress even when the degree of pure scientific research and achievement is remarkably high.

One consequence of the notion of embodied technical progress being dependent upon the act of investment was the development of the so-called 'vintage growth model', where the capital stock is distinguished according to its age profile and where the more recent capital assets are the most productive. The pace at which existing capital assets are scrapped and replaced may depend in part upon the provision of depletion and accelerated depreciation allowances. To the extent that the latter are policy variables, therefore, it may be possible to influence the age profile of a nation's capital stock and hasten technological advance – or at least the pace at which innovating changes are incorporated into productive processes. By the same token, if there are factors weakening the incentive to replace existing assets, as for example the maintenance of an over-valued exchange rate which deters investment in the export sectors and which limits the inflow of external venture capital, then a nation's capital stock may possess an outdated age profile reflected in low productivity per head and limited technological advance.

The Importance of Labour and Labour Allocation

The preceding argument has emphasised the importance of technical change. However, it should be stressed that the meaning of technical change employed above is that of a residual factor which explains any upward shift of the production function – in short, anything not accounted for by increased capital per capita. Once this is recognised, then it is clear that consideration must be given to the labour input and in particular to any factor which accounts for increased labour productivity not embodied in increased investment.[8]

There are two factors which specifically need to be taken into account. The first has become known as the learning process which relates the impact of job experience to labour productivity. Stated simply, this thesis maintains that the amount of labour input per unit of output declines as the total volume of output increases for any given product. The learning process is not of course without limit and the limit in many cases arises through a change of product; nonetheless, it remains an example of a peculiar economy of scale which raises overall productivity exogenously and is therefore independent both of capital accumulation and advances in technology.

Secondly, a change in aggregate productivity per capita may be achieved merely by the transfer from low to high productivity occupations, without any augmentation of the total factor input and without any technological advance. Such a change is closely related to the transfer of resources out of agriculture and non-agricultural self employment into manufacturing. Indeed, in the case of less advanced economies some of the labour employed within the agricultural sector may possess zero or near zero marginal product and its transference into more productive usages is often looked upon as a prerequisite for continuing development. There is no doubt that the ratio of agricultural output to GNP is closely correlated (inversely) with the level of income per capita and indeed such a ratio is sometimes looked upon as a useful index of the development process. This increased productivity through labour re-allocation is sometimes looked upon as being especially significant in accounting for the comparatively poor growth performance of both the United States and the United Kingdon *vis-à-vis* Western Europe. What is alleged is that this source of economic growth has become virtually exhausted for the former two countries;

their ability to contract the agricultural sector is severely constrained in comparison to the economies of Western Europe. The force of this argument, originally propounded by Kaldor (1966), lies not just in the once-and-for-all increase in output per head, but in the associated productivity changes arising from increasing returns in manufacturing whilst agriculture is characterised by diminishing returns. Britain's poor growth performance, in this view, is explained by her having exhausted her surplus agricultural labour upon which highly productive manufacturing activity could draw.[9]

British Growth Performance

We have already warned against attaching too much importance to intra-country comparisons of economic growth upon the grounds that different countries will possess different growth potential. This point is reinforced when Britain's relatively poor post-war growth performance is appraised historically; the growth rate has not deviated markedly since the 1880s. Nonetheless, the fact remains that the UK's post-war growth performance has been extremely disappointing when evaluated in terms of the long-term trend in productive capacity.[10] Moreover, this comparatively poor growth performance, illustrated by reference to table 1, has not just been of concern to successive British governments. It has also concerned those international organisations which have intervened to support sterling and it has also led to a major study sponsored by the Brookings Institution of Washington (Caves 1968). Very broadly, and perhaps most disturbingly, such enquiries have not highlighted any one single factor as being responsible for poor rates of growth; rather they indicate a number of interlinked influences compounding the problems of correcting them. First of all, there appears to be a consensus that Britain's post-war growth performance has stemmed partly from a failure to exploit technical change. Technological progress has been limited, especially when compared to EEC countries (Aukrust 1964), despite the fact that expenditure upon pure research and development has been remarkably high.[11] It is not the lack of advances in knowledge so much

Table 1. *Growth, investment and export performance 1953–76 (average of yearly figures)*

	% change real GNP	*Investment as % of GNP*	*% change in export volumes*
USA	3.23	14.50	5.88
Canada	4.81	22.77	6.02
W. Germany	4.96	23.70	9.99
Netherlands	4.99	23.70	9.38
Sweden	3.67	22.96	7.16
France	4.95	21.93	8.78
Denmark	3.58	20.11	6.77
Australia	4.95	25.42	6.98
Italy	4.96	20.87	12.09
Switzerland	3.56	24.28	7.20
Norway	4.18	29.61	7.70
Belgium	4.07	19.97	9.24
Japan	8.55	30.21	16.18
Austria	5.17	25.09	11.12
UK	2.71	17.26	4.46
S. Africa	4.97	24.53	6.57
Spain	5.94	21.64	11.10
Finland	4.55	26.37	6.63

Source: Adapted from Kern (1978)

as the failure to apply them in investment and innovation which explains the limited pace of technological progress. What is the reason for such reluctance? Here opinions diverge markedly. One school identifies the resistance to change in the conservative nature of British management and the general preference for non-specialised and less professionally qualified management personnel.[12] Others point to the restrictive practices of trade unions and class divisions reflected in overmanning, which places a premium upon labour-intensive techniques where the scope for innovatory changes is more limited. A third body of thought identifies the major limitation with the balance of payments constraint. The peculiar position of sterling in the world economy led to an over-valued rate of exchange for the pound (at least until the 'forced' devaluation of 1967) and resulting balance of payments crises have required recourse to frequent 'stop–go' policies imposed by both Labour and Conservative governments alike. In this view the uncertainty of domestic demand pressure thus generated has produced a reluctance upon the part of industry to invest and innovate. This argument, it will be noted, assumes both that technological change is dependent upon investment and secondly that investment is itself related inversely to the degree of cyclical disturbance. It is on this second point that the 'stop–go' thesis has been subject to attack, for as Whiting (1976) has demonstrated the percentage deviations from trend of UK growth rates have been less than any other major OECD country – yet nonetheless Britain has experienced the lowest rate of growth. However, whilst it is difficult to endorse the 'stop–go' explanation without qualification, the argument gains in credibility when it is linked to the valuation of sterling. Maintenance of an over-valued exchange rate, for essentially historical reasons, leads to an unwillingness to transfer venture capital into the export sector, which becomes increasingly uncompetitive and reinforces the need for even more stringent deflationary policies. If this view is correct, then the termination of sterling's traditional role would suggest more optimistic growth prospects in the future.

More recently Kaldor (1977) has advanced an explanation for Britain's poor growth performance which stresses the vital role of exports. Since the bulk of exports stem from the manufacturing sector and since it is the latter sector which experiences increasing returns to scale, any factor constraining export growth will inhibit productivity changes and hence dictate relatively low rates of economic growth. British exports are constrained by the level of unit labour costs which in turn depend upon labour productivity. But labour productivity itself depends upon the rate of expansion of the manufacturing sector, since it is this sector which reaps economies.[13] In Kaldor's world the UK is caught in a vicious circle of low exports, low manufacturing expansion, low productivity change and hence low exports. Discretionary aids to manufacturing (as, for example, the now defunct selective employment tax) or selective intervention and support of certain industries (determined by the National Enterprise Board) might well be the conclusions to be drawn from this analysis.

A not dissimilar explanation of Britain's comparatively poor growth performance has recently been advanced by Bacon and Eltis (1976, 1978). In their view, Britain's current economic problems stem primarily from the transfer of industrial labour into the expansion of the public sector. The slow growth rate is a direct consequence of the process of de-industrialisation. Adapting a distinction originally made by Johnston (1975), they argue that the British economy is now structurally unbalanced with the industrial sectors producing marketable output suffering a relative decline *vis-à-vis* those sectors producing non-marketable goods and services. The comparative expansion of the public sector has proceeded at an unprecedented pace in Britain's case and has now reached a critical level of imbalance. In part, the blame lies in the relative ease of moving out of recession by stimulating central and local government employment. The labour thereby absorbed into the public sector was thus no longer available to British industry during the resulting upswing of the cycle, and this was contributing to the premature curbing of the boom. The rapid acceleration of public sector wages that occurred during the mid-1960s served to intensify the impact by increasing the tax burden generally, but – in real terms – relatively severely upon the industrial sectors.

The strength of this argument is reinforced when productivity changes are taken into account, because these will normally be greater for those sectors producing marketable output. Bacon and Eltis claim that over the period 1961–73 the percentage growth rate of the non-industrial sector[14] was in the order of 32% – approximately double that of France and Germany and roughly three times that of Italy and the United States. Nonetheless, the argument is at best *simpliste,* since *a priori* resources may be more productive when employed in the public sector.[15] Moreover, as demonstrated by Peacock and Ricketts (1978), no clear correlation emerges between the growth rate of GDP and the growth rate of governments' share in GDP for the major OECD countries.

A further leading explanation for Britain's poor growth performance points to the misallocation of capital investment. Whilst the overall investment/GNP ratio in the UK is not particularly high, it is not notably out of line with the USA or other advanced European economies, as indicated in table 1. However, there is evidence to indicate that the productivity of capital employed is low by international standards (Bacon and Eltis 1976, 1978). In part, this springs from considerable opposition to multi-shift working, with the result that expensive capital assets often stand idle for considerable periods of time. In addition, public sector investment, which has been maintained often at the expense of investment in the private sector, has been directed into sectors possessed of high capital–output ratios. In recent years this tendency has been reinforced by selective structural policies designed to ease the adjustment problems of labour-intensive industries faced with secular decline in the wake of increased competition, particularly from third world nations. Investment in textiles, steel and shipbuilding industries provide recent examples, where doubtless regional considerations have influenced the allocation of capital investment.

In conclusion, then, whilst there are differences in opinion as to the underlying cause of Britain's post-war growth rate, it would appear that there is a growing consensus that it does not lie solely in the rate of augmentation of factor inputs, but rather in the manner in which such inputs are combined and allocated. Such a conclusion implies that higher growth rates will depend not solely upon economic policies but also upon social attitudes and institutions. It is a sad fact of contemporary British life that capital and labour are not viewed as co-operative factor inputs in the augmentation of national output, but rather as competing claimants upon a fixed national cake. Such attitudes are not conducive to economic growth.

Finally, two further comments appear warranted. First, it would appear that British membership of the European Economic Community has not proved to be the panacea for growth that the advocates of membership proclaimed it to be: in particular, it would appear that the economies of scale argument has been seriously overplayed, as evidenced in the increasing recognition being given to the innovative role of small businesses in initiating the growth process. Second, to what extent are Britain's long-term growth prospects transformed by the exploitation of North Sea oil? There is a growing consensus of opinion to the effect that this sudden fortuitous windfall will terminate Britain's balance of payments problems within a matter of years and in addition will provide the government with substantial revenues from the taxes derived from the oil companies. Whether these additional resources are used to restructure the economy and provide the funds needed by growth-oriented investment strategies, or whether they are dissipated in election appealing tax cuts[16] and government consumption outlays, may well determine the future of Britain's ultimate growth path.

Notes

1. Redistribution may, of course, be desired upon other grounds. It may be noted that economic growth permits redistributive policies to be implemented without necessarily diminishing the absolute living standards of the comparatively well-to-do, and to this extent increases the political acceptability of such policies.
2. An illustrative example from nineteenth century UK experience is provided by the stark poverty forced upon hand-loom operatives in the textile industry arising from the introduction of the power loom.
3. The relationship between the increase in factor inputs and the resultant increase in output indicates, *ceteris paribus*, whether increasing diminishing or constant returns to scale apply.
4. One country which has enjoyed phenomenally high growth rates (often exceeding 10%) in the post-war period is Japan, where the investment/GNP ratio has been remarkably high. In 1970 Japan invested 28% of her national income – approximately double the UK ratio (HMSO 1974).
5. The principal determinant of the division between replacement and net investment is the age profile of the capital stock. Here, considerable intra-country differences emerge. In the 1950s and early 1960s for example, the age profile of capital in the German Federal Republic was much younger than in either the UK or the USA.
6. Particularly in the public sector where investment has been maintained or even increased with the onset of recession.

7. Not least, the assumption that capital is paid its marginal product. Furthermore, the relevant variable to test the contribution of capital is not the change in the capital stock as such, but the change in the effective utilisation of the capital stock. Solow did indeed attempt to deal with this question by assuming an equal percentage unemployment of capital as of the labour force; an admittedly arbitrary assumption which highlights some of the difficulties encountered in empirical work of this nature.
8. The quality and hence productivity of labour is enhanced by education. The resulting upward shift of the aggregate production function may thus be best described as technical advance embodied in investment in human resources.
9. It should be noted that Kaldor no longer maintains this view that the shortage of labour to the manufacturing sector constitutes the main constraint on UK growth performance. He now believes the main factor to lie in the slow rate of growth for British exports, thus switching from a resource-constrained to a demand-induced view of the growth process. See Kaldor (1975). The latter view gains endorsement from Parikh (1978).
10. In the short run actual increases in output have been impressive, but they mislead with respect to the sustainable growth rate since they arise from the quickening utilisation of hitherto unemployed resources under the influence of expansionary monetary and fiscal policies.
11. Expressed as a percentage of GNP, expenditure upon research and development in the UK was some fifty per cent greater than comparable expenditure in the United States. Cf. Caves (1968).
12. This view is buttressed by evidence indicating that American managed firms located in the UK and employing British labour belonging to British trade unions, earn on balance a higher return upon capital than their British owned counterparts. See Dunning (1966).
13. The argument relies crucially upon the existence of increasing returns to scale in industry, the so-called Verdoorn Law (Verdoorn 1949), which posits a positive relationship between the rate of growth of manufacturing output and rate of growth of productivity. The evidence in support of the law is at best contentious as evidenced by Rowthorn (1975).
14. Excluding agriculture.
15. The Bacon–Eltis thesis is reminiscent of the Smithian distinction between productive and unproductive labour, with the latter being considered coterminous with public sector employment.
16. Admittedly, certain tax reductions might be judged beneficial to economic growth if they exerted a significant impact upon incentives and altered attitudes to risk-taking.

References

Aukrust, O., 'Factors in economic development: A review of recent research', *Weltwirtschaftliches Archiv*, Band 93, No. 1, 1964.

Bacon, R. and Eltis, W., *Britain's Economic Problem: Too Few Producers?* 2nd edn, Macmillan 1978.

Caves, R.E., *Britain's Economic Prospects*, George Allen and Unwin 1968.

Denison, E.F., *Why Growth Rates Differ: Postwar Experience in Nine Western Countries*, Brookings Institution 1967.

Dunning, J.H., 'US subsidiaries in Britain and their UK competitors', *Business Ratios*, Autumn 1966.

The Regeneration of British Industry, Cmnd 5710, HMSO 1974.

Johnston, J., 'A macro-model of inflation', *Economic Journal*, June 1975.

Kaldor, N., *Causes of the Slow Rate of Economic Growth of the United Kingdom*, Cambridge University Press 1966.

Kaldor, N., 'Economic growth and the Verdoorn Law', *Economic Journal*, December 1975.

Kaldor, N., 'Capitalism and industrial development: Lessons from British experience', *Cambridge Journal of Economics*, June 1977.

Kern, D., 'An international comparison of major economic trends', *National Westminster Bank Quarterly Review*, May 1978.

Mishan, E.J., *The Costs of Economic Growth*, Staples Press 1967.

Mishan, E.J., *The Economic Growth Debate – An Assessment*, Allen & Unwin 1977.

Parikh, A., 'Differences in growth rates and Kaldor's Laws', *Economica*, February 1978.

Peacock, A.T. and Ricketts, M., 'The growth of the public sector and inflation' in F. Hirsch and J.H. Goldthorpe (eds), *The Political Economy of Inflation*, Martin Robertson 1978.

Rowthorn, R.E., 'What remains of Kaldor's Law?', *Economic Journal*, March 1975.

Samuelson, P.A., 'The new look in tax and fiscal policy', *Federal Tax Policy for Economic Growth and Stability*, US Government Printing Office 1966.

Samuelson, P.A., 'Fiscal and financial policies for growth' in *A Symposium on Economic Growth: Proceedings*, The American Bankers' Association 1963.

Solow, R.M., 'Technical change and the aggregate production function', *Review of Economics and Statistics*, August 1967.

Verdoorn, P.J., 'Fattori che regolano lo sviluppo della producttivita del lavoro', *L'Industria*, 1949.

Whiting, A., 'An international comparison of the instability of economic growth', *The Three Banks Review*, March 1976.

Suggestions for Further Reading

Allen, G.C., *The British Disease*, Hobart Paper No. 57, Institute of Economic Affairs 1976.

Bacon, R. and Eltis, W., 'Stop–go and de-industrialisation', *National Westminster Bank Quarterly Review*, November 1975.

Cairncross, Sir Alex (ed.), *Britain's Economic Prospects Reconsidered*, George Allen and Unwin 1971.

Fores, M., 'Britain's economic growth and the 1870 watershed', *Lloyds Bank Review*, January 1971.

Kravis, I., 'A survey of international comparisons of productivity', *Economic Journal*, March 1976.

Maddison, A., 'Explaining economic growth', *Banca Nazionale del Lavoro Quarterly Review*, September 1972.

Peaker, A., *Economic Growth in Modern Britain*, Macmillan 1974.

Shaw, G.K., *An Introduction to the Theory of Macroeconomic Policy*, 3rd edn, Martin Robertson 1977, Chapter IX.

13. The international monetary system: retrospect and prospect

GEORGE ZIS
Lecturer in Economics,
University of Salford

International trade allows countries to specialise in the production of those goods in which they enjoy a comparative cost advantage. If the world economy is to derive all the gains that follow from trade, there must exist a set of international monetary arrangements conducive to a system of multilateral payments. The rules and regulations governing the operations of the International Monetary Fund (IMF), and through it specifying the norms of conduct for member countries, are such a set of international monetary arrangements. During the post-1945 period a system of multilateral trade and payments was firmly established. The importance of the contribution of the IMF system to this achievement is generally accepted. However, recurring international monetary crises exposed the weaknesses of the original system and have led governments to seek an alternative, more enduring, set of international monetary arrangements.

This chapter, in describing the evolution of international monetary relations since 1945, examines the reasons leading to the breakdown of the original IMF system in 1971 and assesses the impact of the various forces impinging on the efforts to negotiate and, eventually, agree upon the main features of a new and more viable international monetary system.

Alternative Exchange Rate Systems

The principal task of any international monetary system is to provide for the maximum possible harmony between the interests of the world economy and those of the individual country. But the country which chooses to pursue its domestic economic objectives in collaboration rather than in conflict with the rest of the world necessarily accepts that the conduct of its economic policy be subject to internationally agreed constraints. If these constraints are so severe as to result in the domestic objectives becoming subordinate to the interests of the world economy, then sooner or later individual countries will attempt to redress the balance and in the process of doing so the prevailing international monetary system will disintegrate. If, alternatively, international monetary relations are based on a set of ill-defined and ambiguous rules and regulations, then the individual country will have an incentive to pursue its domestic economic objectives with little or no regard for the international repercussions of its policies. Again the international monetary system that imposes no constraints on the formulation of domestic economic policies is unlikely to be particularly durable. But while economic nationalism may conceivably yield benefits to the individual country in isolation, if all governments are simultaneously to determine their policies on purely domestic criteria, then all countries will suffer — as none will be in the position to enjoy the gains accruing from the international specialisation in production associated with a multilateral system of trade. It follows, therefore, that there is no inherent incompatibility between the interests of the world economy and those of the individual country, although temporary conflicts may arise reflecting the individual economy's response in adjusting to a real or monetary disturbance. The task of the international monetary system is to assist the country whose interests temporarily diverge from those of the international economy to adopt policies that facilitate domestic adjustment without being disadvantageous for the rest of the world.

For much of the post-war period the primary function of international monetary rules and regulations was deemed to be the promotion of exchange rate stability. It was recognised that exchange rate stability was necessary if post-war trade was to expand and, therefore, contribute to the attainment of the objectives of full employment and high rates of growth. To assess the potential capability of alternative international monetary systems to promote exchange rate stability, it is first necessary to consider how exchange rates are determined.

Assume, for simplicity, that the world is divided into two countries, Britain and the US; there are no capital flows between them and their governments abstain from intervening in the foreign exchange market. British importers are willing to supply sterling in exchange for dollars to pay for US goods. US importers exchange dollar for sterling to pay for British goods. Thus the demand for British goods implies a demand for sterling, while the British demand for US goods implies a supply of sterling. Private demand for and supply of sterling will, therefore, determine its price in terms of the dollar. In the absence of government intervention in the foreign exchange market, the exchange rate will continuously be in equilibrium; and assuming no change in UK or US economic policies the equilibrium exchange rate will remain unchanged, implying that the price of sterling in terms of both UK and US goods will alter at the same rate. This implies that the difference in the rates of growth of the supply of dollars and the demand for dollars in the US is equal to that for sterling in the UK. In other words, the rate of inflation in the UK is equal to that in the US.

Let us now trace the impact of a change in monetary policy in the UK on the sterling exchange rate. Assume that to begin with money supply growth rates in both countries are equal to the respective growth rates in the demand for money. Suppose now that the UK authorities increase the rate of growth of the money supply. Monetary disequilibrium emerges in the UK, which causes a positive rate of inflation. If monetary equilibrium is to be restored, the price of sterling has also to change in terms of US goods. Given no change in US economic policies the exchange value of sterling against the dollar will fall. It further follows that if the UK authorities persist with the new rate of growth of the money supply, then sterling will continuously depreciate in terms of the dollar. If, alternatively, the UK authorities reverse their monetary policy and reduce the money supply growth rate to the rate of growth of the demand for money, then the exchange rate will cease to alter with the new equilibrium exchange rate implying, of course, a depreciation of sterling relative to the dollar in comparison with the original exchange rate.

Note that the above analysis does not imply that the equilibrium exchange rate will alter only in response to a change in the money supply growth rate. The equilibrium exchange rate is determined through the interaction of the demand and supply of money. Thus any policy measure or disturbance that affects the demand for money will result in the equilibrium exchange rate changing, assuming that there is no offsetting change in the rate of growth of the money supply.

It is evident, therefore, that under an international monetary system in which exchange rates are freely determined without any government intervention, exchange rate stability will emerge only if countries pursue convergent monetary policies. But under freely determined exchange rates discretionary demand management policies become more attractive for the policy makers and governments are more likely to pursue expansionary macroeconomic policies. Given that the intensity of the domestic pressures exerted on national governments varies across countries and over time within any individual country, and since the response of policy makers to these pressures differs among countries and alters within a country over time, it follows that national economic policies will tend to diverge rather than converge. Consequently, under a system of flexible exchange rates there will emerge a tendency for continual changes in the equilibrium exchange rates. Unless these changes are perfectly predictable, exchange rate uncertainty will result in trade, as an economic activity, becoming more costly. Thus, some economists argue that a system of flexible exchange rates is undesirable because of its capacity to promote exchange rate instability which discourages the development and growth of international trade. This view was broadly accepted by the countries negotiating the features of the post-war international monetary system, particularly the US. Flexibility of exchange rates was rejected on the grounds that it implied a degree of national autonomy in economic policy making that was unlikely to result in exchange rate stability. The objective, therefore, to promote a rapid expansion of trade on a multilateral basis would be jeopardised. Instead it was decided to achieve exchange rate stability through fixed exchange rates. The main argument for a system of fixed exchange rates is that it so links economies with each other as to encourage trade among them, just as the existence of a single currency within a country facilitates transactions among the regions of that country. However, if such a system is to have the desired effects, certain conditions must be met.

As we have already seen, if the rate of growth of the money supply exceeds the rate of growth of the demand for money in a country, assuming monetary equilibrium in the rest of the world, then the country's currency will depreciate in terms of all other currencies. If the exchange rate is to remain unchanged, the government must intervene in the foreign exchange market and absorb the excess supply of the national currency. But for governments to maintain fixed exchange rates there must exist some internationally acceptable money which they can use to purchase the excess supply of their currency, or be prepared to accept in exchange for their currency when excess demand emerges. This internationally acceptable money can either be a commodity, e.g. gold, or a national currency, e.g. sterling or dollars, or an asset created by an international institution, e.g. IMF drawing rights, which all countries are prepared to use.

We now consider the process of equilibrium under a system of fixed exchange rates. Assume for simplicity zero rates of growth and inflation throughout the world, with no country experiencing a balance of payments deficit or surplus. Suppose that the UK alone increases its money supply. The restoration of monetary equilibrium requires that the domestic price level rises sufficiently so as to eliminate the excess cash balances held by UK citizens. But if that were to happen, the implication would be that the price of sterling in terms of UK goods declined, while it remained unchanged in terms of goods produced abroad. Clearly this could be but a temporary phenomenon. UK citizens will substitute foreign goods for domestic products. That is, the UK will develop a balance of payments deficit leading to a fall in its foreign exchange reserves and, therefore, to a decrease in the UK money supply. As aggregate demand for domestic products declines because of the monetary consequences of balance of payments deficit, the domestic price level will begin to fall. It will continue to do so and the balance of payments deficit will persist until the entire increase in the money supply is exported through the balance of payments. At that point the domestic price index will have returned to its original level, with the demand for money now being equal to the supply of money implying the restoration of balance of payments equilibrium. The country's money supply will have decreased to its original level, with the decrease in the country's foreign exchange reserves being exactly equal to the original increase in the money supply. Note that the elimination of excess cash balances, in this example, proceeded first by an increase in the domestic price level and then by a combination of a balance of payments deficit and domestic prices that were above their equilibrium level.

Implicit in the above analysis is the assumption that the UK is so small relative to the rest of the world that it could not affect world prices through its monetary policies. However, for the sake of illustration assume that the UK money supply accounts for 50% of the world money supply. If the UK increases its money supply by 20%, this would imply a 10% increase in world money supply. As the rest of the world develops a balance of payments surplus with the UK , other country's money supplies would begin to increase significantly and foreign prices would increase. Restoration of general equilibrium would involve a 10% increase in world prices. Thus the UK will have experienced a 10% rise in the domestic price index with a loss of reserves amounting to half the original increase in the domestic money supply. Therefore, for a given disturbance, the smaller the country is, the larger will be the required aggregate balance of payments deficit for monetary equilibrium to be restored.

In practice the adjustment process does not take place in quite such a straightforward manner as the hypothetical examples predict. Consider the following more 'realistic' case. Goods may be divided into traded and non-traded ones.

The prices of the former are determined at the world level, while those for the non-traded goods are determined by domestic forces. Assume that there prevails general equilibrium in the world economy, with the rate of growth of the money supply in each country being equal to the domestic rate of growth of the demand for money. Postulate an increase in the rate of growth of the money supply in the UK and no change in monetary policies in the rest of the world. In response to the emergence of excess aggregate demand, the prices of the non-traded goods will begin to rise. But the prices of traded goods will remain unaffected, given the size of the UK relative to the world economy. The UK will therefore develop a balance of payments deficit. Further, there will emerge a positive rate of inflation in the UK, reflecting the change in the prices of the non-traded goods, in contrast to the (assumed) zero rate of inflation in the rest of the world. But given the different price response of the two categories of goods to the increase in the money supply growth rate, UK citizens will substitute traded for non-traded goods resulting, initially, in an increase in the balance of payments deficit in comparison to the deficit immediately after the rise in the money supply growth rate. So long as the UK pursues the higher money supply growth rate, its balance of payments will remain in deficit and will continue to experience a rate of inflation higher than the rest of the world. However, the larger the proportion of aggregate domestic expenditure devoted to traded goods at any time, the larger will be the balance of payments deficit and the smaller will be the difference between the domestic and world rates of inflation.

The distinction between traded and non-traded goods is not immutable: it may be argued that as trade expands and the world economy becomes more integrated, more goods will pass into the traded goods category and, consequently, the proportion of aggregate expenditures on traded goods will rise. In turn that would imply that as trade expands, the larger will be the impact on a country's balance of payments of any given, real or monetary, disturbance. Thus, if governments are to maintain fixed exchange rates, they will require a higher volume of foreign exchange reserves. We may then conclude that if a system of fixed exchange rates is to function smoothly, it is necessary that it ensures that the volume of international liquidity grows at a rate which is in line with the expansion of world trade.

Next, let us again assume that Britain increases its money supply growth rate while economic policies in the rest of the world remain unchanged. The ensuing emergence of excess aggregate demand will induce an output response, especially in the non-traded goods sector where prices will be rising. Unemployment will, therefore, fall below the natural rate and there will prevail a positive rate of inflation, assuming that there was a zero rate of inflation prior to the increase in the money supply growth rate. Of course, simultaneously Britain will develop a balance of payments deficit. If in the next period the rate of growth of the money supply is reduced to the original one, the balance of payments disequilibrium will gradually be eliminated, price stability will be restored, equilibrium relative prices between traded and non-traded goods will be re-established and unemployment will return to the natural rate. Suppose, however, that the government persists with the increased money supply growth rate. Eventually the expected rate of inflation will begin to adjust to the actual rate of inflation and the level of unemployment will increase towards the natural rate. There would be no convincing rationale for such a policy. Instead, it would be more persuasive to postulate that the government seeks to maintain the lower rather than the natural rate of unemployment. However, if this is to be achieved, it follows that the rate of growth of the money supply must accelerate. This, in turn would imply that the balance of payments deficit will increase, therefore sustaining larger foreign exchange reserve losses. But no country has an unlimited amount of international liquidity at its disposal. If the UK is to maintain its exchange rate, sooner or later it will have to initiate such measures as to eliminate its balance of payments deficit and to allow unemployment to rise to the natural rate. Indeed, if the reserve losses were to be partially or fully reversed, then domestic unemployment would have to rise above the natural rate. However, allowing unemployment to rise to or above the natural rate may be regarded, for various reasons, as undesirable and, consequently, UK policy makers may opt for imposing barriers to the movement of goods and capital, in the form of tariffs, quotas, exchange restrictions, etc. But the adoption of such measures, as a means of curing a balance of payments disequilibrium, is totally at variance with the main argument for a system of fixed exchange rates, which is that it facilitates the expansion of international trade. We may, therefore, conclude that if a system of fixed exchange rates is to function smoothly and have the desired effects, it must contain provisions ensuring that countries initiate corrective measures before the balance of payments disequilibria become so acute as to undermine the viability of the system.

The speed with which a country takes action to correct a balance of payments deficit will depend on the volume of foreign exchange reserves at its disposal and the stringency of its international obligations. Countries that attach top priority to the objective of full employment will prefer a set of arrangements that result in an abundant supply of international liquidity. On the other hand, countries that regard a low or zero rate of inflation as their principle objective will opt for a system of fixed exchange rates that prevents countries from delaying the introduction of measures aimed at restoring balance of payments equilibrium. Unless a generally acceptable compromise can be reached, then national governments will succumb to domestic pressures and, in effect, pursue divergent economic policies. The more diverse the domestic objectives of governments are, the more likely it will be that at some stage some countries will choose a devaluation or revaluation of their currency as a means of effecting adjustment in their balance of payments.

No set of international monetary arrangements can ensure the irrevocable fixity of exchange rates if countries adopt divergent monetary policies in the pursuit of different economic objectives. But if complete certainty in the international value of a currency is lacking, then economic agents will attempt to anticipate changes in exchange rates. A country running a persistent balance of payments deficit will come to be expected to devalue its currency. Such expectations will induce economic agents to move their funds into a country whose currency is expected to at least maintain its international value. If the expected devaluation does materialise, then economic agents can repatriate their funds and thus make a profit. If, on the other hand, the national authorities of the deficit country do succeed in maintaining the exchange rate, then people who acted on their expectation will have suffered no loss above the costs of tranferring their funds from country to country.

We may, therefore, conclude that divergent monetary policies not only lead to balance of payments disequilibria, but also that they are not conducive to the promotion of confidence in the international value of currencies.

In summary, the three requirements that must be fulfilled for a system of fixed exchange rates to operate smoothly are: provisions must be made for an adequate rate of growth of international liquidity; the system must ensure that countries speedily respond to the emergence of balance of payments disequilibria; and the system must promote confidence in the international value of currencies, particularly of the major ones.

The IMF System

The IMF was created to provide a forum for consultations among member countries aiming at the promotion of international monetary co-operation, the lack of which was seen as an important cause of the ills of the inter-war period. International co-operation was seen as the necessary precondition for the monetary arrangements embodied in the IMF system to form the basis of a multilateral system of payments which would be conducive to the rapid expansion of trade. The central feature of the system was the commitment of member countries to maintain fixed exchange rates. We may, then, turn to considering how the IMF system was to meet the three requirements of a smoothly functioning system of fixed exchange rates.

The liquidity requirement was to be fulfilled by the IMF making available international credit facilities to the member countries. These IMF Drawing Rights were to supplement national gold holdings, thus ensuring that the liquidity needs of a growing world economy would be met. Also, under IMF rules the price of gold could be increased, which would be equivalent to an increase in the world stock of international liquidity.

Briefly, the IMF was to contribute to the solution of the liquidity problem in the following way. A quota subscription was specified for each member country; usually the member country subscribed 25% of its quota in gold and the rest in its own currency. The size of the quota determined the country's voting strength and drawing rights. Member countries could purchase currencies from the IMF in exchange for their own currency, the limit being determined by the country's quota and the level of the IMF's holdings of the currency of the country. Member countries could automatically borrow from the IMF an amount equal to their gold subscription. If they wished to borrow more, which would have implied that the IMF held balances in excess of the quota of the borrowing country's currency, the approval of the IMF Executive Board was required. For most countries the upper limit of drawings was reached when the IMF's holdings reached 200% of the quota.

The pool of currencies with the IMF was to be made available to member countries facing balance of payments difficulties. Increases in international liquidity were to be provided by increases in member countries' quotas in gold holdings.

Member countries were requested to define the price of their currencies in terms of gold and were obliged to maintain a 1% margin on either side of the declared parity. Given that all countries' currencies were tied to gold, the price of any individual currency in terms of the other currencies was thus automatically determined. Countries were committed to defend their declared exchange rates and under the IMF rules they could devalue or revalue their currency only if confronted with a 'fundamental disequilibrium' in their balance of payments and after they had secured the agreement of the IMF. What precisely was meant by 'fundamental disequilibrium' is something that was never clarified, though a country with a persistent and increasing surplus or deficit in its balance of payments would have been thought of as facing 'fundamental disequilibrium'.

By incorporating rules, albeit ill-defined, under which countries could alter their exchange rates, the IMF was hoping to provide some solution to the adjustment problem which would not inevitably lead to a conflict between the external and internal objectives of a country. Further, in order to contribute towards easing the adjustment problem, provisions were made under which the IMF could declare a currency 'scarce'. In such an event, countries would have been permitted to discriminate against trade with the country whose currency was declared 'scarce'.

Finally, under IMF rules countries were allowed to impose controls on short term capital movements if such controls were deemed necessary by the national authorities for the maintenance or restoration of confidence in the international value of the country's currency.

The IMF System in Practice

A complex of reasons led to recurring international monetary crises during the 1960s, which culminated in the breakdown of the IMF system in August 1971. Failure by the IMF to solve the liquidity problem, and the impact of this failure on countries' monetary policies, could be argued as being the principal reasons that led to increasing doubts as to the viability of the original system and to the search, since 1971, for a new set of international monetary arrangements.

As already indicated, a prime function of the IMF was to provide international liquidity to supplement gold holdings. A role, but only a minor one, for reserve holdings in the form of sterling and dollar balances was envisaged, but the emphasis was on gold and IMF drawing rights as the main components of international liquidity. However, the IMF failed to provide the international liquidity that an increasingly integrated world economy needed. The implications of the IMF's failure were accentuated by the fact, not surprising in retrospect, that increases in gold production were not sufficient to meet the expanding demand for international liquidity. The vacuum thus created was filled by the emergence of the dollar as a key currency, US deficits becoming the main source of additional international liquidity.

The failure of the IMF to provide the additional international liquidity is illustrated by the fact that while during the period 1951 to 1971 world monetary reserves rose by $80 billion, countries' reserve position in the IMF increased by only $5.2 billion. In terms of the contribution towards the aggregate volume of world liquidity, IMF reserve positions represented less than 6% in 1971 and they never exceeded 10%.

The contribution of gold to international liquidity declined in importance throughout the period and by the end of 1971 gold holdings amounted to only 30% of total world reserves. Indeed, after 1965 gold holdings fell in absolute terms. Of the $80 billion increase in world aggregate reserves between 1951 and 1971, $63 billion was due to the expansion of foreign exchange reserves. In 1951 foreign exchange reserves amounted to approximately 30% of the total international liquidity – but to nearly 60% by the end of 1971. The major part of countries' foreign exchange reserves was held in dollar balances. Some countries chose to hold their reserves in sterling balances. The dominance of the US economy and its large gold holdings were the main factors which led to the supremacy of the dollar as an internationally acceptable currency. Countries were willing to accumulate dollar balances, confident that they could be converted to gold if desired, an attitude which lasted until the mid-1960s.

US deficits, by providing the required additional liquidity, were important in creating an environment conducive to the expansion of the world economy. Be that as it may, the failure of the IMF to solve the liquidity problem, combined with the inadequate increases in gold production and the emergence of the dollar as the main key currency, was the basic cause of the instability and ultimately of the breakdown of the IMF system.

The holding of dollar balances as a form of international liquidity allows countries to economise on the use of gold. However, an international monetary system which operates on the basis of gold and a national currency as the main components of international liquidity is inherently unstable. This instability arises from two sources: first, the impact of the demand and supply of gold, and second, from the problems of a national currency being used as international money, its acceptability as such being dependent on its reserve backing in gold.

The world economy experienced high rates of growth during the post-1945 period. Not surprisingly, this growth led to an increase in private demand for gold. The fact that the price of gold was fixed in an inflationary period when the prices of all other commodities were rising, reinforced the increase in the demand for gold. However, on the supply side, the fixed price of gold and the resultant change in relative prices implied that the production of gold became less profitable. The emergence of private excess demand for gold led to the expectation that the central monetary authorities would raise the price of gold. Such expectations further stimulated private demand for gold. Central monetary authorities' reluctance to raise the price of gold resulted in their position changing from being net buyers to becoming net sellers of gold after 1965 in order to maintain the fixed price of gold at $35 per ounce.

The high rate of post-war growth of the world economy and the fixed price of gold in a period of rising prices which stimulated demand and discouraged production, resulted in the emergence of private excess demand for gold. This led to the expectation that the central monetary authorities would be forced to raise the price of gold. At the same time, the willingness of countries to accumulate dollar balances rested on their confidence in the ability of the US government to convert dollar balances into gold at the fixed price. The fall in the ratio of the US gold holdings to dollar liabilities which followed from the US balance of payments deficit, gradually led the world to suspect that the US would not be able to maintain the dollar price of gold. From the early 1960s some countries, notably France and Germany, sought as a matter of policy to restrict their dollar reserves and convert dollar balances into gold holdings. Thus between 1958 and 1967 France's gold holdings increased from $0.8 billion to $5.2 billion, Germany's from $2.6 to $4.2 billion, Italy's from $1.1 to $2.4 – while US gold holdings decreased from $20.6 to $12.1 billion.

By the mid-1960s, therefore, the co-existence of gold and dollars as the main components of international liquidity was becoming a source of instability. Confidence in the dollar was rapidly decreasing, generating speculative flows of short-run capital in the expectation that major countries would not be able to maintain their exchange rate. The failure of the IMF system to provide a solution to the liquidity problem was leading directly to the emergence of a confidence problem engulfing not only individual currencies' international prices, but also the prevailing international monetary arrangements. The world economy had three options: to raise the price of gold and stimulate its production, to move on to a dollar standard system, or to create a new international asset.

The international role of the dollar was at the centre of the controversy of what the solution to the liquidity problem required. The emergence of the dollar as a reserve currency permitted the US to run balance of payments deficits without being under the pressures that other deficit countries were to eliminate their external disequilibrium. Similarly, surplus countries were resentful of the position of the US as they were open to inflationary impulses emanating from the American economy. Thus a number of countries argued for the elimination of US deficits, with some of them, France being the most vociferous, advocating an increase in the price of gold. The US opposed any devaluation of the dollar against gold for reasons of national prestige and also because the chief beneficiaries would be the major producer countries, the Soviet Union and South Africa. At the same time, the US argued that the elimination of its balance of payments deficit would be detrimental to the world economy if it preceded the establishment of a new scheme guaranteeing the adequate growth of international liquidity.

After 1965 the instability of the international monetary system increased, primarily as a result of the expansion of the US money supply in order to finance the escalating war in Vietnam and domestic social programmes. The consequences were an accelerating rate of inflation both in the US and in the world as a whole, together with increasing contrast between the balance of payments deficits of the US and the surpluses of Germany and Japan. Increasing transfers of short-term capital between countries exacerbated the instability of the system. To counteract these 'hot money' flows, countries developed various *ad hoc* arrangements, notably 'swap' arrangements whereby central banks agreed to lend balances to one another and to accept others' currency up to some agreed level.

Prolonged international negotiations on the most desirable means of solving the international liquidity problem culminated in an agreement, in 1967, to create a new international asset, the Special Drawing Rights (SDRs). Any member of the IMF has the right to participate in the SDR scheme. SDRs are allocated on the basis of countries' quotas. Any country participating in the scheme undertakes to provide its currency, when so instructed by the IMF, in exchange for SDRs. A country cannot refuse to accept SDRs unless its total holdings reach three times its allocation. Any country using SDRs is charged a rate of interest, set originally at 1.5%, while the country providing its currency in exchange for SDRs receives a payment at the same rate of interest. Countries participating in the SDRs scheme are obliged to maintain their average holdings of SDRs over a period of five years to a level equivalent to at least 30% of their average cumulative net allocations. Thus, if a country uses more than 70% of its SDRs allocation it has to reconstitute its SDRs holding by providing its currency for other participating countries. Countries using SDRs are not obliged to submit their policies for the approval of the IMF, this being a major difference between SDRs and IMF drawing rights.

The SDR scheme was greeted with widespread scepticism. In particular the IMF negotiations had concentrated on the problem of a *shortage* of international liquidity, whereas the chief problem was the *composition* of international liquidity – in particular the co-existence of the dollar and gold. The introduction of SDRs represented the creation of a third international asset to be used alongside gold and dollars and accentuating rather than solving the difficulties stemming from the availability to countries of alternative methods of holding their foreign assets. Although countries were not allowed to use SDRs to change the composition of their reserves, this stipulation is seen to be of dubious relevance if we consider the case of a deficit country. Nothing could prevent such a country from financing its balance of payments deficit by running down its dollar balances. By abstaining from using SDRs, deficit countries could easily alter the composition of their reserves.

Not unrelated to the composition problem, interest payments were thought of as a means of making SDRs more attractive than gold. Given that the interest rate was originally fixed at only 1.5% and the capital gains which would result from an increase in the price of gold were in line with what the demand and supply of gold would imply, it was hardly likely that SDRs would become acceptable as a substitute for gold and thus permit a decrease in the international role of the latter. The SDRs scheme was further criticised for not taking into consideration the special needs of developing countries. Allocation of SDRs on the basis of countries' quotas implied that the industrial countries received the major share.

The special problems of sterling during the late 1960s resulted in the Basle Agreement of 1968. Even after the 1967 devaluation, the holders of sterling balances displayed a lack of confidence in sterling. Thus, in September 1968 the UK agreed to guarantee the dollar value of official sterling balances in exchange for an undertaking by sterling area countries to hold a specified minimum proportion of their foreign exchange reserves in the form of sterling balances. At the same time, the UK reached an agreement with the major industrial countries and the Bank for International Settlements for $2 billion to be made available to the UK for use in support of sterling, if sterling balances declined below an agreed level. The Basle Agreement was for a period of three years and it was subsequently renewed. Towards the end of 1974 the UK government announced that the sterling guarantee arrangements were to be terminated.

A further prop to the fixed exchange rate regime was erected in 1968 with the introduction of a two-tier gold market. The maintenance of gold at $35 an ounce proved impossible in the face of increasing prices for all other commodities. Speculative purchases of gold were encouraged by France's official support for a higher gold price. Under the impact of these pressures, in March 1968 the major countries announced that they would cease to operate in the gold market with the aim of maintaining the gold price at $35 per ounce. Thus the price of gold in the private market was freed to vary as demand and supply forces dictated. However, the price of gold was to stay at $35 per ounce for transactions among central monetary authorities.

The devaluation of sterling, the agreement on the SDRs scheme, the Basle Agreement, the increasing use of swap arrangements and the freeing of the price of gold in the private market, were not sufficient to restore confidence in the IMF system. Individual currencies came under increasing speculative pressures, while expectations regarding a rise in the official price of gold gathered momentum. In 1969 the French franc was devalued and the German mark revalued, and in August 1971 the US, facing a large and deteriorating balance of payments deficit largely reflecting outflows of short-run funds in anticipation of a dollar devaluation, announced that it was suspending the convertibility of its currency into gold. The dollar was to float, its price in terms of other currencies being determined by demand and supply in the foreign exchange market.

The Search for a New International Monetary System

The crisis that followed the US decision to suspend the dollar convertibility was 'resolved' in December 1971 when the countries comprising the Group of Ten agreed on a new set of exchange rates, the US devaluing the dollar in terms of gold by raising the price of the latter from $35 to $38 per ounce. Further, the IMF announced that member countries would be allowed to move within margins of 2.25% instead of 1% on either side of the newly agreed parities.

Any hopes that the new set of exchange rates was to last were proved unfounded by June 1972, when the UK authorities announced that sterling would be allowed to float. In January 1973 the announcement of a record US trade deficit threw the whole international monetary system into turmoil. Speculation against the dollar rapidly gathered momentum and general uncertainty over exchange rates intensified when it was revealed that the US was to continue to have a large budget deficit. Germany and Japan experienced particularly heavy capital inflows. The decision in February to devalue the dollar by a further 10% in terms of gold, raising its price from $38 to $42.22 per ounce, was not sufficient to curtail speculation. In March the EEC countries decided to maintain fixed exchange rates among their currencies, but not *vis-à-vis* other countries. The UK and Italy did not participate in the joint float; instead they let their currencies move independently. Thus, after March 1973 the world moved to a system of fluctuating exchange rates, central monetary authorities abstaining from systematic interventions in the foreign exchange markets.

With the breakdown of the IMF system, the need to reform the rules governing international monetary arrangements became urgent enough to attract the continuous attention of policy makers. In June 1972 the Committee of Twenty was formed with the task of presenting a set of proposals which would form the basis for the radical reform of the international monetary system. Despite the apparently irretrievable breakdown of the system of fixed exchange rates, the Committee proclaimed in March 1973 that the new system should be based on 'stable but adjustable par values'. Proposals were presented to the annual meeting of the IMF in September for a return to fixed exchange rates with the SDR as the principal reserve asset and the requirement that countries moving into balance of payments disequilibrium would initiate internal policies to correct such tendencies.

The Committee of Twenty was instructed to proceed and prepare a considered set of proposals by July 1974. However, the decision of the oil producing countries to raise the price of oil by nearly 400% in the winter of 1973 and the political implications of the embargo imposed by the Arab producers resulted in the negotiations for a reformed international monetary system becoming more complex. Nationalistic tendencies, especially among industrialised countries, emerged as countries sought to minimise the fall in their real standard of living that could not be prevented following the increase in the relative price of oil. Countries were more inclined than ever before to determine their policies on purely domestic criteria. In the circumstances, governments were hardly willing to enter into new commitments with respect to their exchange rate policies. Flexible exchange rates suddenly became attractive. One of the immediate consequences of the oil crisis was a renewed demand for gold to be retained and its price increased against all currencies. Countries argued that if their gold holdings were to be valued at market prices, which by February 1974 had passed the $180 per ounce mark, that would facilitate the financing of their deficits. Such considerations led to the decision of December 1973 which allowed governments to sell gold in the private market, thus reversing the 1968 agreement.

In January 1974 the Committee of Twenty abandoned its efforts to agree upon the establishment of a new monetary system and, in its Annual Meeting of 1974, the IMF concluded 'that it will be some time before a reformed system can be finally agreed and fully implemented'. Flexible exchange rates were to stay, at least for the time being, and attention turned to considering how best the international monetary system could function during this transitional period. In August 1974 the IMF announced a new facility making available to member countries, for a limited period of time, funds amounting to SDR 2.8 billion, with the specific aim of assisting them to finance deficits arising from the increase in the price of oil. Further, in September of that year the IMF created a new facility for medium-term assistance to member countries facing special balance of payments difficulties arising from structural changes in their economies.

In October 1974 the Interim Committee was established to recommend reforms which would enable the IMF to continue to play a role towards the maintenance of a multilateral system of payments. In January 1976 a set of proposals by the Committee were accepted by the Group of Ten countries and became embodied in the Proposed Second Amendment to the Articles of Agreement which came into force on 1 April 1978. The Second Amendment legitimised prevailing exchange rate practices. The amended Article IV now permits 'other exchange arrangements of a member's choice'. That is, countries are now allowed to fix the price of their currencies against anything they wish *except gold.* They can do so with reference to another currency, or to a basket of several currencies, or to the SDR, or they can engage in mutual pegging. Further, countries can choose whatever margins of intervention they like, if they decide to peg their currencies. Alternatively, countries can allow their exchange rate to change on the basis of a rule, they can abstain from any systematic intervention, or they can let the exchange rate be freely determined. Any exchange rate policy is therefore now compatible with the constitution of the IMF. The main constraint placed upon countries is that they must not engage in foreign exchange operations aimed at gaining a competitive advantage at the expense of the rest of the world. There are provisions for countries' co-operation to reduce erratic exchange rate fluctuations, while Article IV permits the eventual return to the original exchange rate system, provided that countries with 85% of the total vote declare themselves in favour of such a return. However, countries desiring to continue with floating exchange rates would be allowed to do so, even if there were a general return to the original exchange rate system.

The Second Amendment reiterates the objective of establishing the SDR as the principal reserve asset of the international monetary system. Thus it liberalises and extends the conditions under which the SDR can be used. Consistent with this objective, the Second Amendment institutionalises the valuation of the SDR in terms of a basket of currencies. This practice was initiated in June 1974, until when the value of the SDR was determined in terms of gold. Further, consistent with the aim of establishing the SDR as the principal reserve asset, the IMF has sought to reduce the role of gold. Thus the official price of gold was abolished. In May 1976 the Executive Directors of the IMF announced a four year gold sales programme, according to which one sixth of the IMF's gold (25 million ounces) would be sold at the former official price of $35 an ounce directly to all member countries and one sixth would be sold at public auction for the benefit of developing countries. The major countries agreed not to attempt to peg the price of gold and that the total stock of gold in their and the IMF's possession would not be increased.

The first gold auction was held in June 1976. But even before then the US had started to sell gold in the private market in an effort to dampen the rising price of gold and to encourage the gradual demonetisation of gold. US gold sales were resumed, after a brief interval, during 1978 in response to the weakening position of the dollar. Rather than to arrest the rising price of gold, the intention was to take advantage of the high gold prices in order to finance its balance of payments deficit. By late 1979 the price of gold had exceeded $500 per ounce.

Looking back at the 1970s one cannot avoid the conclusion that the world economy failed to reform the international monetary system. There is no evidence that we are experiencing the gradual demonetisation of gold. It could be argued, on the contrary, that the role of gold is increasing in importance. There is little or no likelihood of the SDR becoming the principal reserve asset in the foreseeable future. There is no evidence of countries adopting more convergent monetary policies or in succeeding in co-ordinating their objectives. Thus, as exchange rates move erratically and unpredictably, there are growing tendencies among countries to resort to protectionist policies.

Disenchantment with the actual experience with flexible exchange rates since 1973, and the desire to eliminate the consequences of exchange rate unpredictability, led to the decision of the EEC member countries, except the UK, to establish the European Monetary System, which came into effect in March 1979. Each of the eight participating countries fixed the value of its currency against all other currencies and against the composite European Currency Unit (ECU), which is defined as a basket of fixed amounts of all EEC currencies. In the European Monetary Fund countries deposited 20% of their *gold* and dollar reserves. In exchange countries received unconditional drawing rights denominated in ECUs which they can use to finance intra-EEC settlements. It is significant to note that the creation of the European Monetary System implies the formal return of gold as a reserve asset in international monetary arrangements. Further, the price of gold, relevant to the operation of the European Monetary System, is market determined.

Conclusion

The failure of the IMF system cannot be interpreted as evidence against the proposition that a system of fixed exchange rates is not only desirable but also viable. What that failure demonstrated was that a system of fixed exchange rates based on the use of a national currency as international money is both unstable and inflationary. The 'system' of floating exchange rates since 1973 has proved less than successful. Exchange rate fluctuations have been larger and more unpredictable than anticipated by the proponents of such a system. It is evident that current practices can be only temporary if the world is not to relapse into the bilateralism of the inter-war period. Given the failure of the IMF member countries in general to negotiate viable reforms, it may well be the case that through the success of the European Monetary System the world may gradually be led to a new and durable international monetary system.

Suggestions for Further Reading

Johnson, H.G., *Further Essays in Monetary Economics*, Allen and Unwin 1972, Chapters 7, 8, 11 and 15.

Vaubel, R., *Choice in European Monetary Union*, Ninth Wincott Memorial Lecture, Occasional Paper 55, Institute of Economic Affairs, 1979.

Williamson, J., *The Failure of World Monetary Reform 1971–74*, Nelson 1977.

Index